THE "HOW TO" GRANTS MANUAL

THE "HOW TO" GRANTS MANUAL

Second Edition
Successful Grantseeking Techniques for Obtaining Public and Private Grants

David G. Bauer

American
Council on
Education

NEW YORK

Macmillan
Publishing
Company

Collier Macmillan Publishers
LONDON

Macmillan Publishing Company
A Division of Macmillan, Inc.
866 Third Avenue, New York, N.Y. 10022

Collier Macmillan Canada, Inc.

Library of Congress Catalog Card Number: 87-37226

Printed in the United States of America

printing number
1   2   3   4   5   6   7   8   9   10

Library of Congress Cataloging in Publication Data

Bauer, David G.
    The "how to" grants manual : successful grantseeking techniques
  for obtaining public and private grants / David G. Bauer. — 2nd ed.
        p.   cm. — (The American Council on Education/Macmillan series
  on higher education)
    Bibliography: p.
    Includes index.
    ISBN 0-02-902431-5 (Macmillan)
    1. Fund raising.   2. Grants-in-aid.   3. Corporations, Nonprofit.
  I. American Council on Education.   II. Title.   III. Series: American
  Council on Education/Macmillan series in higher education.
  HG177.B38 1988
  658.1'5224—dc19   87-37226
                                                              CIP

Contents

PART THREE: PRIVATE FUNDING SOURCES

Preface

This *"How To" Grants Manual* is a compilation of years of effort and experience to systematize the process of grant seeking for nonprofit agencies in the United States. Having instructed over five thousand grant seekers in hundreds of seminars, I am sensitive to the problem of you controlling grant seeking, instead of having the grant seeking control you. Whether you are a full-time one-person grants office, a part-time grants person, or have a staff of twenty, this manual is intended to assist you in improving the investment return of your grants effort.

This book will save you hours of precious time and increase your monetary return by thousands of dollars. By applying this systematic approach to organize your proposal efforts, you will project a more professional image to funding sources.

Special thanks must be given to the American Council on Education, the State University of New York College of Technology, and Capitol Publications for the opportunities they have provided by assisting in the development and sharing these techniques.

This manual will give you increased insight into the competitive grants marketplace. The system outlined in this manual provides techniques that I know will work to help you obtain the grants you desire. Although the grants marketplace changes almost daily, this manual will enable you to locate and secure funds, whether they be federal or private, because the techniques for success resist change and the system will keep you up-to-date.

To assist you in organizing the grantseeking techniques outlined in this manual, a software package consisting of four diskettes is available from David G. Bauer Associates, Inc. Please refer to price list at the end of the book.

In order to reduce the time spent on researching possible funding sources for projects that involve higher education, I suggest you locate the companion piece to this manual, *The Complete Grants Sourcebook for Higher Education* (New York: ACE/Macmillan). If your grants quest involves the health area, consider investing in *The Complete Grants Sourcebook for Nursing and Health Research* (New York:ACE/Macmillan). While you will discover some similar techniques and worksheets in the books, these sourcebooks represent thousands of hours of research to help locate the best funding sources. Incorporation of the techniques in this book will increase your chances of success with funders. If instructing others in grantseeking is of interest to you, you will find the ten cassette videotape training program, WINNING GRANTS, invaluable. Contact David G. Bauer Associates, Inc. for a preview tape. Please refer to the price list at the end of the book.

May your grantseeking efforts be productive.

Introduction

Why Seek Grants? Is All the Effort Worth It? Who Needs Grants?

Understanding the importance of grant seeking to nonprofit organizations in the United States requires some knowledge of the marketplace. The following points should be kept in mind:

- It is estimated that there are 750,000 to 1,000,000 Not-for-Profit organizations in the U.S.

- Over 350,000 nonprofit organizations (NPOs) that are considered "gift supported" are competing for grant funds in the United States.

- New federal regulations allow not-for-profits and profit-making companies to compete for the same dollars, which makes the grant-seeking process more competitive. There are even "Small Business Set-Asides" in the grants arena, which makes it more difficult for nonprofits to secure their "fair share" of necessary funds to maintain their existence.

- In 1981 "Reaganomics" forecasted a cut of 25 billion dollars in direct grants to NPOs by 1985. The reduction was 80% correct. (40B in 1980 to 22B in 1985)

Recent trends have shown an increase in the federal grants marketplace to a 1986 high of $27B. But the current grant dollars are still less than they were in 1980.

To be competitive in the grants world requires knowledge and insight into what is happening in the grant-funding area and why. Each of the major areas of grant funding are dealt with in detail in this book.

The importance of the written proposal or grant to the not-for-profit world is staggering:

- *$20 to 30 billion* of the federal government budget is awarded through a grants mechanism—be it a block grant or a categorical grant.

- *$5.17 billion* went to nonprofits in 1986 from private foundations in the form of grants.

- *$4.50 billion* went to nonprofits from corporations, a similar award procedure.

Nonprofit organizations turn to the grants mechanism for everything from bricks and mortar, new projects, and extension of services to paying last year's phone bill deficit.

The grants mechanism provides the funding source with the key to unlocking the world's largest reserve of collective and individual genius and pitting that collective intelligence against any one of the multitude of problems that plague the world of modern man. To unlock this reserve, a funding source announces its intention to direct funds toward specific areas or concerns that the funding source feels should be addressed.

The NPO (Non Profit Organization) uses its resources to develop an approach to solving the stated problem or areas of concern. How you locate the grant opportunities that are *right* for your organization, and how you can bring the process to a positive conclusion are the concerns of this manual.

This resource manual and its systematic approach are based upon a "winning approach" to grant seeking. The funding sources have a certain perspective on what they want for their money. This perspective is based upon their values and how they believe the monies they are charged with dispensing will impact the problem. Whether they are corporate board members, foundation trustees, or government officials, they have interpreted their charge or job through their own beliefs and values.

The key to using this book is to understand that the grants system is reflective of producing a match between what the funding source wants and what your organization can provide. *Note* that I did not say what you *need*; not many people care about what *you need*, unless it matches with what *they need*.

This manual will help you pinpoint what you need and develop strategies on how to develop the interest of others in projects or grants that would benefit both of you.

This requires more analysis before you write your proposal and more tailoring of your proposal to each funding source. The result is well worth the extra effort.

Rather than investing time in a grants effort that generates a 2 percent success rate, you can improve your time investment and obtain a 50 percent success rate through this systematic approach. The "secret ingredient" in this system is confidence—*yes*, confidence.

Following these steps will provide you with the knowledge that you need when approaching each funding source.

You will avoid a hastily prepared approach that is based on your needs and not on those of the funding source. You will not send the same proposal to a list of funding sources, you will develop a tailored approach. Or, as a women in my grants class said: "I used to go after grants with a shotgun; now I use a rifle and spend time aligning my telescopic site."

Successful grant seeking involves doing your "homework." This book is dedicated to providing the direction and shortcuts to do the work of grant seeking in as time-efficient a manner as possible.

While many grant seekers *begin* with the proposal, the systematic approach of this manual does not address the actual proposal until Chapter 15. The purpose of this book is to increase the probability of getting your proposal awarded and most successful veteran grant seekers agree that much of the work required for a funded proposal is done *before* the proposal is written.

This manual is organized upon the following key concept: your ability to communicate with a potential funder, show them your ideas and approaches to the solution of their problem, and co-opt or draw them into the decision on which approach to utilize will dramatically increase your grants success rate.

There are several theories that can be used to substantiate why a pre-proposal contact with the funding source results in success. One theory that is particularly useful in explaining how to be more successful is Festinger's Theory of Cognitive Dissonance.

Dissonance is defined as the static that is produced in individuals when they are presented with information (facts) that is not in agreement (matched) with what they have decided is true (reality). Since each person bases his or her reality on their beliefs or values, we are then influenced by those values and view, or compare, the world to what we *believe to be true.*

This means that a potential funder has an existing value system of which you must be aware. Failure to be sensitive to this value system and neglecting to view your project from the funder's perspective can cause dissonance. This means that your preferred solution to the problem may meet with a negative response to your request—not because it would not produce the anticipated results, but because the funding source has a problem accepting that approach because of the static it produces in themselves.

This theory explains why it is important to learn about your funders before you approach them for funds. You can reduce the probability of causing dissonance (static) by planning. You can increase your success by knowing the funder's values and:

- taking a person with you who has similar values to that of the funding source;

- wearing the "right" clothing; and

- selecting an approach they would like.

While it is not always possible to contact funding sources before you develop your proposal, funders leave a trail of information about their values. You can find out what they value by:

- reviewing who and what they have funded, and
- analyzing their choices in selecting staff (reviewers, etc.).

Finally, as you read this text, remember how your value system works to provide you with selective discrimination to avoid producing dissonance. You may decide that you do not like what you are reading in this manual. Before you question the facts presented herein or the validity of this systematic approach, ask yourself if you are experiencing cognitive dissonance. Your success in the "grants world" will depend on how sensitive you are to the funder's values.

Remember the Golden Rule: "She or he who has the gold rules."

Note: When you match your project with an interested funder, think seriously of the reduction of dissonance with how the funder perceives you, your proposal, and your organization. Expressing your rights, freedoms and opinions may conflict with the "Golden Rule."

MAY YOUR GRANTS EFFORTS BE REWARDING!

THE "HOW TO" GRANTS MANUAL

PART ONE

How To Get Ready To Seek Grant Support For Your Organization

CHAPTER 1

Organizing a Proposal-Development Workbook

The steps necessary to produce a grant application are very logical and follow a definite order. Many people seeking grants find the process complex and difficult to deal with because they are overwhelmed with the totality of the task or end result. As a result of this feeling, they avoid approaching proposal development until it is too late to do an adequate job.

Allen Lakein, in his book, *How To Get Control of Your Time and Your Life* (New York: New American Library, 1974), discusses a theory that you can utilize to get your grant-writing process under control and organized. His "Swiss Cheese" concept divides a difficult task into parts. Lakein's example of a mouse confronted by the job of carrying away a huge piece of cheese is analogous to the feeling a grant seeker has when presented with the prospect of creating a grant proposal—*overwhelmed!*

To avoid this feeling, Lakein suggests that the mouse would best be advised to divide the big piece of cheese into parts. Avoid being overwhelmed by the whole task by completing the smaller parts. By eating holes and dividing the cheese into manageable parts you get "Swiss Cheese."

Bauer Associates have applied this concept to your grant-seeking efforts by creating a set of Swiss Cheese tabs (see Fig. 1.1). These tabs are similar to Lakein's mouse eating holes in the cheese. We have divided the task of developing a proposal into thirty (30) steps. By addressing each step in the grant-seeking process, you organize your approach, control the process, and lower your anxiety level.

This manual is based on this concept. Take your proposal a piece at a time and the process will not overwhelm you. The Swiss Cheese Book approach can save you *50 percent* of the time involved in proposal preparation.

I have found it a great help in making the grants process more understandable and manageable. Make a Swiss Cheese Book for each of the major areas for which your organization is planning to seek funding through utilizing a grants mechanism.

For example, a nonprofit organization working with senior citizens might have several Swiss Cheese Books/Proposal Organizing Workbooks to address:

- Transportation

- Health

- Nutrition

- Recreation

Your Swiss Cheese Book/Proposal Development Workbook should be a three-ring binder with tabs dividing up the task of a full-scale proposal. To follow the above example, when you read a research article on nutrition for the elderly, make a copy or summarize it and place it under the tab for "Documenting Need/Needs Assessment."

When a politician visits your center and expresses a concern for the elderly, get a letter of support for your work and put this politician on an advisory committee. File a copy of the endorsement under the tab "Advocates," and the name, address, and telephone number under "Advisory Committee."

FIGURE 1.1. Proposal Development Workbook (Swiss Cheese Book).

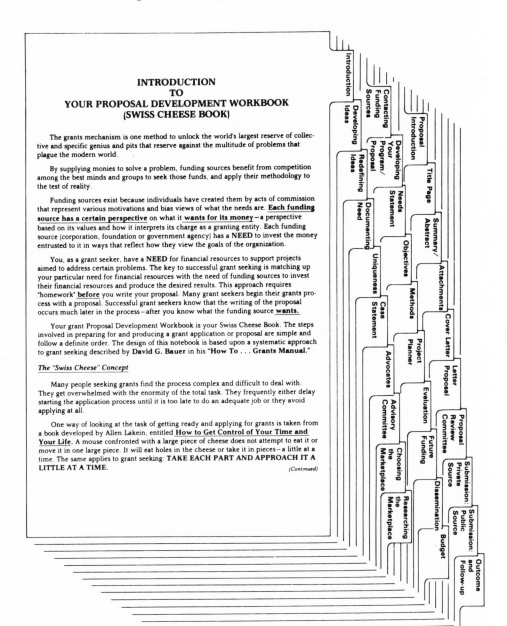

Review the list of tabs after you have read this manual. You may want to eliminate or combine some areas to tailor the concept to your organization. (Sets of thirty tabs can be purchased from Bauer Associates at a reasonable cost.)

SUGGESTED TABS

1. Organizing A Proposal Workbook
2. Developing and Evaluating Proposal Ideas
3. Redefining Proposal Ideas to Find More Funding Sources
4. Documenting Need/Needs Assessment
5. Uniquenesses/Capitalizing on Your Differences
6. Your Case Statement
7. Advocates: How to Use Them
8. Advisory Committee: How to Develop Community Support

In addition, you will want tabs for the research and contacts in the marketplace you choose.

FOR GOVERNMENT FUNDING SOURCES

14. Federal Grants Research Form
15. Selecting the Appropriate Government Funding Program
16. How to Contact Government Funding Sources
17. The Project Planner

FOR PRIVATE FUNDING SOURCES

23. How to Record Research and Information
24. Private Funding Source Research Tools
25. Locating and Selecting the Appropriate Private Funding Sources
26. How to Contact a Private Funding Source
27. The Letter Proposal
28. Submission and Who to Contact on Follow-Up

Your Proposal Development Workbook acts as a file for your proposal ideas. A potential funding source will be very impressed if you respond to a question by referring to your Proposal Development Workbook instead of a tattered pile of file folders and loose pages of notes.

One grant seeker using this successful process, called our office to tell us how great it was to see the look on a potential funder's face when she was asked, "Why should we give the money to your organization when there are hundreds of others who are asking for this grant?" She opened her Proposal Development Workbook to the tab on uniquenesses and presented a list of fifty reasons why her organization was uniquely suited to carry out the proposed project—with the best five reasons circled.

The Proposal Development Workbook is one step in the process of making your grants effort more cost- and time-effective. If you thought that proposal preparation was a Herculean task—last-minute, forty-eight-hour miracle—think again. This manual and its usefulness are based on the assumption that proposal preparation is an organized approach that utilizes adequate development time and provides support to the mission and the image of the organization.

Those grant seekers who prepare proposals overnight pose a threat to the image of your organization in the eyes of a funder, and develop the fear of proposal preparation in your staff.

This manual uses time-proven steps to allow you to improve your image with funding sources (known as "positioning" in marketing talk, but it really works when you present your organization as an honest, organized, well-planned agency—even if it is not totally true). One hastily written proposal (overnight wonder) with budget transpositions and typographical errors will affect your image negatively for many years.

Organizing your Proposal Development Workbook is a process that, once initiated, promotes development of project ideas, location of funding sources, and writing proposals. It is a proactive process.

Finding a funding opportunity and developing a proposal is a *reactive process* that puts you under someone else's time frame and adds to the existing pressure that deadlines normally create.

The grants process can be *made* to work for you and your organization.

CHAPTER 2

Developing and Evaluating Proposal Ideas

The underlying theme or philosophy of this manual is based on the concept that when you ask someone (funder) for support (grant), you must look at your organization and your request from their perspective. It is the "Golden Rule"—not the one you were taught in grade school, but the rule for grant seeking: "He or she who has the gold rules."

The least we can do is try to determine what the grantor values, likes, and dislikes, and avoid those areas that may be potentially negative, while we highlight the areas that make us look competent to the grantor.

Most grant seekers write the proposal first, which does not allow sufficient flexibility to tailor or select alternative approaches (solutions) to the problem. A funder, while very definitely concerned about the problem, may find your approach (solution) very unpalatable.

The process outlined in this chapter recommends that you develop several alternatives to solve the problem (perform your research, develop your model, or solve your space problems, etc.).

By providing the funding source with several approaches, you develop credibility and present an image of analysis as a basis for your approach—*not a bias and preference of your project staff.*

The worksheets in this chapter will provide you with three useful tools:

1. Idea generation;
2. A system to summarize your best ideas and assess organizational commitment to the project; and
3. Cost/benefit analysis of your best ideas/approaches.

One of the best techniques for developing sound proposal ideas and alternatives is to *brainstorm* the idea with your staff and peers. This has the added benefit of tapping the collective genius of the group. You build support for the proposal since you invited your staff to share in the idea generation. Thus, the project becomes "our" project and your staff will be more willing and eager to work at night and on weekends to meet the deadlines (when numerous proposals are worked on).

Brainstorming is a simple technique of quickly generating a long list of creative ideas. To obtain maximum benefit from this idea-generating process, break your participants into groups of five to eight individuals, and:

1. Appoint a neutral group leader to facilitate the process (encouraging and prodding other members, checking the time).
2. Appoint a recorder.
3. Set a time limit (ten minutes will be plenty).
4. State one question or problem (e.g., reducing student dropouts, increasing attendance, keeping pregnant teenagers in school, increasing student interest in certain subject areas).
5. Ask group members to generate and present as many answers or possible solutions to the problem as possible, within a time limit.
6. Encourage group members to "piggyback" on each other's ideas (suggesting a new idea that adds to one already given).
7. Record all answers; combining those that are similar.

Note: One crucial rule of brainstorming is to avoid any evaluation or discussion of ideas until the process is over.

An important rule in brainstorming is that the recorder can ask to have an idea repeated, but should allow no comments by others (e.g., "We can't do that!" or "That's stupid!").

Brainstorming/Wish List Summary Form for
Proposed Project

This worksheet could be subtitled "Pre-proposal Summary." When you have ideas you would like funded, project directors can fill out "Idea Summary Forms," rather than write full-scale proposals. These forms can then be discussed by a "Proposal Review Committee," staff, or the administrators, and returned for modification.

There are many benefits to this:

- Projects can be quickly summarized; *more ideas* for projects are generated.

- The increase in the number of ideas lends itself to an *increase in the number of fundable projects.*

- There is a *greater chance of combining two or three good ideas into one "great" one.*

- Because project designers have not invested a great deal of time in writing a proposal for their idea, they are less *defensive when their project summary is criticized or modified;* subsequent improvements are therefore easier to make.

Many organizations find it useful to copy this form in bulk on both sides of one sheet of paper, and then distribute copies to their staff. This can be of benefit when proposals must be approved before they can be written. This sheet also has the advantage of becoming a valuable way of coordinating contact with funding sources. Many grant-seeking organizations find themselves unknowingly discredited by unauthorized staff contact with funding sources. While these contacts are usually made by zealous, well-intentioned staff members, the mistakes staff may make and the first impression they may leave are a potentially indelible source of embarassment.

This form can be used to insure that the individuals who are required to sign your proposal at submittal time know (in advance) that the proposed project is coming.

I recommend that you have your key people (person) make comments concerning areas they question or object to in the right-

PRE-PROPOSAL REVIEW AND APPROVAL FORM

PROBLEM AREA: A POSSIBLE SOLUTION IS:	COMMENTS

Resources Needed (approximately)
 	
1. Total Estimated Dollar Cost: $_____
 	
2. Matching or Inkind Commitment: $_____
 	
3. Estimated Time Needed For Proposal Process: _____
    Pre-proposal Date _____
    Contacting Funders (completed B) ___:_____
    Proposal Submission _____
    Project Start-up _____
 	
4. Individuals in Charge: (Project Director)
    _____
 	
    Co-workers _____
 	
    _____
 	
5. How Does This Project Relate To The Mission Or
    Goal Of Agency:
    _____
 	
    _____
 	
SUMMARIZE:
 	
    Objectives:
 	
    Methods:	

PRE–PROPOSAL REVIEW AND APPROVAL FORM (Cont.)

PROBLEM AREA: A POSSIBLE SOLUTION IS:	COMMENTS

Estimate Non–Personnel Resources Needed:
 	
Travel: _____
 	
Supplies: _____
 	
Printing: _____
 	
Equipment: _____
 	
Other: _____
 	
6.   Estimated Equipment Costs: $_____
 	
7.   Facilities Needed: _____
 	
     Square Feet: _____
 	
     Desired Location: _____
 	
     Special Considerations: _____
 	
     _____
 	
     _____
 	
     _____
 	
8. Project Personnel Needed: _____	

Title	Salary Range	Name (if known)	

hand margin of the form. Then have them initial the form—giving their consent or approval to proceed. This insures that the time, money, and resources spent in the proposal-preparation process will not be met with a negative response and result in a failure to have your proposal signed when it is completed.

This process allows your decision makers to comment on:

- Matching funds commitment;

- Space and resource allocations;

- Coordination of contact and use of funding sources;

- Organizational mission, etc.

The explanation of how this project relates to the mission or purpose of your organization is of critical importance. Funding sources are wary of groups that write proposals simply to "get" money. It may be advisable to review the chapter on "Case Statement." Several organizations give prospective grant seekers a copy of the "Case Statement" or mission statement when they distribute a pre-proposal review form.

Cost/Benefit Analysis Worksheet

An important aspect of any fundable idea is its economic feasibility. Funding sources want to know that you've chosen methods that will produce the best results for the least amount of money. The cost/benefit analysis worksheet will assist you in demonstrating economic accountability.

Column One. Complete this column with brief descriptions of each method you are considering. For example, a project to feed senior citizens could range from a meals-on-wheels program, to congregate feeding, to a food cooperative for the elderly. Choose two or three possible approaches that will fulfill the goals of the project.

Column Two. Record here the estimated price or cost of each idea or set of methods. This figure will be found on your Pre-Proposal Review and Approval Form.

COST/BENEFIT ANALYSIS WORKSHEET

1. SUMMARY OF IDEA AND METHODOLOGY	2. COST	3. # OF PERSONS SERVED	4. COST PERSONS SERVED	5. POSITIVE POINTS	6. NEGATIVE POINTS	7. RATING

14

Column Three. Utilize this column to estimate the number of individuals, persons, or clients who will be affected by a particular methodology (idea or approach).

Column Four. Enter the estimated cost per person or client served. This is essential, since funding sources are wary about sponsoring projects that possess an unrealistic cost per individual served. Projects with a high cost per person have great difficulty securing funding and are considered a waste of money by many funders.

Column Five. This column provides the opportunity to summarize the advantages of each idea of set of methods. This approach has resulted in funders considering the support of a more costly approach because the advantages outweigh the expense.

Column Six. In this column, the disadvantages or drawbacks to each approach can be highlighted. This increases your credibility with the funder, as you develop their confidence in your honesty.

Column Seven. The seventh column is used to rate each approach. Your objective is to present the problem and several alternative solutions while allowing the funding source to:

- Feel confident that you have analyzed the situation carefully.

- Observe your flexibility and see the pros and cons of each approach.

- Make a choice of the approach they favor (now you have the advantage of writing the approach the funding source agrees to).

You should use this worksheet each time you refine your project ideas. You can also bring a completed "Cost/Benefit Analysis Worksheets" to preliminary meetings with funding officials. They will be impressed by the fact that you considered their financial interest while designing your project.

Remember that many grant officials are executives of profit-making companies. They're very sensitive to cost-efficiency in all investments they make. Take this into account when refining your project ideas; it will help you win more grant funds.

CHAPTER 3

Redefining Proposal Ideas To Find More Funding Sources

Most grant seekers have a myopic view of their proposal idea. They define the idea in a narrow perspective—like looking at the world with tunnel vision. They fail to see that their project can be related to many funders. To expand your funding horizons, think of the project in as many ways as possible to uncover potential funding sources that may not be obvious when you look at only one way of defining the project.

Look at the project from at least four perspectives or categories and analyze possible connections to the project:

1. *Subject Areas,* the most common perspective: Does the project deal with education, labor, etc.?
2. *Constituency Group:* What type of constituency or target groups could benefit from the project?
3. *Type of Grant:* Can you do a pilot project instead of a needs assessment?
4. *Project Location:* How you define the geographic boundaries of the project affects the funding sources greatly.

REDEFINING YOUR PROJECT

PROJECT:

Education

_____ Elementary and Secondary   _____ Vocational

_____ College   _____ Continuing

_____ Adult   _____ Other:

Relationship/Connection to your project:

Humanities

_____ Art   _____ Opera

_____ Museum   _____ Theater

_____ Music   _____ Other:

Relationship/Connection to your project:

REDEFINING YOUR PROJECT (Cont.)

PROJECT:

Sciences

_____ Physical Science - astronomy and space,
          earth science _____

_____ Life Science - nutrition, environmental,
          agriculture _____

_____ Social Sciences - anthropology, sociology

_____ Business - labor, unions, management

Relation/Connection to your project:

Constituency Groups

_____ Youth   _____ Other:

_____ Women   _____

_____ Handicapped   _____

_____ Native American   _____

_____ Blacks   _____

_____ Hispanics   _____

_____ Orientals   _____

_____ Elderly   _____

Relation/Connection to your project:

REDEFINING YOUR PROJECT (Cont.)	
TYPE OF GRANT - Look at these kinds of grants and check any that may be useful in funding all or part of your project.	EXPLAIN RELATION/CONNECTION OF YOUR PROJECT - How can you use this type of funding?
_____ Block - Federal funds to state agencies. _____ Research - What parts of your grant can be defined as pure or applied research. _____ Consortium - Team up with another organization in your field. _____ Construction - Bricks and mortar. _____ Continuing Education - Will this project and results be useful to a college as Continuing Education?	_____ Demonstration - Proving or demonstrating a new approach or method. _____ Discretionary - Some funding sources have funds to use at their discretion if you show them a reason to fund. _____ Planning - Can your project be more successful if you get a grant to plan an approach to the problem? _____ Training - Does your project have components that call for education/training of participants, staff, volunteers? _____ Equipment - What types/kinds and amount of equipment will be needed. _____ Other
PROJECT LOCATION - Many funders are interested in your project as it relates to their geographical interests.	EXPLAIN RELATION/CONNECTION TO YOUR PROJECT
_____ City - Community Foundations, etc.: City Government _____ Community-wide - Corporate and Special Interest Foundations; County Government. _____ County - Borough	_____ State - State Governments Sources; Block Grant From Federal Level _____ Regional - Federal and State Regional Commission/ Offices _____ National - Federal Sources and Foundations and Corporations with national scope.

Carefully examine each of these categories. Each time you discover another way to look at the project, you will have uncovered additional funding sources that may become interested in your project.

In viewing the worksheets, check the subcategories that might apply to the project and use the accompanying work space for notes.

The final step is explaining the connection or relationship to the project. There is space on the worksheet for this activity.

CHAPTER 4

Needs Assessment

This section is vital to your decision to proceed and invest your time and effort into developing this proposal any further. Most grant writers make statements like, "Everyone knows the need for—!"

The needs assessment is critical to your ability to create a motivating and interesting proposal. Many grant seekers place undue emphasis on the development of the methodology, or how you will solve the problem.

First, a funding source must clearly see that there is a *pressing problem or need that must be addressed.* The needs-assessment section (pp. 22–25) will provide the back-up for the development of a convincing and motivating needs statement in a final proposal.

At this point, you make a copy of any pertinent article, study, quote, or statistic that is related to the problem area you will address. Developing the needs assessment is analogous to a lawyer developing background information for a case. This information will be reviewed and certain data selected for use. A good lawyer will select from this data base the information that will sway a particular jury toward his or her side of the argument.

The purpose of the needs assessment is to provide you with a command of the facts to document the need. You will select infor-

NEEDS ASSESSMENT

TYPE OF APPROACH	ADVANTAGES	DISADVANTAGES
1. Key Informant – Solicit information from individuals whose testimony or description of what exists for the client population or state-of-affairs is credible – either by their position in the community or through their experience and/or expertise. Includes: elected officials, agency heads (police chiefs, juvenile delinquency, parole officers, etc.). Funders may value their opinions/insights.	○ easy to design ○ costs very little ○ you control input by what you ask and whom you ask and whom ○ excellent way to position your organization with important people (shows you're working on common problem/concern)	○ Most funding sources know you have selected and included comments of those individuals sympathetic to your cause. You may be leaving out parts of the population who have not been visible and caused problems that were noticed, commented on.
2. Community Forum – Host or sponsor public meetings. You publicize the opportunity to present views of populace. You also invite key individuals to speak. Funder may like the grass roots image this creates.	○ easy to arrange ○ costs very little ○ increases your visibility in the community ○ promotes active involvement of the populace	○ Site of forum has proformed effect on number and type of representation. ○ You can lose control of the group and have a small vocal minority slant results or turn meeting into a forum for complaints.

NEEDS ASSESSMENT (Cont.)

TYPE OF APPROACH	ADVANTAGES	DISADVANTAGES
3. Case Studies/Examples – An excellent approach to assist the funder in appreciating what representative members of the client population are up against. Select individuals from the needs population or client group and provide analytical, realistic description of their problem/situation, their use of your services, need for them, etc.	° easy to arrange ° costs very little ° increases sensitivity to the client's "real world" ° very moving and motivating	° Your selection of a "typical" client may be biased and represent a minority of cases. ° You must describe one "real" person – not a composite of several put into one "example." The anonymity of the person must be insured.
4. Statistical Analysis – Most funders like to see a few well chosen statistics. With this approach, you utilize existing data: ° census data/records ° Govt. studies/reports ° reports and research articles to develop a statistical picture of the needs population	° there is an abundance of studies and data ° little cost to access data ° allows for flexibility in drawing and developing conclusions ° analysis of data is catalytic in producing more projects and proposals as staff "sees" the need	° can be very time-consuming ° bias of staff show up in studies quoted ° feelings on funder's part that you can prove anything with statistics ° if original data has questionable validity, your extrapolation will be inaccurate.

NEEDS ASSESSMENT (Cont.)

TYPE OF APPROACH	ADVANTAGES	DISADVANTAGES
5. Survey – Very commonly used approach to gathering data on the needs popula- tion, this approach has usefulness even when the survey is carried out with volunteers and with limited statistical validity. Accurate surveys may entail control groups, establishing random samples, and use of computers and statistical analysis. However, acknowledgment by you that the results of your survey cannot be extrapolated beyond the sample group will prove more than adequate in most situations.	° high credibility with funders ° excellent flexibility in design of survey to get at problem areas and document exactly what you want to document	° takes time to do survey properly

NEEDS ASSESSMENT WORKSHEET

WHAT INFORMATION DO WE NEED TO DOCUMENT THE PROBLEM?	WHICH APPROACHES TO NEEDS ASSESSMENTS ARE BEST FOR US AND/OR PREFERRED BY FUNDER:				
	KEY INFORMANT: _____ COMMUNITY FORUM: _____ CASE STUDIES: _____ SOCIAL INDICATORS: _____ SURVEY: _____				
DATA TO BE GATHERED	HOW IT WILL BE GATHERED	WHO WILL DO IT	DATE DUE	COST	CONSORTIUM AGENCIES INVOLVED

mation from this data base that is necessary to develop a needs statement depending on the known viewpoints and biases of those who will read and act on the proposal.

The key to needs assessment is *choosing the approach*. There are five basic needs-assessment approaches:

1. *Key Informant:* testimony from people who know about the problem.
2. *Community Forum:* public meetings to get testimony on the problem.
3. *Case Studies:* example of clients in a need population.
4. *Social Indicators:* use of data from public records to depict need.
5. *Survey:* random selection of population to answer questions related to need.

The worksheets on the previous pages will help you decide which one to adopt for your organization. Information is provided for each approach, followed by some questions to assist you in choosing the best one.

It will enhance your "fundability" or ability to attract funds for this project if you provide the funding source with well-documented needs for the project.

The needs assessment should be done prior to contacting the funding source or writing the proposal.

The information from your needs assessment should provide an accurate and compelling need that must be addressed. Most proposals lack "urgency," they sound like, "If you can't afford to fund the project this year, how about next year?" The urgency is reflective of the immediacy of the need. The funding source should feel that they must fund the project now, or things will be worse by next year.

Take a few minutes to look at the various types of needs assessments to determine the approach that is right for you. You may decide that you need to write a small grant first to fund the needs assessment. This is made easier by telling the funding source that they will be ultimately responsible for all the funds that result from this excellent needs statement that will attract other funders in a final proposal.

Please note that some funding sources do not talk about needs, but refer to a search of literature in the field, or review of related literature or studies. These are a form of approach #4, social indicators. The key here is to do a thorough search of studies so that you appear to be the "expert." There are several computerized searching tools you can review in the research section. You must use the most recent studies to show you have "state-of-the-art" knowledge.

One problem encountered in this review of studies is that of causing dissonance in the funding source or the individual they hire to review your proposal by citing researchers you prefer or feel are the most influential in the field, when they favor some other researcher.

CHAPTER 5

Capitalizing on Your Differences

Many grant seekers forget that the funding source has to choose among many prospective grantees and that the successful grantee must *stand out* from the rest of the competition. How can you increase your ability to project an image that puts you "a cut above the rest"?

One method is to show the funding source that you are different from "the crowd." You are the logical choice to fund because you are *different* from others in your field. Your differences, or uniqueness, make you the logical choice for investment of their grant dollars.

Many of our seminar participants have a great deal of trouble here. They respond with "I'm just another college, hospital, association for _____." This is generally not true. Examine what you do that is different from the others; your staff, location, building, special areas of interest, and the like. You could make being similar to many others a uniqueness by explaining that you are uniquely suited for funding because:

- We are similar in make-up to *x* percent of the others in the United States;

- A pilot project done here could be replicated in other similar organizations in the United States.

These are rather weak uniquenesses. A little time spent on this chapter and its exercises for developing a list of those special qualities that your organization can capitalize upon will be a very worthwhile investment.

Keep the information you develop here in your Proposal Development Workbook (Swiss Cheese Book). It will then be ready when needed in writing letters or proposals, and in making personal contacts.

In order to be prepared with answers to the question, "Why should we give the money to your organization instead of another in your field?," brainstorm a list of responses to the question. Use the following activity to add a little excitement and flavor to a staff meeting, board meeting, or with a volunteer group or advisory committee.

The Uniqueness Exercise

This exercise will result in:

- A list of those factors that make your organization unique.

- The ability to select those uniquenesses that have particular appeal to a funding source.

- A staff that refocuses on your unique qualities, placing you above the "others."

This exercise can be successful with a variety of groups. It is especially useful to do this with:

- staff

- volunteers

- clients

- board members

Exchanging the lists among the groups will develop more unique characteristics.

EXERCISE INSTRUCTIONS

1. Give the group Sheet A (p. 31); remind the group of the rules for brainstorming from Chapter 2; set a time limit for brainstorming. Use Question 1 or 2 and record the answer.

2. Combine the answers to Question 1 or 2 provided by individuals and/or groups.

3. Ask each person to look at the list and:

- rank-order their preferences 1 to _____?

- give each individual ten points and request them to allocate their ten points over the entire list; this will produce a weighted list.

Use your completed list to select uniquenesses that will convince a funder that their money will go farther with you. For example:

- Your staff has _____ years' experience.
- Your buildings are centrally located.
- Special equipment is available.
- Your needs population and geographics are broad.

In addition to use in the grants area, your uniquenesses are valuable in:

- training and recruiting staff, board members, and volunteers;
- developing case statements (Chapter 6);
- direct mail, wills and bequests, other fund-raising techniques.

SHEET A: OUR UNIQUENESSES

Our organization has many unique qualities. These positive qualities can be utilized to convince a funding source that they are investing in the right individuals when they grant your organization money.

This exercise will result in a combined list of qualities that make you stand out from the competition for grant funds. Your leader will tell you when to begin recording your responses to Question 1.

Question 1: *What makes our organization/college good at what we do?*

Question 2: *Why will a funding source (donor) give a grant to us instead of some other organization in our field (what makes us a good investment—what are the advantages of funding us)?*

CHAPTER 6

Your Case Statement

Your case statement, or mission statement, is a key ingredient in presenting your case for funding or in the awarding of a grant to your organization. When you present your application for funding, your approach is that:

- There is a compelling need.

- Your organization is uniquely suited to carry out the project.

- It is your purpose or mission to carry out this project—verified by your "case statement."

The case statement provides the funding source with written documentation that the purpose (reason to exist) of your organization and this project are a perfect match.

Your case statement consists of:

1. *How and why your organization got started*—(what social problems or reasons for starting existed). *Note:* societal need today is more valuable than number of years you've existed. One funding source remarked to me that the organizations she had the greatest doubts about were those that have been around a long

WORKSHEET

1. How and Why Your Organization Got Started.

   Year _____ Prime Movers/Founders _____

   Societal Need: _____

   _____

2. Today – Changes From Original Mission: _____

   _____

   Societal Need Changes: _____

   _____

   Current Priorities: _____

   _____

   Clients: _____

   Staff: _____

   Buildings: _____

3. <u>Future</u>: Where Will Your Organization Be Five Years From Now? Change
   in Mission: _____

   _____

   Changes in Need: _____

   _____

   Changes in Facilities and Staff: _____

   _____

4. <u>Optional</u> – What Opportunities Exist or Will Exist To Move You Toward
   Your Plans/Goals.

   A. _____

   B. _____

   C. _____

time. She felt that they generally were bureaucratic, had a tendency to lose sight of their mission or purpose, and generally had more "dead wood" on the payroll.

2. *What is your organization doing today?* Have you deviated from the past? Why? What effect has the passage of time had on

your mission and reason for being? What are the current priorities, programs, clients, staff, buildings, and uniquenesses (Chapter 5)?

3. *Where are you going in the future?* What is your five-year plan? Ten-year plan? Or longer, if you have one? Since funding sources are investing in you, they want their project to be placed with a winner who will still be around when the funding runs out.

Show the funding source that you are worthy of funding and that the project that they have invested in will continue to benefit people due to your long-range planning and ability to secure future funding to carry on.

The worksheet on page 33 is designed to assist you in determining the factors that should be included in your case statement. If you already have a case statement, review it to see if you can update or tailor the statement for the grants marketplace.

If you have a ten-page mission statement, use this worksheet to edit it and reduce it to one concise page.

CHAPTER 7

Advocates

How to Use Them

The politics of grant seeking is a fascinating area that spells M-O-N-E-Y for those that master the art and develop their political skills. Do not be frightened! The politics of grant seeking is understandable and can be an organized process.

Many people develop a sick feeling in the pit of their stomach when the word politics is used, so we will use the term *advocates.* Those people who know your organization and identify with your cause, mission, or your staff need to know how they can be of service to you. *They can always say no!*

This chapter suggests that you consider exploring the area of advocacy and how you can help people help you. The worksheets develop a systematic approach so that you know who your contacts are. You may find that there are supporters you did not even realize you knew.

You will develop a list of the people you can utilize as advocates. This list will be valuable since you can then select people to:

- write endorsement letters (see worksheet, p. 40);

- talk to funding sources for you; set up appointments;

- utilize advocates' expertise (finance, marketing, etc.);
- accompany you to meet with potential funders.

Use the worksheets below to increase your advocacy potential. Several organizations have placed the results of this process on a microprocessor. When a potential funding source is located through research, the data base is consulted to see if you have any advocates who know the funding source. There may be:

- members on both your organization's and the funding source's boards;
- an advocate who can get you "in" to talk to funder;
- an advocate who could write a letter to a "friend" on the board.

One successful method in using your advocates is to divide them into two major categories:

- *Inside your organization:* Employees, board of trustees, advisory committee members, volunteers, former staff, former clients, and the like.
- *Outside your organization:* Associations and groups you belong to, experts in the field, politicians, religious leaders, community leaders, and so forth.

Next, using those individuals who are inside your organization, follow these steps:
1. Pass out the advocacy worksheet (see p. 37) to the individuals you have identified (this may be done in a group or individually).
2. Read the section explaining how the information they provide will be used; you will have better results.
Note: Several organizations have had very good results when introducing this advocacy concept attached to a major project of the organization that has widespread support. It may be necessary to list several of your most logical funding sources and ask the clear question:

Do you know any of these funding executives or board members?

LIST: _____

_____

_____

3. Record the information in your computer and/or files.
4. When a match between a potential funder and an advocate is made, call your contact person and discuss the possibility of having him or her help you in meeting the funding source or board member/trustee.

When you locate a funding contact using the Webbing Form (p. 38) ask the person completing the form to set up an appointment for you with the funder, through the contact. If appropriate, ask the person making the appointment if he or she can come with you to the meeting. This will add credibility to your presentation.

Keep all returned forms on file and update periodically. This is a good activity for volunteers to handle. Expand your advocates and you expand your universe of potential funders with whom you are able to communicate. Bauer Associates has available an inexpensive computer program for your microprocessor that allows for storing and using this information. Care must be taken to safeguard this information. Through use of a small, personal computer, you can safeguard the program and data by performing your own security. Make a copy and store it in a safe place.

Use of larger central computing facilities greatly reduces security. *Remember:* you are storing personal information that is *privileged,* and you must not allow any access to it, or you violate your advocate's trust.

Use the Advocate Planning Sheet on p. 39.

Draft of Possible Advocacy Worksheet

We are requesting your assistance in completing this survey of potential ways that you may wish to assist _____ in continuing our mission to _____. In particular, our organization's ability to attract grants from funding sources is increased by 300 percent

POSSIBLE WEBBING FORM

YOUR NAME: PHONE #:

ADDRESS:

1. What foundation or corporation boards are you or your spouse on?

2. Do you know anyone who is on a foundation or corporation board?

3. Does your spouse know anyone on a foundation or corporation board?

4. Do you know any government funding contacts? (Have you served on any
    government committees?)

5. Have you ever helped a not-for-profit organization get a grant? (Who
    and When?)

                NOTE: It is optional to ask for personal data.

6. Fraternal groups, social clubs, service organizations that you are
    involved in.

Other questions you may ask include: educational background, military
background, religious affiliation, political preference, job title and
description, and information on ability to travel for business.

(greatly) if we can talk informally with a funding official (or board
member) before we submit a formal proposal.

We are asking you to help us identify those linkages that you
may have with a potential funding source. If our research indicates that a funding source you have identified has a record of

ADVOCATE PLANNING SHEET

PROJECT TITLE: _____ PROJECT DIRECTOR: _____

Select from this list the ways to utilize advocates that will advance this project.

° Endorsement Letters   ° Set up your appointment
° Testimonials   ° Accompany you to see funding source
° Letters of Introduction   ° Go see funder for you

TECHNIQUES FOR THIS PROJECT	ADVOCATE TO BE USED	WHO WILL CONTACT ADVOCATE AND WHEN	DESIRED OUTCOME	DATE COMPLETED

providing grant support for one of (your organization's) projects we would:

• Contact you and explain the project.

• Discuss how you could assist us, for example:
  a. by writing an endorsement letter,
  b. in getting to talk to the funder.

• Have your complete approval before any action was taken.

This information is critical to allow us to utilize every advantage we can find in this very competitive marketplace. A simple phone call can result in our proposal actually being read, not left in a pile. In considering our need, remember our pledge to never use your name or linkage without your consent.

These linkages are worth hundreds of thousands of dollars each year from foundations, corporations, and the government.

Thank you for your cooperation.

Endorsement Letter Worksheet

An advocate may not provide you with a useful endorsement letter unless they know what you are looking for. A well-intentioned endorsement that focuses on the wrong aspects of your project causes turmoil because:

- You may not be able to include the endorsement in your proposal, which may prove embarrassing.

- It is difficult to correct the letter, return it with comments, and ask for another.

To avoid these problems, give the advocate a basic summary or outline of what "they" might consider including.

Note: put in any pertinent facts or statistics, and once they are stated in the endorsement letter, they are a fact that you can quote (e.g., using your program graduates has increased services by 20 percent with no increase in cost).

Include:

- Facts/statistics.
- Length of time they have worked with you (number of hours, awards earned).
- Summary of their committee work and their major accomplishments (give away any credit you can).

The advocate should be able to retype and sign the "outline."

Be sure to include the advocates' addresses and any instructions that the funding source may require.

CHAPTER 8

Advisory Committees

HOW TO DEVELOP
COMMUNITY SUPPORT

Some funding sources require that you demonstrate community support for your proposal. The funding source may want to see this support in the form of advisory committees, resolutions, and minutes of meetings or letters of endorsement.

The following worksheets are designed for you to review as you consider community support and how it will increase your fundability.

By using your Proposal Development Workbook (Chapter 1) for community support, you can put together an advisory committee and benefit from their input on brainstorming project ideas, needs-assessment techniques, letters of endorsement, and other helpful tasks. Many grant writers start the process of applying for a grant so near the deadline date that advisory committees are a token and, in most cases, never meet or provide input. It is not uncommon for funding-source representatives to ask to meet with committee members when they arrive for a site visit. By utilizing the Swiss Cheese Concept, you can deal creatively with this area of community support and have *legitimate* minutes of *actual* meetings with your committee.

41

HOW TO DEVELOP COMMUNITY SUPPORT

PROJECT TITLE: _____ PROJECT DIRECTOR: _____

_____ DATE: _____

#	TECHNIQUES	APPLICABILITY TO THIS PROJECT	WHO WILL CALL MEETING	MEMBERS OF COMMITTEE	DATES
1	ADVISORY COMMITTEE brainstorm uniquenesses of your organization (chapter 5)				
2	ADVISORY COMMITTEE work on setting up needs assessment (brings them closer and more aware of the need, more commitment)				
3	Use your ADVISORY COMMITTEE to brainstorm your project ideas				

HOW TO DEVELOP COMMUNITY SUPPORT (Cont.)

#	TECHNIQUES	APPLICABILITY TO THIS PROJECT	WHO WILL CALL MEETING	MEMBERS OF COMMITTEE	DATES
4	Use your committee to develop a public relations package and produce it (printers, media representative) NEWSPAPER COVERAGE for your organization -- press releases, interviews, etc. RADIO - TELEVISION COVERAGE public-service announcements on talk shows, etc.				
5	Have an artist perform or an open house for key people* in the community				

*Public officials, Congresspeople, potential advocates, and others.

CHAPTER 9

Choosing the Correct Marketplace

Many prospective and oftentimes overzealous grant seekers launch their research efforts too quickly. The approach that maximizes your grants potential requires the kind of planning that is described in the preceding chapters. Developing funding that will promote a professional image for your organization requires an approach to researching funding sources that:

- Is based upon a win-win attitude. Your research must provide the depth of information so that you know your project meets the funding soruce's needs (values) while moving your organization ahead toward meeting its mission and providing benefits to people (clients); the funder wins; your organization wins; and your clients win.

- Provides you with the confidence to present yourself as worthy of funding. You will have done your research "homework." You will have taken the time to find the "right" funder. The funder will see that you are confident and hear it in your voice.

You are not going to send a mass-produced copy of a proposal to hundreds of funding sources. You will have a tailored approach based on your research.

To locate funding sources that are interested in you and your proposal idea, compare your project to the funding source's interests. Different types of categories of funding sources have *distinct funding characteristics.*

After your project has been redefined, you can begin to narrow down the search for the correct funding source. How do you know where to go, which type of funding source is the "right" one to approach? Since we know that certain factors predetermine how a funding source will "view the world," you must match or compare your proposal idea with those likely to be thought of by the funding source as *outstanding*—"just what they are looking for."

Look at each of the following types of marketplaces for your grant/contract before you spend time researching individual funding sources.

General Grants Marketplace Information

I have administered a grants marketplace quiz as a pre-test assessment instrument to over seven thousand grantseekers who have attended Bauer Associates' training seminars since 1975. These grantseekers were not randomly selected or representative of *all* grantseekers. They varied widely in grants expertise and background. What is interesting and surprising is that the guesses to the quiz are less accurate today than they were in 1975. Why is this, when today's grantseekers are exposed to an influx of information about grants and funding sources through the general media, professional journals, newsletters, and conferences? It is my supposition that news sources may, in fact, be the contributing factor to the current misconceptions in the grants marketplace.

Grantseekers and those whom they work for read publications that make announcements concerning non-profit groups that attract above average grants. The awards that make the news are usually "exceptions to the rules." Unfortunately, however, they are often interpreted by well meaning, motivated grantseekers as the "norm" and are used to shape their views of the marketplace. Judging the marketplace by what makes the headlines inflates conceptions concerning grant giving and decreases one's expectations of some funding categories, while increasing others.

In the late 1970s the Filer Commission Report estimated that government grant support was equal to support from private philanthropy (about 40 billion dollars each). Since that time, the marketplace has experienced many changes.

- The federal government reduced its total grants contribution to non-profit organizations to an estimated 1987 level of 30 billion. This is a 10 billion decrease.

- Private philanthropy has grown from the 1979 level of 43.69 billion to a 1986 level of 87.22 billion.

This dramatic shift in funding for non-profit organizations has resulted in confusion and the development of grants and fund-raising strategies that are founded on misconceptions, rather than facts. Private philanthropic support of non-profit organizations has demonstrated a consistent pattern of growth that has survived years when inflation rose faster than giving, and others when giving was slightly higher than inflation. What is important to grantseekers is the change that has occurred, and how it affects grantseeking strategies.

- Federal funding through grants has declined from a 1980 high of 40 billion, to a 1984 low of 22–25 billion, to a 1987 level of 30 billion.

If the government grants marketplace had followed the same growth as private philanthropic giving (they were equal in 1980), there would be 80 billion in federal grants in 1987, not 30 billion. This analysis is given so that there is little misunderstanding. *The federal grants mechanism has not increased the deficit or aggravated inflation,* and is currently operating 10 billion below the 1980 level.

The decrease in government grant funding created an initial overreaction on the part of non-profit organizations. Many grantseekers only knew that government funding was cut. Therefore, the number of applications for government grants declined, even though, at its lowest level in 1984, government funds were three times the level of private philanthropy. While the private area has grown steadily, the actual percentage of private funds that are distributed through the grants mechanism has remained relatively stable, and is much less than grantseekers, or their supervisors, realize.

- The total grant marketplace for corporate and foundation grants in 1986 was 9.67 billion.

- Government grant support for non-profit organizations is 300% greater than private support.

Unfortunately, many executive directors and board members of non-profits do not know the marketplace facts. With misconceptions about the marketplace, the strategies of the grantseeker may be misdirected, and he or she may not receive the resources needed to succeed. Remember, sound grantseeking strategies reflect a knowledge of the grants marketplace.

The Government Marketplace

Seek federal funds first! The marketplace facts already presented provide the basis for this deduction.

- The federal government is the largest single grantor in the world (30 billion/year).

- Some foundations and corporations will fund only those grantseekers who have exhausted the possibility of a federal grant.

HISTORICAL PERSPECTIVE

The federal government has utilized the grants mechanism since the United States was founded. The term *land grant college* refers to the early attempts of the federal government to encourage the state to develop a system of higher education that would provide a focus for education and agriculture. The federal government developed much of its current role as a grantor during the post Korean War period. The Russian accomplishment in space, Sputnik, encouraged the government to make grants available to foster education and research.

The government grants mechanism as we know it increased in usage with the Kennedy and Johnson administrations. Most grants under their "New Frontier" and "Great Society" programs were administered on the federal level. Early programs were of the project-grant type and followed a categorical funding pattern (explanation to follow).

When national concern looked to the social issues of the 1960s, the grants mechanism was employed to encourage research and develop model projects that dealt with the disadvantaged, elderly, minority groups, handicapped, etc. The 1970s saw the grants mechanism utilized to make advances in health care, and to address problems such as drug and alcohol abuse, smoking, cancer, etc.

In the 1970s, however, there began a growing trend toward local and regional distribution of federal government grant dollars. This "New Federalism" or "Revenue Sharing" indicated a trend away from categorical grants to formula and block grants (explanation to follow). The election of Ronald Reagan heightened this trend.

The Reagan administration signaled a decline in government involvement in utilizing the grants mechanism for initiating, directing and sustaining change in American society.

First, the administration called for a reduction of 40 billion dollars in domestic grants. Although there were repeated attempts to accomplish the virtual elimination of grants altogether, Congress did not allow cuts below the 20 to 22 billion dollar level. However, grant funds were cut almost in half.

Second, the Reagan administration attacked the categorical-grants funding mechanism. The administration's philosophy of "the government governs best which governs least" could not support a federally controlled system of categories and project areas controlled by Washington bureaucrats. Instead, the Reagan administration capitalized on "New Federalism" concepts and growing conservatism to institute the most dramatic change in the grants mechanism in U.S. history, the block grant (explanation to follow).

PROJECT GRANTS AND CATEGORICAL GRANTS

These grant opportunities are designed to promote proposals within defined areas of interest. They address a specific area with which a federal program is concerned, for example, drug-abuse prevention, nutrition education for the elderly, or research on certain types of idsease. The government decides what problems need to be corrected and you, the prospective grantee, design an approach to solve or reduce the problems.

Project grants are given out by various agencies under congressionally authorized programs. Grants are awarded to the organizations that submit the best proposals that meet announced program guidelines. Most programs require outside review panels to evaluate the project. Because project design is left to the grant seekers, this has been the most popular kind of government grant. Since these grants fall under definite categories for funding, a whole series of categorical grants developed, with each grant category having its own federal office to administer it.

Government funding agencies using the categorical and project grants approach require grant seekers to fill out long, standardized applications. This makes it difficult, but not impossible, to tailor proposal contents to the needs of the granting agency. These applications differ in format from agency to agency, and are generally tedious, complicated, and time consuming. Once they are submitted, there is generally a long review process, staff review for mechanical details, and peer review of proposal content. Project and categorical grants require frequent reports and accurate project records.

FORMULA GRANTS

The term "formula grants" refers to granting programs under which funds are allocated according to a set of criteria (formula).

This mechanism has been used to infuse money into the economy; CETA (Comprehensive Employment Training Act) and the 1983 "jobs bill" are examples.

Criteria for allocation may be census data, unemployment figures, number of handicapped, veterans, and the like, that a state, city, or region may have. The formula grants programs are generally area-specific such as the nursing capitation grants of the 1970s. Each cap or head in a specific program is counted in the formula and the allocation is divided accordingly.

The funds may go through an intermediary, such as a state, city or county government, before reaching the nonprofit groups. The formula grants mechanism is another example of the "New Federalism" that started developing in the early 1970s. While the general rules are developed at the federal level, the rules can be interpreted, and local input can considerably alter the federal program. The concept of local control and input into how federal funds should be spent resulted in mandated review by local political panels to insure that the programs that groups applied to the federal government for were desired at the local level (an extension of the Federalism concept).

BLOCK GRANTS

The block-grant concept was founded on the premise that it was not the purview of the federal government to force the states to follow categorical grant program priorities. The categorical programs were "blocked" or synthesized into groups of related programs and the funds sent to the states for them to "grant" to those areas and projects that the states gave priority to.

The "block grant" movement caused mass confusion in the grants world as grant seekers had to figure out who had the funds and what would be funded. In most cases, the states received more decision-making power but less money than they did under categorical grants. The block grant mechanism allowed the federal government to reduce staff formerly used to administer programs, but elimination of staff was hampered by the fact that many grant programs had a research component that could not be handed over to the states. The federal government was fored to direct the research component to avoid duplication and to coordinate research. The year 1986 marked the decline of the "block grant" mania of the early Reagan years and witnessed the return of categorical funding mechanisms.

Virtually all of the new grant programs introduced in 1986–1987 were categorical grants, and most grant experts agree that this trend will continue.

CONTRACTS

In recent years the differences between a grant and a contract have become harder to discern. Indeed, after hours of negotiation with a Federal Agency on your grant, you may end up with a contract officer with whom you have to finalize your budget. The basic difference between a grant and a contract is that a contract tells you precisely what the government wants done and you bid on accomplishing the task. You must prove that you have the ability to perform the contract at an acceptable price. There is decidedly less flexibility in creating the approach to the problem or work tasks with a contract than there is with a grant.

Contracts are publicized or advertised in a different way from grants. They are governed by different rules, and are awarded on a lowest-bid basis from those contractors deemed qualified to do the specified work.

The contracts "game" requires a track record and expertise. The best way to break into this marketplace is to identify a successful bidder to approach as a possible subcontractor. This way, you gain experience, confidence, and contacts.

The statistics quoted in this chapter *do not* include the government contracts monies. The variety and number of government contracts are staggering. The amount of money that the government spends on contracts stretches the imagination. Recent exposés on the thousand-dollar-part that can be purchased in a hardware store for fifty cents are an indication of the problems of administering the contract estimates and the contractors.

There are several types of contracts, including fixed cost, cost reimbursable, and those that allow the contractor to add on additional costs incurred during the contract. Contracts have been increasingly pursued by nonprofit groups in recent years. The problems that nonprofits encounter in bidding on contracts have been reduced through developing separate profit and nonprofit agencies to avoid problems of security agreements, academic freedom, patent, copyrights, and the like.

Shifts in funds away from domestic grant programs and large increases in Defense Department budgets have led many non-profits to begin contracting in the defense area to pursue many of their programs and research. This is a task for the experienced grantseeker only.

STATE GOVERNMENT GRANTS

Federal block grants to states place grant funds closer to you, require less long distance travel, and allow you to use your local politicians to make your case heard. These advantages are counterbalanced when you consider that states set their own priorities for the grants, add additional restrictions, and bring in to play a review system of state bureaucrats and more political appointees. (*Note:* Although states have their own monies, granting programs and rules, if state granting programs utilize block-grant monies from the federal government, the states guarantee that the eventual user of those funds will follow all federal rules, circulars, compliances, etc.)

The Foundation Marketplace

There are approximately 24,859 private foundations in the United States with 48.2 billion dollars in assets. Though these figures may seem staggering to the novice grant seeker, there is some consolation in the following:

- 8.2% of the foundations (2,038) give 56% of all grants.

- Grants payments increased by 22.3% in 1986 while the number of grants awarded increased by only 6.6%.

- The average grant size of a foundation with $20 to $100 million in assets is in the $20,000–$25,000 range.

- Only 40,000 grants for more than $5,000 were given last year by 444 foundations.

- 444 foundations granted 2 billion of the total 5.17 billion.

Therefore, a small percentage of the foundations have most of the assets and a relatively high average grant size. What about the other 20,000+ foundations? Consider: the remaining foundations have an average grant size of less than $2,000 and they award hundreds of thousands of grants each year.

Foundations increased their grant giving by 15.9% in 1986. This increase was due to the increase in foundation assets and dividends paid. Foundations must give away 5% of the market value of their assets each year. Most did not plan on the dramatic increase in stock portfolios and have a "grace" year to adjust to the 5% figure. For example, W.K. Kellogg's assets increased 91%; Danforth Foundation's assets increased 57%; and Carnegie will award an extra 10 million in grace year 1986 due to a 26.5% gain in assets in 1985.

Selecting the right foundation marketplace and requesting a logical grant size from a potential funder involve having knowledge of the types of foundations. Each type or category of foundation will be outlined with pertinent characteristics described. At the end of this chapter, you will see how this information is utilized to develop an easy-to-use funding matrix. This matrix will serve as a convenient guide to which criteria will be valued for each type of the five basic classifications of foundations:

1. Community Foundations;
2. National Foundations (multipurpose);
3. "Special-Purpose" Foundations;
4. Family Foundations;
5. Corporate Foundations.

COMMUNITY FOUNDATIONS

This group of 300 foundations represents the newest and fastest growing area in the foundation marketplace. The main purpose of community foundations is to provide a grants mechanism to address problems and areas of interest that affect the geographic area the foundation was created to serve.

These foundations have no connection with the United Way fund drives and are not in competition with their neighboring United Way organizations. Actually, community foundations are frequent grantors to agencies supported by the United Way. While both groups seek to enrich the community and address its problems, the community foundations' usual mechanism for building their funding base is to establish endowments. In this way, local citizens can leave a bequest to the community foundation that will insure that the interest from the bequest stays in the community for which the individual has a concern. This way of developing assets is very different from the United Way approach of payroll deduction, cash contribution, and corporate solicitation. Their assets are approximately 3.3 billion dollars and are growing daily. As the name implies, these foundations are primarily interested in the local needs of their communities and have been designed to promote this limited geographic area. The primary beneficiary of community-foundation grants is the health area, followed by social welfare, education, and arts and culture.

Most community foundations have been initiated by public-spirited citizens who leave money in a bequest to the foundation for specific types of local projects. Since the monies are held separately for donor interests, the majority of this group are classified as public charities. The foundation can abide by donor wishes or reflect changes in the needs and interests of the community. The community foundation's reason to exist is to deal with local need. They will fund causes that other foundations would not think of funding. If your organization's purposes relate to local need, even last year's deficit can be fundable if it means keeping you in business. You can get funding for a needs assessment. You can approach these foundations with the argument that a good needs assessment will result in attracting monies from other sources to the community. Convince the community foundation that their needs-assessment grant will be responsible for all the funds that are generated from your higher-quality proposal.

If you are not sure if there is a community foundation in your area, write:

The Council on Foundations
888 7th Avenue
New York, NY 10019

If the answer is no, get the council's book on how to start one in your area. Better than that, get a grant to start one. You will never be sorry, and your community will benefit for many years—and you gain another prospective funding source.

The five largest community foundations are:

	ASSETS	GRANTS
1. New York Community Trust	$500,000,000	$39,000,000
2. Marin Community Foundation	$430,000,000	new
3. Cleveland Foundation	$415,000,000	$18,673,500
4. Chicago Community Trust	$237,418,306	$23,396,743
5. Permanent Charity	$176,846,561	$12,188,669

(*Note:* There are several community foundations that define "community" in a variety of geographic parameters; for example, the California Foundation, Rhode Island Foundation, and Oregon Foundation use large state areas, while others may use city limits.)

NATIONAL GENERAL-PURPOSE FOUNDATIONS

When you think of foundations, the names Rockefeller Foundation and Ford Foundation usually come to mind. Although these large foundations number only a few hundred, they have two-thirds of all assets among the 24,859 foundations and account for over 50 percent of the grant dollars. Some foundations in this group have a philanthropic interest in one or more subject areas, give across the United States, and have a more general scope to their giving pattern and interests than most of the other types of foundations.

This group prefers proposals that have the potential to impact on a broader scale. They prefer model, creative, innovative projects that can demonstrate the way for other groups to replicate the approach and solve their problems. Since they like to promote change, they do not fund deficits, operating income, or the many necessary but not highly visible or creative functions of your organization.

SPECIAL-PURPOSE FOUNDATIONS

Several hundred foundations fall into the "special-purpose" category. How you define "special-purpose" could increase this number by thousands. For our definition, "special-purpose" includes those foundations whose funding record consistently supports a specific area of funding and their funding represents a significant contribution in that specific area. For example, the Robert Wood Johnson Foundation specializes in the health area. The key is to fit your group and project into the area of specialization. This group evaluates your request according to the potential impact your grant will have on its special area of interst.

FAMILY FOUNDATIONS

There are 20,000+ foundations in this category. They are hard to categorize by interests, but represent the values of family groups or members. These family members may be living or those whose interests have been memorialized by creation of a foundation. Most family foundations have geographic preferences and may act as small-scale, special-purpose foundations. Many are operated by family members who change their giving patterns and funding priorities frequently.

This group of foundations is the most susceptible to the influence of board members, their friends, and popular "causes." Your ability to link your organization to "friends" of the foundation is very important to insure that your proposal at least receives attention. Since these foundations can and do change their priorities it is helpful to have a contact who keeps you informed about the current year's funding goals.

CORPORATE FOUNDATIONS

The number of corporations that utilize a corporate foundation to administer their charitable contributions and grants programs is increasing. While exact figures are unavailable, in a 1983 Conference Board survey of 467 companies, half reported having a foundation.

While much can be said about the role that a corporate foundation plays in comparison to regular corporate giving, the fact is recognized that the ability to develop and stabilize a corporate philanthropy program is enhanced through a corporate-foundation structure. Corporate foundations have frequently donated more money than they received. The ability to utilize foundation assets in times of reduced corporate profits leads to a more uniform and stable approach to corporate social philanthropy than the "see-saw" effect of relying solely on a percentage of company profit.

Since corporate foundations are an extension of the profit-making company, they tend to view the world as any company would. Many funds grant only in areas where they have factories or a special interest in the community. The corporation must see a benefit in funding your project. Making the grant benefit the corporation, the workers, or the ability of the corporation to attract high-quality personnel to the community are some of the concerns that corporations may exhibit in making grant choices. In many cases, there is little difference between corporate giving and corporate-foundation giving. Some corporations make grants through both mechanisms.

CORPORATE PHILANTHROPY

There are over 2.3 million for-profit corporations in the United States. There are many misconceptions concerning the giving patterns of these corporations.

- Only 35% of the corporations make corporate contributions to nonprofit organizations.

- Of those that do contribute, less than 10% make grants of over $500 a year.

Careful selection of corporations is suggested to avoid the embarrassment that can be caused by asking for a grant from a corporation that has never given one, or has never granted one of the size you are requesting.

Corporations contributed 4.5 billion to nonprofit organizations in 1986. This was 2.3 percent more than in 1985. With inflation at 1.1 percent, this still represented a real increase of 1.2%. This is a marked change from the 1985 increase of 15.8%.

Corporate contributions had been forcasted to show little growth, or possibly a decline. Consider these factors:

- Corporate pre-tax income dropped by 22.5 billion from 1985 to 1986.

- *Fortune* magazine reported 600,000 fewer employees by the end of 1986 in Fortune 500 companies.

- New tax laws encouraged 3,397 mergers and acquisitions worth 190 billion.

The mergers have created an atmosphere that removes corporations from their original ties with communities and have resulted in a decrease in corporate investment by the merged companies.

WHY DO CORPORATIONS GIVE?

Corporations give for a variety of reasons:

1. Some give based on a feeling of social philanthropic responsibility.
2. Some give tax-exempt gifts of money and products to help themselves:

- Buy improved relationships with employees, the community, and the union.

- Gain marketplace advantages through product research opportunities and the positioning of products in lucrative areas.

Corporate giving can usually be described in a "this-for-that" syndrome. Corporations purchase what they want. They do not usually give away money; they invest it. For example:

- Education received 38.3% of corporate contributions. Education provides the trained workers.

- Health and welfare received 29.2%. Health and welfare provide direct benefits to employees and have the potential to lower health costs.

- Civic and community affairs received 16.5%. They provide visible support to the community.

Corporations have a giving pattern that is related to the geographic concerns of their workers and factories. You can learn far more about their profitability and their contributions through purchasing a share of two of their stock than in purchasing expensive books on corporate philanthropy. Ask your Chamber of Commerce for a list of the corporations in your area. They are listed in order of the number of employees. Select those companies you can relate to by programs that benefit workers or research that relates to their products.

To approach corporate funding sources, you must relate your request to:

- Help in attaining corporate goals: manpower training; availability of resources.

- Employee or management benefits: health programs; cultural programs; recreation facilities.

- Improvement of the environment around the corporation: programs that affect transportation, communication, ecology.

- Improved corporate image: better reputation in the community.

When you evaluate your potential for getting corporate grants, determine what these "returns on investment" are, and emphasize them in your presentations to corporate funding officials.

Another interesting aspect of corporate philanthropy is what might be called the "school of fish syndrome." Corporations do not like to be the first to fund a project. They are afraid to leave the protection of the "school of fish." They are extremely sensitive to what their competition is doing. This can work in favor of the successful grant seeker. Once one corporation gives you a grant, others will tend to follow (to be in the "school of fish"). In addition, if a corporation grants to another organization in your field, your chances of getting a grant from a competing corporation increase. Corporations do not want to be first to take a chance, but then again, they do not want to get left behind.

CORPORATIONS

Compared to foundations and government-granting agencies, corporations have very unstructured application procedures. Personal contact, crucial to success in any grant solicitation, is especially important here. Corporate grant seeking almost always involves personal contact, followed by a businesslike proposal, and completed through negotiation with decision-making executives. You must appeal to the business sense of every corporate grant maker you contact; always show them in concrete terms how their grant will benefit the firm.

Summary of Grants Marketplace

Now you have a basic idea of the type of funding sources that make up the grants marketplace. You need a *Time-Saving Tool* to help you select the correct marketplace and also to give you an idea of the strengths and weaknesses of your project as you approach each potential funding area.

You now know from the general description of the marketplace that the federal-grants area must be approached first. You must play the odds that favor the 30-billion-dollar marketplace.

Do not forget to track the possible block grants down from the federal level to the local or state level.

The greater the potential for developing a model that impacts a large area or great number of people, the more interest you will generate from federal and state funding sources. After you have reviewed the funding potential with the government sources or you have found that you are ineligible for funding from these sources, you will want to try the private-sector marketplace.

The private-sector marketplace can be approached logically after utilizing the worksheet that follows. List your project on a copy of the worksheet and rate your project by how closely it meets the criteria for each type of funding.

PRIVATE-SECTOR SUPPORT

FOUNDATIONS/CORPORATIONS

Project Title: _____

	COMMUNITY FOUNDATION	NATIONAL FOUNDATION	SPECIAL PURPOSE	FAMILY FOUNDATION	CORPORATE SOURCES
"THE NEED"	Local needs only	National needs, widespread	Need in their "specialty"	Geographic concerns usually	Needs of workers or product concerns
"YOUR PROJECT METHODS"	No experiments - time tested, proven approaches	Unique, cost-effective	Viewed as special to this area	Depends on what the board likes	Proven safe project methods, more unique research protocols
YOUR FRIENDS -- CONTACTS WITH FUNDERS	Very important local contacts	Important	Important, especially in field of interest	Very important -- gives you hidden agenda	Very important -- gives money to those they trust
GRANTS EXPERIENCE	Credibility and need can overcome lack of experience	Important, like to work with others	Not as important as the potential contribution	Not critical	Important -- expect experience

PART TWO

Government Funding Sources

CHAPTER 10

Researching the Government Marketplace

Public funding, or government funding, is comprised of:

- *Federal funds:* grants and contracts that are received directly from federal agencies by your organization.

- *State funds:* These consist of: (a) state granting programs that distribute funds generated from state revenues other than federal revenue-sharing monies; and (b) state block grant programs that distribute federal revenue sharing and block grant funds.

- *County/borough and city funds:* these provide grants to your specific area. They consist of funds from the parking meter fund to pass through monies from state and federal government.

How do you research and track these funds? The worksheet entitled Federal Research Tools (pp. 66–67) outlines some of the more useful resources for locating these funds.

65

FEDERAL RESEARCH TOOLS

NAME	DESCRIPTION	WHERE TO GET IT	COST
Catalogue of Federal Domestic Assistance (202)275-3054	The official information on all government programs created by law. It does not mean funds have been appropriated. (See sample entry in Figure 10.1)	Supt. of Documents U.S. Government Printing office, Washington, D.C. 20402	$30.00/yr.
Federal Assistance Program Retrieval System (FAPRS)	A retrieval system that uses key words to match with federal granting programs to give the user the CFDA programs that are related to the desired grants area. (See sample entry.)	Call your congressperson and ask how to do a FAPRS search. *They may do it for you at no cost.	*
Federal Register (202)275-3054	Official news publication for the federal government; makes public all meetings, announcements of granting programs, regulations and deadlines. (See sample entry in Figure 10.2)	Supt. of Documents, U.S. Government Printing Office, Washington, D.C. 20402	$340.00/yr.
U.S. Government Manual	Official handbook of the federal government. Describes all federal agencies and gives names of officials. (See sample entry in Figure 10.30	Supt. of Documents U.S. Government Printing Office, Washington, D.C. 20402	$13.00/yr.

FEDERAL RESEARCH TOOLS (Cont.)

NAME	DESCRIPTION	WHERE TO GET IT	COST
Agency Newsletters and Publications, RFP's & Guidelines	Many federal agencies publish newsletters to inform you about the availability of funds and program accomplishments. You can receive application materials, requests for proposals. (See sample in Figure 12.1)		Usually Free
Federal Executive Telephone Directory (202)333–8620	Includes names, addresses, and phone numbers of federal government agencies and key personnel	Federal Telephone Directory, 1058 Thomas Jefferson St., NW, Washington, D.C. 20007	$140.00/yr
Commerce Business Daily (202)275–3054	The mechanism to announce the accepting of bids on government contracts. (See Figure 10.4)	Supt. of Documents, U.S. Government Printing Office, Washington, D.C. 20402	$173.00/yr.
Congressional Record (202)275–3054	Day–to–day proceedings of the Senate and House of Representatives; includes all written information for the record. (All grant-program money appropriated by Congress).	Supt. of Documents, U.S. Government Printing Office, Washington, D.C. 20402	
Listing of Government Depository Libraries	Provides locations of large public and university libraries that receive government publications (e.g., CFDA).	Chief of the Library Department of Public Documents U.S. Government Printing Office, Washington, D.C. 20402	

Approaching Federal Funding

You need to keep in mind that grant seeking follows an orderly progression. You use your Pre-Proposal Review and Approval Form (p. 11) to begin your search for funding. From the idea and from your redefinition of your idea, you develop a list of key words to use in your search.

Since almost all federal funding documents use key words and subject areas as a way to find granting programs, use your redefinition sheets and the Federal Grants Research Form (pp. 69–70) to assist you.

As you look at examples of the research on federal and state funding sources, you will see that the information to complete these research sheets is readily available. Do not stop with the first few sources that sound or look good. Remember that you want the best funding source. Complete your research.

Federal Grants Research Form

Choosing a federal grant prospect requires persistence. Personal contacts must be made, gathered, and recorded. With even a few proposals, the information you were sure you would remember gets lost in the confusion.

The Federal Grants Research Form allows you to keep track of the grant programs you set out to investigate. Copy this form and pass out a sufficient number to your grants researchers so that your data gathering will be consistent and complete.

The key to providing your organization with federal funding is a combination of determination, hard work, and homework. The homework consists of systematic research, record keeping, and follow-up. There are several ways one can look at this research and record-keeping function:

1. If anything happens to you, your contacts and your projects will be able to live on.
2. As one grant seeker reported in a grants seminar, "The only way I can extort my unusually high salary is to keep all the

FEDERAL GRANTS RESEARCH FORM

	Source & Date
Project Title _____	
CFDA # _____ Title _____	
Federal Agency _____	
Authorizing Legislation # _____	
Information Contacts: Federal/State	
Name _____ Title _____	
Address _____	
Telephone _____	
Regulations/Guidelines Sent for: _____ Rec'd: _____	
Application Kit Sent for: _____ Rec'd: _____	
Restrictions that must be observed	
_____	
Eligibility _____	
_____	
Formula/Matching Requirements: _____	
Past Years' Peer Reviewers Sent for: ___ Rec'd: ___	
Comments on Peer Reviewers Analyzed & Attached: ___	
_____	
List of Agency Grantees requested (date) ___	
Rec'd: ___ Observations-type of recipient ___	
_____	
Financial Data: Obligation Levels	
19___ $ _____ 19___ $ _____	
19___ $ _____ 19___ $ _____	

(Cont.)

research and contacts in my head. They pray that nothing happens to me back at my organization."

You can decide which of these two diverse approaches you prefer to side with.

FEDERAL GRANTS RESEARCH FORM (Cont.)

Trend: Up _____   Down _____   Stable _____ | Source & Date

Average Grant Size $ _____   Grant Range _____ to_____

Deadline Dates: 19 _____   19 _____

Number of Proposals Req'd: _____ Bound: _____

Time Frame for Decision: _____

_____

Record of Contacts About This Program:

Date	Our Person	Federal Contact	Outcomes

How to Use the Catalogue of Federal Domestic Assistance (CFDA)

STEP 1: LOOK AT THE INDEXES

- *Agency Program Index*—difficult to deal with; gives you code of types of funds each agency program funds.

- *Applicant Eligibility Index*—allows you to look up a program to see if you are an eligible applicant (you must know the program first; this is not a great help).

- *Deadline Index*—look up the deadline dates for programs to see if they have a multiple deadline system.

- *Functional Index*—programs can be divided by the function they provide in each program area.

- *Popular Name Index*—lists programs by common usage name (the name most often referred to by agencies and applicants); this is good to check when you don't find a federal program under what you thought its name was.

- *Subject Index*—this is the most commonly used index, since most people express their interests in this way (according to subject).

STEP 2

Using redefinition sheets and key words, look for programs that would be interested in your project idea. Briefly outline the best ones on research sheets. Be sure to write down the CFDA number that references the program. (Familiarize yourself with the Federal Grants Research Form and the following guidelines for "Reading the CFDA."

READING THE CFDA

Samples of the catalogue (see Fig. 10.1) have been selected to demonstrate the features of each program you have located through the indexes. In the first example, CFDA Number 45.128 PROMOTION OF THE HUMANITIES—EXEMPLARY PROJECTS AND HUMANITIES PROGRAMS FOR NONTRADITIONAL LEARNERS, reader aides have been placed in the left margin. These numbers will not appear on any

FIGURE 10.1.   Sample CFDA entries.

Huey Long. (3) Scripting of a series on the life and work of Henry Ford.

CRITERIA FOR SELECTING PROPOSALS: (A) The Media Program seeks to transmit the vital work of scholarship and learning in the humanities to a wide and general audience. (B) Projects must address a well defined subject area within the humanities that clearly affords the opportunity to move beyond the presentation of information to the examination and interpretation of informing theses, countervailing arguments, and fundamental concepts. (C) Projects must involve substantive use of the appropriate scholarly resources in the humanities in a definitive and objective manner and provide for full and effective collaboration between scholars and highly skilled professional producers, directors, and writers drawn from either the commercial or noncommercial sectors of the broadcast and filmmaking industries. (D) The proposed format of the project should be clearly thought out, imaginative, and attractive for general audiences. (E) Projects must include a budget that is appropriate to the significance and scope of the project and the experience of its principal personnel. (F) Projects must be designed to reach a broad or national adult public audience or, in the case of radio projects, a local, regional or national audience, and must provide both in a plan for and some assurance of secondary non-broadcast distribution and long-term utilization. (G) The Media Program joins the other programs of the Endowment in soliciting proposals of themes suitable for commemorating the Bicentennial of the U.S. Constitution in 1987 and the Columbian projects which encourage the understanding of American history and the understanding of foreign cultures. (H) The Media Program continues to encourage the submission of proposals intended to create humanities programming for youth of junior high and high school age. (I) The Media Program also encourages the submission of proposals for radio and television biographies of "American Lives".

45.111 PROMOTION OF THE HUMANITIES— EXEMPLARY PROJECTS AND HUMANITIES PROGRAMS FOR NONTRADITIONAL LEARNERS

FEDERAL AGENCY: NATIONAL ENDOWMENT FOR THE HUMANITIES, NATIONAL FOUNDATION ON THE ARTS AND THE HUMANITIES

AUTHORIZATION: National Foundation on the Arts and the Humanities Act of 1965; Public Law 89-209 as amended; 20 U.S.C. 951 et seq.

OBJECTIVES: To support activities that improve the teaching of the humanities through faculty development, and sharing of institutional resources. Activities may include institutes, workshops, conferences, or other collaborative projects. Most projects are planned and implemented by college and university faculty, cultural institutions, or professional associations. Others constitute assistance to assist institutions that wish to improve the quality of education new audiences by increasing the rigor, coherence, and accessibility of instructional programs.

TYPES OF ASSISTANCE: Project Grants.

USES AND USE RESTRICTIONS: Grant funds may be used for workshops, conferences, humanities institutes, multi-institutional faculty development projects; and other forms of collaboration that promote significant and broadly applicable improvements in the teaching of the humanities; less frequently grants are made for the preparation of bibliographies and other teaching materials. Grant funds may also be used for consultants, workshops, curriculum development, course materials and released time for additional training in the humanities for faculty members. The development of teaching materials will be limited to those projects that meet the highest standards of scholarship and that do not compete with the private sector. Materials may include bibliographies, audiovisual materials, teachers guides, or other products that assist but do not substitute for intensive study of the humanities. Funds may not be used for construction costs, nonessential permanent equipment, general operating expenses, or educational research.

ELIGIBILITY REQUIREMENTS:

Applicant Eligibility: State and local governments; sponsored organizations; public and private nonprofit institutions/organizations; other public institutions/organizations; Federally recognized Indian tribal governments; Native American organizations; U.S. Territories; non-government-general; minority organizations; other specialized groups; and quasi-public nonprofit institutions.

Beneficiary Eligibility: State and local governments; sponsored organizations; public and private nonprofit institutions/organizations; other public institutions/organizations; Federally recognized Indian tribal governments; Native American organizations; U.S. Territories; non-government-general; minority organizations; other specialized groups; and quasi-public nonprofit institutions.

Credentials/Documentation: Costs will determined in accordance with OMB Circular No. A-21 for educational institutions and OMB Circular No. A-122 for nonprofit organizations.

APPLICATION AND AWARD PROCESS:

Preapplication Coordination: Informal inquiry with office, followed by submission of preliminary draft six weeks in advance of the application deadline is urged. Use of program guidelines provided by the agency is essential. The standard application form as furnished by the Federal agency and required by OMB Circular No. A-102 must be used for this program.

Application Procedure: Submission of a proposal accompanied by an application form. This program is subject to the provisions of OMB Circular No. A-110.

Award Procedure: Applications are reviewed by subject area specialists, panels of scholars, and other appropriate individuals. Awards are made by the Chairman of the National Endowment for the Humanities after recommendation by the National Council on the Humanities.

Deadlines: Exemplary Projects: December 1 and May 1. Humanities Programs for Nontraditional Learners: April 1 and October 1.

Range of Approval/Disapproval Time: Approximately six months.

Appeals: None, but applicant may reapply with a revised proposal.

Renewals: Applications for renewal must compete against new applications and present a full evaluation of prior activities. Applications for renewal must also show continued demand and new audiences.

ASSISTANCE CONSIDERATIONS:

Formula and Matching Requirements: This program has no statutory formula. Cost sharing by applicant is encouraged. Source: Program Guidelines. Contact: See Headquarters Office below.

Length and Time Phasing of Assistance: Funds must be expended during the grant period. Funds are released as required. Grants generally cover a period of 6 months to 3 years. Projects for Nontraditional Learners: 6 months to 3 years.

POST ASSISTANCE REQUIREMENTS:

Reports: Progress reports are required at least annually but no more frequently than quarterly. Cash reports are required quarterly. Final progress and expenditures reports are due within 90 days after completion or termination of project support by NEH.

Audits: In accordance with the provisions of OMB Circular No. A-128, "Audits of State and Local Governments," State and local governments that receive financial assistance of $100,000 or more within the State's fiscal year shall have an audit made for that year. State and local governments that receive between $25,000 and $100,000 within the State's fiscal year shall have an audit made in accordance with Circular No. A-128, or in accordance with Federal laws and regulations governing the programs in which they participate.

Records: Documentation of expenditures and other fiscal records must be retained for three years following the submission of the final expenditure report.

FINANCIAL INFORMATION:

Account Identification: 59-0200-0-1-503.

Obligations: (Grants) FY 86 $4,126,000; FY 87 est $4,319,000; and FY 88 est $3,725,000.

Range and Average of Financial Assistance: As appropriate to the scope and purposes of the project.

PROGRAM ACCOMPLISHMENTS: In fiscal year 1986, 101 applications were received, of which 40 were funded. In fiscal year 1987, approximately 42 grants are likely to be funded, out of a total of 106 applications.

REGULATIONS, GUIDELINES, AND LITERATURE: 45 CFR 1100 and 1105. Applications and guidelines as well as a publication entitled "Overview of Endowment Programs, January 1987" are available upon request from the National Endowment for the Humanities, Room 409, Washington, DC 20506. Available from the Superintendent of Documents, U.S. Government Printing Office, Washington, DC 20402, is the Endowment's official publication, "Humanities," by subscription (6 issues annually, $14.00 domestic, $17.25 foreign).

INFORMATION CONTACTS:

Regional or Local Office: None.

Headquarters Office: Exemplary Projects and Nontraditional Programs, National Endowment for the Humanities, Room 302, Washington, DC 20506. Telephone: (202) 786-0384.

RELATED PROGRAMS: 45.127, Promotion of the Humanities—Humanities Instruction in Elementary and Secondary Schools; 45.150, Promotion of the Humanities—Central Disciplines in Undergraduate Education.

EXAMPLES OF FUNDED PROJECTS: (1) A university sponsors a six-week institute for twenty-five college and university teachers on the literary and historical contexts of the Essays of Montaigne. The participants are faculty dealing with great authors in undergraduate world literature courses, with comparative literature, or with interdisciplinary courses focusing on a given period, such as the Renaissance. Faculty participants continue to develop professionally and intellectually within their general interests. (2) A professional association conducts a two-year project to clarify and strengthen the role of linguistics in the undergraduate curriculum. Following thorough study of courses and programs in linguistics, the association will develop model curricula for implementation and evaluation in several institutions. (3) A university plans a series of co-curricular workshops for advanced graduate students engaged in research and writing of the dissertation. The workshops include faculty and students from a wide range of research interests in the humanities. They enable graduate students to maintain intellectual involvement with broad issues and current questions in their own and related fields, ensuring breadth as well as depth in the last years of graduate study. (4) A university offers three regional workshops to disseminate information about humanities programs for nontraditional students. The workshops will provide information about outstanding programs, enable discussion of key issues concerning adult students and the humanities, establish a network of program directors, and disseminate information about available resources in establishing humanities programs for nontraditional learners.

CRITERIA FOR SELECTING PROPOSALS: Proposals are read and evaluated on their promise for improving the teaching and learning of the humanities in colleges and universities. Intelligence and imagination in conception, intellectual substance, thoroughness of planning, strength of staff, degree of commitment, involvement of participants, demonstration of need, and other factors are considered. See the program guidelines for specific criteria.

45.113 PROMOTION OF THE HUMANITIES— PUBLIC HUMANITIES PROJECTS

FEDERAL AGENCY: NATIONAL ENDOWMENT FOR THE HUMANITIES, NATIONAL FOUNDATION ON THE ARTS AND THE HUMANITIES

AUTHORIZATION: National Foundation on the Arts and the Humanities Act of 1965; Public Law 89-209 as amended; 20 U.S.C. 951 et seq.

OBJECTIVES: To support humanities projects addressed to out-of-school audiences. All projects must draw upon resources and scholars in the fields of the humanities. Priorities include: projects undertaken by humanities institutions or by national or regional organizations which bring humanities programming to public audi-

ences; proposals related to the forthcoming Columbian Quincentenary, projects in intellectual history, classics, philosophy, history, theory and criticism of the arts, and the interpretation of literature.

TYPES OF ASSISTANCE: Project Grants.

USES AND USE RESTRICTIONS: The reimbursement of personnel and other costs related to the planning, production or presentation of a project are eligible for support. Support is not offered for performance costs in the arts. Out of school projects for junior high and high school youth are encouraged.

ELIGIBILITY REQUIREMENTS:

Applicant Eligibility: State and local governments; sponsored organizations; public and private nonprofit institutions/organizations; other public institutions/organizations; Federally recognized Indian tribal governments; Native American organizations; U.S. Territories; non-government-general; minority organizations; and other specialized groups; quasi-public nonprofit institutions.

Beneficiary Eligibility: State and local governments; sponsored organizations; public and private nonprofit institutions/organizations; other public institutions/organizations; Federally recognized Indian tribal governments; Native American organizations; U.S. Territories; non-government-general; minority organizations; and other specialized groups; quasi-public nonprofit institutions.

Credentials/Documentation: Costs will be determined in accordance with OMB Circular No. A-87. OMB Circular No. A-21 for educational institutions, and OMB Circular No. A-122 for nonprofit organizations apply.

APPLICATION AND AWARD PROCESS:

Preapplication Coordination: A preliminary proposal should be submitted to the office listed below eight weeks in advance of the deadline for staff comment and assessment of the project's eligibility. Such a proposal should define the subject matter of the project and its relationship to the humanities. It should also convey a clear sense of the project's intended audience, presentation methods, personnel, and a general estimate of costs. The standard application forms as furnished by the Federal agency and required by OMB Circular No. A-102 must be used for this program.

Application Procedure: Application forms and proposed guidelines are available upon request. This program is subject to the provisions of OMB Circular No. A-110.

Award Procedure: Applications are reviewed by subject area specialists, panels of scholars, and other appropriate individuals. Awards are made by the Chairman of the National Endowment for the Humanities after recommendation by the National Council on the Humanities.

Deadlines: September 18, 1987, for projects beginning after April 1, 1988, and March 18, 1988, for projects beginning after October 1, 1988.

Range of Approval/Disapproval Time: Within six months after deadline.

Appeals: None, but applicant may reapply.

Renewals: Renewals may be granted and are processed as a new application.

ASSISTANCE CONSIDERATIONS:

Formula and Matching Requirements: This program has no statutory formula. Cost-sharing by applicant is encouraged. Source: Program Guidelines. Contact: See Headquarters Office below.

Length and Time Phasing of Assistance: Ordinarily not longer than 18 months to 2 years. Planning grants are usually 3 to 12 months in duration. Funds must be obligated during the grant period.

POST ASSISTANCE REQUIREMENTS:

Reports: Progress reports are required at least annually but no more frequently than quarterly. Cash reports are required quarterly. Final progress and expenditures reports are due within 90 days after completion or termination of the project.

Audits: In accordance with the provisions of OMB Circular No. A-128, "Audits of State and Local Governments," State and local governments that receive financial assistance of $100,000 or more within the State's fiscal year shall have an audit made for that year. State and local governments that receive between $25,000

FIGURE 10.1. *(continued)*

and $100,000 within the State's fiscal year shall have an audit made in accordance with Circular No. A-128, or in accordance with Federal laws and regulations governing the programs in which they participate.

Records: Documentation of expenditures and other fiscal records must be retained for three years following the submission of the final expenditure report.

FINANCIAL INFORMATION:

Account Identification: 59-0200-0-1-503.

Obligations: (Grants) FY 86 $2,154,000; FY 87 est $2,000,000; and FY 88 est $2,128,000.

Range and Average of Financial Assistance: $15,000 to $200,000; $60,000.

PROGRAM ACCOMPLISHMENTS: During fiscal year 1986, 109 applications were received and 20 grants were made to colleges, universities and national organizations. The awards supported major regional and urban projects, programs designed to reach new audiences within the humanities and projects which combined research for public purposes with discussion programs. In fiscal year 1987, Public Humanities Projects expects to receive 100 applications. It is anticipated that about 20 awards will be made. In fiscal year 1988, Public Humanities Projects expects to receive 150 applications. It is anticipated that about 21 awards will be made.

REGULATIONS, GUIDELINES, AND LITERATURE: 45 CFR 1100 and 1105. Applications and guidelines as well as a publication entitled "Overview of Endowment Programs, January 1987" are available upon request from the National Endowment for the Humanities, Room 409, Washington, DC 20506. Available from the Superintendent of Documents, U.S. Government Printing Office, Washington, DC 20402, is the Endowment's official publication "Humanities" by subscription (6 issues annually, $14.00 domestic, $17.25 foreign).

INFORMATION CONTACTS:

Regional or Local Office: Not applicable.

Headquarters Office: Public Humanities Projects, Division of General Programs, National Endowment for the Humanities, Room 426, Washington, DC 20506. Telephone: (202) 786-0271.

RELATED PROGRAMS: 45.104, Promotion of the Humanities—Humanities Projects in Media; 45.125, Promotion of the Humanities—Humanities Projects in Museums and Historical Organizations; 45.137, Promotion of the Humanities—Humanities Projects in Libraries; 45.140, Promotion of the Humanities—Interpretive Research/Projects.

EXAMPLES OF FUNDED PROJECTS: (1) A State humanities resource center received a grant in support of a traveling exhibition and a series of public lectures on the roles played by black Americans in the State. In addition to panel text, the portable display of photographs and facsimiles of documents in further interpreted by a booklet of essays written by scholars. (2) A symphony orchestra has received support for a series of free programs conducted by a humanities scholar who also serves as the symphony's resident music adviser. Through pre-concert lectures, radio interviews, and lecture-demonstrations, audiences are provided a summary of current musicological scholarship on the works to be performed by the orchestra. (3) Support was given to a university medical center for a 3 year series of symposia, lectures and other public events aimed at various audiences found in a major urban medical center, including patients, medical students and hospital staffs. The series of programs is carefully designed to focus on a set of issues found at the intersection of medicine and the humanities.

CRITERIA FOR SELECTING PROPOSALS: Activities supported by Public Humanities Projects are expected to focus upon ideas or themes from the disciplines of the humanities. In doing so they may enhance the appreciation and interpretation of cultural works; the illumination of historical ideas, figures, and events; and an understanding of the humanities disciplines. Additional criteria would be the degree to which a project will help to disseminate the work of humanities scholars to public audiences; and the degree to which the suggested personnel for the project have appropriate training in the humanities.

45.115 PROMOTION OF THE HUMANITIES— YOUNGER SCHOLARS

FEDERAL AGENCY: NATIONAL ENDOWMENT FOR THE HUMANITIES, NATIONAL FOUNDATION ON THE ARTS AND THE HUMANITIES

AUTHORIZATION: National Foundation on the Arts and the Humanities Act of 1965; Public Law 89-209, as amended; 20 U.S.C. 951 et seq.

OBJECTIVES: To support noncredit humanities projects during the summer by college students and advanced high school students. Projects must be closely supervised by a humanities scholar.

TYPES OF ASSISTANCE: Project Grants.

USES AND USE RESTRICTIONS: Grants are awarded for the research and writing of a paper, in one or more of the fields included in the humanities: history, philosophy, language, linguistics, literature, archaeology, jurisprudence, art history and criticism, and those aspects of social sciences which are philosophical or historical in nature. Funds are not awarded for purchase of equipment, construction, performance or creative work in the arts, or for the general educational or training expenses of individuals, thesis work, foreign travel, or any work abroad. No academic credit may be sought for work conducted under a Younger Scholars grant.

ELIGIBILITY REQUIREMENTS:

Applicant Eligibility: Individuals are eligible who are U.S. citizens, native residents of U.S. territorial possessions, or foreign nationals who have been residents in the U.S. for at least three years immediately preceding the date of the application. A college student who is below the level of senior or any high school student may apply. If they are over 21, they must be enrolled as full-time college students pursuing an undergraduate degree at the time of application. Applicants may not have received a bachelor's degree, nor expect to receive one before October 1, 1988.

Beneficiary Eligibility: High school students and college students below the level of senior. Applicants may not have received a bachelor's degree nor expect to receive one, before October 1, 1988.

Credentials/Documentation: Cost will be determined in accordance with NFAH 3009 for individuals.

APPLICATION AND AWARD PROCESS:

Preapplication Coordination: None.

Application Procedure: Application forms and guidelines will be made available upon request and should be requested at least one month before the deadline by writing to the office below. This program is subject to the provisions of NFAH 3008.

Award Procedure: Applications are reviewed by subject area specialists, panels of scholars, and other appropriate individuals. Awards are made by the Chairman of the National Endowment for the Humanities after recommendation by the National Council on the Humanities.

Deadlines: November 2, 1987, for projects to be undertaken in the Summer of 1988.

Range of Approval/Disapproval Time: Variable; average four months.

Appeals: None, but applicant may reapply with a revised proposal.

Renewals: Grants are not renewed.

ASSISTANCE CONSIDERATIONS:

Formula and Matching Requirements: This program has no matching requirements. Source: Program Guidelines. Contact: See Headquarters Office below.

Length and Time Phasing of Assistance: Younger Scholars Grants are given for a nine week period between June 1 and August 31. Funds are released at the beginning of the grant period, and must be expended during that period.

POST ASSISTANCE REQUIREMENTS:

Reports: Final progress reports are due within 30 days after completion or termination of project by NEH.

Audits: Subject to audit by Endowment auditors or their representatives.

Records: Documentation of expenditures and other fiscal records must be retained for three years following the submission of the final expenditure report.

FINANCIAL INFORMATION:

Account Identification: 59-0200-0-1-503.

Obligations: (Grants) FY 86 $338,000; FY 87 est $400,000; and FY 88 est $378,000.

Range and Average of Financial Assistance: $1,800 or $2,200.

PROGRAM ACCOMPLISHMENTS: In fiscal year 1986, 983 applications were received and 167 awards were made. In fiscal year 1987, 1,000 applications are anticipated and 200 awards will be made. In fiscal year 1988, approximately 1,000 applications are anticipated with about 190 awards.

REGULATIONS, GUIDELINES, AND LITERATURE: 45 CFR 1100 and 1105. Applications and guidelines as well as a publication entitled, "Overview of Endowment Programs, January 1987" are available upon request from the National Endowment for the Humanities, Room 409, Washington, DC 20506. Available from the Superintendent of Documents, U.S. Government Printing Office, Washington, DC 20402, is the Endowment's official publication "Humanities" by subscription (6 issues annually, $14.00 domestic, $17.25 foreign).

INFORMATION CONTACTS:

Regional or Local Office: Not applicable.

Headquarters Office: Division of Fellowships and Seminars, Younger Scholars Program, Room 316, National Endowment for the Humanities, Washington, DC 20506. Telephone: (202) 786-0463.

RELATED PROGRAMS: None.

EXAMPLES OF FUNDED PROJECTS: (1) A high school student interested in the constitutional separation of church and State examined the influence of Voltaire, Rousseau, Paine and Jefferson on the thought of James Madison. Madison's ideas, he argued, are embodied in the First Amendment to the U.S. Constitution. (2) A high school graduate provided a reassessment of the French composers Cesar Franck, Ernest Chausson and Vincent D'Indy through a close analytical and stylistic study of their symphonic works, tracing the influence of Franck in French music. (3) An undergraduate student of religion examined the cultural values associated with Islam and traced their impact on the political systems of three Islamic nations: Egypt, Saudi Arabia and Turkey. (4) An undergraduate student of history investigated the intellectual origins of nationalist theory in Catalonia during the nineteenth century. She studied the writings of Catalan nationalist theorists and examined how they were influenced by earlier theories of the nation-state including those of Herder and Fichte, Michelet and Renan, Proudhon and the American federalists. (5) A high school student examined the influence of Montesquieu's, "The Spirit of Laws," on the doctrine of separation of powers in the U.S. Constitution. (6) A college student examined two of Shakespeare's plays, Othello and Macbeth, from the standpoint of three different contemporary schools of thought in literary criticism.

CRITERIA FOR SELECTING PROPOSALS: Applications should discuss the degree to which the project is firmly grounded in a discipline or disciplines of the humanities; the logic of its defined scope and plan of work; the appropriateness of the advisor's training and knowledge in the humanities for the project; the suitability of the applicant's academic record and background for the project; and the contribution the project will make to the young person's intellectual development.

45.116 PROMOTION OF THE HUMANITIES— SUMMER SEMINARS FOR COLLEGE TEACHERS

FEDERAL AGENCY: NATIONAL ENDOWMENT FOR THE HUMANITIES, NATIONAL FOUNDATION ON THE ARTS AND THE HUMANITIES

AUTHORIZATION: National Foundation on the Arts and the Humanities Act of 1965; Public Law 89-209 as amended; 20 U.S.C. 951 et seq.

OBJECTIVES: To provide opportunities for teachers in five-, four-, and two-year colleges to work during the summer in their areas of interest under the direction of distinguished scholars at institutions with library resources suitable for advanced study and research. Seminars offered in this program deal with significant works or topics in the humanities.

TYPES OF ASSISTANCE: Project Grants.

USES AND USE RESTRICTIONS: Grants are to support seminars in the humanities and selected fields of the social sciences and are awarded to the host institution. These seminars will be held during the summer under the direction of distinguished scholars at institutions with libraries suitable for advanced research. College teachers participate in seminars and pursue individual programs of study and research of their own choosing. The focus of the seminars is primarily substantive, reinforcing the participants' commitment to teaching and to research. Grants to participate in seminars will not be awarded to persons enrolled or actively engaged in work leading toward a degree. Faculty members of departments that grant a Ph.D. are ordinarily not eligible as participants in the seminars.

ELIGIBILITY REQUIREMENTS:

Applicant Eligibility: Distinguished scholars and teachers at institutions with libraries suitable for significant research in the humanities or with specialized holdings in the area of the seminar and with facilities adequate for hosting the seminars.

Beneficiary Eligibility: Teachers in five-, four-, and two-year colleges and other persons qualified to do the work of the seminar.

Credentials/Documentation: For educational institutions, costs will be determined in accordance with OMB Circular No. A-21.

APPLICATION AND AWARD PROCESS:

Preapplication Coordination: Informal inquiry is encouraged for prospective directors. The standard application forms as furnished by the Federal agency and required by OMB Circular No. A-102 must be used for this program.

Application Procedure: Proposal instructions are available from the headquarters office. This program is subject to the provisions of OMB Circular No. A-110.

Award Procedure: Applications are reviewed by subject area specialists, panels of scholars, and other appropriate individuals. Awards are made by the Chairman of the National Endowment for the Humanities after recommendation by the National Council on the Humanities.

Deadlines: March 1, 1988, for seminar directors for summer of 1989; March 1, 1988, for teacher participants for summer of 1988. Similar deadlines in future years.

Range of Approval/Disapproval Time: About seven months for seminar directors, about one month for teacher participants.

Appeals: None, but director/applicant may request a critique of the proposal and reapply.

Renewals: Reapplication permitted.

ASSISTANCE CONSIDERATIONS:

Formula and Matching Requirements: This program has no statutory formula. Source: Program Guidelines. Contact: See Headquarters Office below.

Length and Time Phasing of Assistance: Approximately 14 months. Time phasing: October 1988 to September 1989. The seminar itself lasts six or eight weeks during the summer. Funds must be expended during the grant period. Funds are released as required.

POST ASSISTANCE REQUIREMENTS:

Reports: Cash reports are due quarterly. A final narrative report assessing the results of the seminar and final expenditures report are required from the seminar director within 90 days after completion or termination of grant period. In addition, reports are required from the college teachers participating in the seminar assessing the value of the seminar for their professional development.

Audits: In accordance with the provisions of OMB Circular No. A-128, "Audits of State and Local Governments," State and local governments that receive financial assistance of $100,000 or more within the State's fiscal year shall have an audit made for that year. State and local governments that receive between $25,000 and $100,000 within the State's fiscal year shall have an audit made in accordance with Circular No. A-128, or in accordance

FIGURE 10.1. *(continued)*

with Federal laws and regulations governing the programs in which they participate.

Records: Documentation of expenditures and other fiscal records must be retained for three years following the submission of the final expenditure report.

FINANCIAL INFORMATION:

Account Identification: 59-0200-0-1-503.

Obligations: (Grants) FY 86 $3,722,000; FY 87 est $4,095,000; and FY 88 est $3,660,000.

Range and Average of Financial Assistance: $65,000 to $90,000; $77,500.

PROGRAM ACCOMPLISHMENTS: In fiscal year 1986, 137 applications were received and 56 seminars were held. In fiscal year 1987, 147 applications were received and 51 seminars were held. In fiscal year 1988, approximately 160 applications will be received and approximately 50 seminars will be held.

REGULATIONS, GUIDELINES, AND LITERATURE: 45 CFR 1100 and 1105. Applications and guidelines as well as a publication entitled, "Overview of Endowment Programs, January 1987" are available upon request from the National Endowment for the Humanities, Room 409, Washington, DC 20506. Available from the Superintendent of Documents, U.S. Government Printing Office, Washington, DC 20402, is the Endowment's publication, "Humanities," by subscription (6 issues annually, $14.00 domestic, $17.25 foreign).

INFORMATION CONTACTS:

Regional or Local Office: Not applicable.

Headquarters Office: Summer Seminars for College Teachers, Division of Fellowships and Seminars, National Endowment for the Humanities, Room 316, Washington, DC 20506. Telephone: (202) 786-0463.

RELATED PROGRAMS: 45.115, Promotion of the Humanities—Younger Scholars; 45.121, Promotion of the Humanities—Summer Stipends; 45.143, Promotion of the Humanities—Fellowships for College Teachers and Independent Scholars; 45.151, Promotion of the Humanities—Summer Seminars for Secondary School Teachers; 45.152, Promotion of the Humanities—Travel to Collections.

EXAMPLES OF FUNDED PROJECTS: (1) "American Courts: A Bicentennial Perspective"; (2) "The Oral Tradition in Literature"; (3) "Shakespeare and Politics" (4) "Classical and Christian Roots of Anti-Semitism"; (5) "Music and Technology".

CRITERIA FOR SELECTING PROPOSALS: In the evaluation of proposals to direct Summer Seminars, the following criteria are considered: (1) The prospective director's quality as a scholar, teacher, and interpreter of the humanities, as well as interest in undergraduate teaching; (2) the conception, definition, and organization of the proposed seminar; (3) the significance of the proposed topic to the humanities and to undergraduate teaching; and (4) the suitability of the library and research facilities in the field of the seminar, including library collections and other research and scholarly resources, housing availability, and other institutional means of providing and maintaining a collegial setting. Applicants selected to receive stipends to attend summer seminars are those who, in the judgment of the Director and the Director's Selection Committee are able and committed and who can derive the greatest benefit from and make the greatest contribution to the seminar. Preference will be given to those whose primary duties involve teaching undergraduates and who have not recently had the opportunity to use the resources of a major library.

45.121 PROMOTION OF THE HUMANITIES—SUMMER STIPENDS

FEDERAL AGENCY: NATIONAL ENDOWMENT FOR THE HUMANITIES, NATIONAL FOUNDATION ON THE ARTS AND THE HUMANITIES

AUTHORIZATION: National Foundation on the Arts and the Humanities Act of 1965; Public Law 89-209 as amended; 20 U.S.C. 951 et seq.

OBJECTIVES: To provide support for individual faculty and staff members at universities and two- and fouryear colleges and for

others who have made or have demonstrated promise of making significant contributions to the humanities, in order to pursue two consecutive months of full-time study or research on a project in the humanities.

TYPES OF ASSISTANCE: Project Grants.

USES AND USE RESTRICTIONS: The proposed study or research may be such that it can be completed during the stipend period, or it may be part of a long-range project. Applications for the planning of institutional curricula, empirical educational research projects, educational surveys, work in the creative or performing arts, and studies whose content or methods are not those of the humanities are not eligible for consideration.

ELIGIBILITY REQUIREMENTS:

Applicant Eligibility: Applications may come from persons employed by colleges and universities and from others who work in the humanities, from persons with broad interests, as well as scholars working in specialties. Faculty members must be nominated by their academic institutions. Each university, two-year and four-year college in the United States and its territorial possessions may nominate three members of its faculty for Summer Stipends. No more than two of the nominees should be in an early stage of their careers; no more than two should be in a more advanced stage (the rank of associate or full professor). Thus, when an institution submits three nominees for the Summer Stipend competition, two may be Junior and one Senior, or one Junior and two Senior. Applicants with terminating appointments, non-faculty college and university staff members, and persons not employed by colleges and universities are exempt from nomination and may apply directly to the Endowment. Although applicants need not have advanced degrees to qualify, they must have completed their professional training before applying. Active candidates for degrees are not eligible, nor are persons seeking support for work leading toward degrees. Applicants should be United States citizens, native residents of United States territorial possessions, or foreign nationals who have been residing in the United States for at least the three years immediately preceding the date of application.

Beneficiary Eligibility: College and university faculty and staff and independent scholars.

Credentials/Documentation: None.

APPLICATION AND AWARD PROCESS:

Preapplication Coordination: Faculty members must be nominated by their academic institutions.

Application Procedure: Application forms are available after August 15 from each institution or from the headquarters office, listed below. Applications are submitted to the headquarters office.

Award Procedure: Applications are reviewed by subject area specialists, panels of scholars, and other appropriate individuals. Awards are made by the Chairman of the National Endowment for the Humanities after recommendation by the National Council on the Humanities.

Deadlines: October 1, 1987, for awards for 1988.

Range of Approval/Disapproval Time: About five months.

Appeals: None, but applicant may reapply.

Renewals: None.

ASSISTANCE CONSIDERATIONS:

Formula and Matching Requirements: This program has no statutory formula and no matching requirements. Source: Program guidelines. Contact: See Headquarters Office below.

Length and Time Phasing of Assistance: Two consecutive months; stipends disbursed in one payment.

POST ASSISTANCE REQUIREMENTS:

Reports: A final report to be submitted within ninety days of the closing tenure date, is required describing the results of the work done during the period of the award.

Audits: As determined by the Endowment.

Records: Not applicable.

FINANCIAL INFORMATION:

Account Identification: 59-0200-0-1-503.

Obligations: (Grants) FY 86 $668,000; FY 87 est $750,000; and FY 88 est $757,000.

Range and Average of Financial Assistance: All awards are for approximately $3,500.

PROGRAM ACCOMPLISHMENTS: For fiscal year 1986, 1,436 applications were received and 223 awards were made. The application to award ratio is approximately seven to one.

REGULATIONS, GUIDELINES, AND LITERATURE: 45 CFR 1100 and 1105. Applications and guidelines as well as a publication entitled "Overview of Endowment Programs, January 1987" are available upon request from the National Endowment for the Humanities, Room 409, Washington, DC 20506. Available from the Superintendent of Documents, U.S. Government Printing Office, Washington, DC 20402 is: the Endowment's official publication "Humanities," by subscription (6 issues annually, $14.00 domestic, $17.25 foreign).

INFORMATION CONTACTS:

Regional or Local Office: Not applicable.

Headquarters Office: Division of Fellowships and Seminars, Summer Stipends, National Endowment for the Humanities, Room 316, Washington, DC 20506. Telephone: (202) 786-0466.

RELATED PROGRAMS: 45.115, Promotion of the Humanities—Younger Scholars; 45.116, Promotion of the Humanities—Summer Seminars for College Teachers; 45.122, Promotion of the Humanities—Regrants/Centers for Advanced Study; 45.140, Promotion of the Humanities—Interpretive Research/Projects; 45.142, Promotion of the Humanities—Fellowships for University Teachers; 45.143, Promotion of the Humanities—Fellowships for College Teachers and Independent Scholars; 45.151, Promotion of the Humanities—Summer Seminars for Secondary School Teachers; 45.152, Promotion of the Humanities—Travel to Collections.

EXAMPLES OF FUNDED PROJECTS: Stipends for 1986 were awarded for the following projects: (1) To complete work for a book on Chinese Buddhist thought; (2) to prepare for publication the results of an investigation on Aristotelian political philosophy; (3) to study the relationship between gender and genre in the work of women poets; (4) to write a history of the Stockyards district of Chicago during the depression, 1929-1941; and (5) to examine the Constitutional theory of Justice Oliver Wendell Homes.

CRITERIA FOR SELECTING PROPOSALS: (1) The quality or promise of quality of the applicant's work; (2) the significance of the applicant's proposal to a specific field and to the humanities in general; (3) the proposal's conception, definition, and organization; and (4) the likelihood that the applicant will complete the project.

45.122 PROMOTION OF THE HUMANITIES—REGRANTS/CENTERS FOR ADVANCED STUDY

FEDERAL AGENCY: NATIONAL ENDOWMENT FOR THE HUMANITIES, NATIONAL FOUNDATION ON THE ARTS AND HUMANITIES

AUTHORIZATION: National Foundation on the Arts and the Humanities Act of 1965; Public Law 89-209 as amended; 20 U.S.C. 951 et seq.

OBJECTIVES: To support interrelated research in well-defined subject areas at independent centers for advanced study, American research centers overseas, independent research libraries and research museums.

TYPES OF ASSISTANCE: Project Grants.

USES AND USE RESTRICTIONS: Independent centers for scholarly research may apply for funds with which to offer one or more fellowships within the framework of their own fellowship programs. The grants are intended to provide funds for fellowship stipends and standard allowances only. They may not be awarded to degree candidates or for study leading to advanced degrees. Fellowship tenure must be at least six and not more than 12 consecutive months in duration. Fellowship recipients must be granted all benefits, services, and accommodations normally accorded other fellows at the center.

ELIGIBILITY REQUIREMENTS:

Applicant Eligibility: Centers for advanced study that are financed and directed independently, or predominantly independently, of institutions of higher education.

Beneficiary Eligibility: Applicants to centers for fellowships should be citizens of the U.S. or foreign nationals who have lived in the U.S. for at least the three years immediately preceding application.

Credentials/Documentation: Costs will be determined in accordance with OMB Circular No. A-122 for nonprofit organizations.

APPLICATION AND AWARD PROCESS:

Preapplication Coordination: Interested centers are encouraged to inquire informally to the Division of Research Programs. (Persons interested in fellowships at centers may obtain a list and brief description of NEH funded centers from the Division of Research Programs. Further information is available from the centers.) The standard application forms furnished by the Federal agency and required by OMB Circular No. A-102 must be used for this program.

Application Procedure: Application guidelines and materials for interested centers to use are available from Headquarters Office. This program is subject to the provisions of OMB Circular No. A-110. (Persons interested in obtaining fellowships at centers must obtain application instructions and materials from the centers.)

Award Procedure: Applications are reviewed by subject area specialists, panels of scholars, and other appropriate individuals. Awards are made by the Chairman of the National Endowment for the Humanities after recommendation by the National Council on the Humanities. This recommendation is based upon an evaluation of the center and its proposal by a group of consultants and by a panel. The evaluation typically includes a visit to the center by the consultant group and an Endowment staff member.

Deadlines: Yearly: December 1.

Range of Approval/Disapproval Time: Six months.

Appeals: None, but applicant may reapply with a revised proposal.

Renewals: Reapplication permitted.

ASSISTANCE CONSIDERATIONS:

Formula and Matching Requirements: This program has no statutory formula. The use of matching funds by applicant is encouraged. Source: Program Guidelines. Contact: See Headquarters Office below.

Length and Time Phasing of Assistance: From 12 to 36 months. Funds must be expended during the grant period. Funds are released as required.

POST ASSISTANCE REQUIREMENTS:

Reports: In addition to a financial report, a narrative report describing the activities of the fellows and evaluating the success of the grant, and narrative accounts of activities from the fellows, are required. Progress reports are required at least annually. A cash expenditures report is due quarterly. Final reports of expenditures are due within 90 days of completion or termination of project support by NEH.

Audits: In accordance with the provisions of OMB Circular No. A-128, "Audits of State and Local Governments," State and local governments that receive $100,000 or more a year in Federal financial assistance shall have an audit made for that year. State and local governments that receive between $25,000 and $100,000 a year shall have an audit made in accordance with Circular No. A-128, or in accordance with Federal laws and regulations governing the programs in which they participate.

Records: Documentation of expenditure and other fiscal records must be retained for three years following the submission of the final expenditure report.

FINANCIAL INFORMATION:

Account Identification: 59-0200-0-1-503.

Obligations: (Grants) FY 86 $832,000; FY 87 est $805,000; and FY 88 est $785,000.

Range and Average of Financial Assistance: $22,000 to $126,814; $52,000.

PROGRAM ACCOMPLISHMENTS: In fiscal year 1986, 16 grants were awarded in response to 16 applications; in fiscal year 1987, it is anticipated that 17 applications will be received and 15 awards made; and in fiscal year 1988, it is expected that 14 of 18 applications will be funded.

REGULATIONS, GUIDELINES, AND LITERATURE: 45 CFR 1100 and 1105. Applications, and guidelines, as well as a publication enof the other examples that follow, nor will they appear in the actual CFDA document.

1. *Federal Agency:* This is the branch of the government administering the program—not much help to you, except as general knowledge or for looking up program and agency in the U.S. Government Manual.

2. *Authorization:* You need this information to fill out some program applications or to look up the testimony and laws creating the funding (for the "hard-core" researcher and grant seeker only).

3. *Objectives:* Good to review these general program objectives to compare to your project. Don't give up if you are off the mark slightly—contact with the funding source may uncover new programs, changes, or hidden agendas.

4. *Types of Assistance:* Good to review and record the general type of support from this source and compare to your project redefinition.

5. *Eligibility Requirements:* Review this section to be sure your organization is designated as a legal recipient. If it's not—find the type that is designated and apply as a consortium or cooperative agreement.

6. *Application and Award Process:* This information should be reviewed and recorded on your Research Worksheet. Don't let the deadline data bother you—if the award cycle has passed you should still contact the agency and position yourself for next year with (a) copies of old application; (b) list of current grantees; (c) a request to be a reviewer.

7. *Assistance Considerations:* Record information on the match you are required to provide. This will be useful in evaluating which funding sources you will apply to as well as assisting you in developing your project planner to see what you can donate or match from your organization.

8. *Financial Information:* This information is useful for seeing what funds the agency program *may* have received. Don't take this as the last word. One entry recently said they had 3 million dollars

for research. When contacted, they had over 30 million dollars to disseminate under this program and similar ones not in CFDA.

9. *Regulations, Guidelines, and Literature:* Record and send for any information you can get on the funder.

10. *Information Contacts:* Record and use to begin the steps outlined in this book on contacting funders. Note name of contact person and phone number. While the person or number may change, you at least have a place to start.

11. *Related Programs:* In some CFDA entries the government may suggest other programs that are similar or related to your area of interest. While these are usually obvious and programs your research may have already uncovered, review them for leads.

12. *Criteria For Selecting Proposals:* While this may appear after related programs or examples of funded projects, your best choice is to review and record but go on to get rules printed in *Federal Register* or get from reviewers.

STEP 3

You will then select the best government funding program (see the Prospect Analysis Form, Chapter 12).

STEP 4

You will contact the federal agency by using the contact person listed under information contacts (#10 above).

The Federal Assistance Programs Retrieval System (Enhanced Version)

The Federal Assistance Program Retrieval System (FAPRS) is a computerized question-answer system that is designed to provide rapid access to federal domestic assistance program information. The system provides information on federal programs that meet the development needs of the applicant and for which the applicant meets basic eligibility criteria. Program information provided by FAPRS is determined from input supplied by the requestor. Input required includes the name of the state, county, city, town, or federally designated Indian tribe for which program information is requested; the population of the city or town; the type of applicant (e.g., state or local governments, federally designated Indian tribes, nonprofit organizations, small businesses, or individuals), the type of assistance under which programs are administered (e.g., grants, loans); and the specific functional categories and subcategories of interest. Based upon the input supplied by the requestor, the output provided by FAPRS consists of: (1) a list of program numbers and titles: (2) the full text of selected programs: or (3) specific sections of the program text.

As originally developed by the Department of Agriculture, FAPRS was designed to aid small, rural, isolated communities unfamiliar with federal assistance programs or unable to locate federal aid programs that have the greatest funding potential. FAPRS has been developed based on the requirements for federal information systems. The following features have been incorporated into the new FAPRS system:

1. Expansion of functional categories and subcategories. As listed in the Functional Index and the catalogue, the enhanced version of FAPRS uses 20 functional categories and 176 subcategories to specify an area of interest.
2. Expansion of the applicant eligibility specification to include twelve government-related and 10 non-government-related applicant types.
3. Specification of the type(s) of assistance desired as one of the search criteria. At present, the catalogue lists up to fifteen types of assistance provided by federal programs.
4. Display of definitions for functional subcategories, applicant types, and types of assistance.
5. Selection of specific sections of catalogue text to be displayed.
6. Formatted display of federal circular coordination requirements for a selected list of programs.

States have designated access points where FAPRS searches may be requested. In addition, bulletins on FAPRS are available from the system to inform users of the addition or deletion of programs, changes to program numbers from one edition of the catalogue to the next, and enhancements and changes to the system. For further information on FAPRS, the location of the nearest state access point, or a list of the time-sharing companies from which interested persons may arrange for direct access to the system, write to the Office of Management and Budget, Budget Review Division, Federal Program Information Branch, Washington, D.C. 20503. Your congressperson will be able to assist you in locating where you can obtain a FAPRS search in your area.

The Federal Register

The *Federal Register* is the newspaper of the federal government. In order for the government to make legal notices on a great variety of federal issues, it must publish notices in the *Federal Register.*

Areas that must be published in the *Federal Register* in the grants area are the creation of new government granting programs and the rules governing both new and old programs. The rules to evaluate the proposal are also printed. The following points will help you in reading the sample entry in Figure 10.2.

1. *Federal Register Purposes and Prices.*
2. *Contents:* this is a detailed accounting of what is in the *Federal Register.*
3. *Reader Aids:* describes services and phone numbers under services. (*Note:* Public Briefings: "The Federal Register and How To Use It." The government sponsors classes around the United States and in Washington D.C. on how to read and understand the *Federal Register.* Call the phone number listed to find the nearest class and plan to attend one.)
4. *CFR Parts Affected during Past Month:* this will help you if you are keeping track of the changes that affect the Code of Federal Regulations.

FIGURE 10.2. A sample of the *Federal Register*.

7-14-87
Vol. 52   No. 134
Pages 26293-26468

Tuesday
July 14, 1987

Briefings on How To Use the Federal Register—
For information on briefings in Boston, MA, see
announcement on the inside cover of this issue.

II   **Federal Register** / Vol. 52, No. 134 / Tuesday, July 14, 1987

FEDERAL REGISTER Published daily, Monday through Friday,
(not published on Saturdays, Sundays, or on official holidays),
by the Office of the Federal Register, National Archives and
Records Administration, Washington, DC 20408, under the
Federal Register Act (49 Stat. 500, as amended; 44 U.S.C. Ch.
15) and the regulations of the Administrative Committee of the
Federal Register (1 CFR Ch. I). Distribution is made only by the
Superintendent of Documents, U.S. Government Printing Office,
Washington, DC 20402.

The **Federal Register** provides a uniform system for making
available to the public regulations and legal notices issued by
Federal agencies. These include Presidential proclamations and
Executive Orders and Federal agency documents having general
applicability and legal effect, documents required to be
published by act of Congress and other Federal agency
documents of public interest. Documents are on file for public
inspection in the Office of the Federal Register the day before
they are published, unless earlier filing is requested by the
issuing agency.

The **Federal Register** will be furnished by mail to subscribers
for $340.00 per year, or $170.00 for 6 months, payable in
advance. The charge for individual copies is $1.50 for each
issue, or $1.50 for each group of pages as actually bound. Remit
check or money order, made payable to the Superintendent of
Documents, U.S. Government Printing Office, Washington, DC
20402.

There are no restrictions on the republication of material
appearing in the **Federal Register**.

Questions and requests for specific information may be directed
to the telephone numbers listed under INFORMATION AND
ASSISTANCE in the READER AIDS section of this issue.

How To Cite This Publication: Use the volume number and the
page number. Example: 52 FR 12345.

THE FEDERAL REGISTER
WHAT IT IS AND HOW TO USE IT

FOR: Any person who uses the Federal Register and Code of
Federal Regulations.

WHO: The Office of the Federal Register.

WHAT: Free public briefings (approximately 2 1/2 hours) to
present:
1. The regulatory process, with a focus on the Federal
   Register system and the public's role in the
   development of regulations.
2. The relationship between the Federal Register and Code
   of Federal Regulations.
3. The important elements of typical Federal Register
   documents.
4. An introduction to the finding aids of the FR/CFR
   system.

WHY: To provide the public with access to information
necessary to research Federal agency regulations which
directly affect them. There will be no discussion of
specific agency regulations.

BOSTON, MA

WHEN: July 15, at 9 a.m.
WHERE: Main Auditorium, Federal Building,
10 Causeway Street,
Boston, MA.
RESERVATIONS: Call the Boston Federal Information
Center, 617-565-8129

FIGURE 10.2. *(continued)*

Contents

Federal Register

Vol. 52, No. 134

Tuesday, July 14, 1987

FIGURE 10.2. *(continued)*

Federal Register / Vol. 52, No. 134 / Tuesday, July 14, 1987 / Contents   V

<table>
<tr><td>

Hartman Garage, 26376

Labor Department
See Employment and Training Administration; Employment
    Standards Administration; Mine Safety and Health
    Administration

Land Management Bureau
NOTICES
Environmental statements; availability, etc.:
    Mark Twain National Forest, MO, 26365
    Rawlins District, WY, 26373

Mine Safety and Health Administration
PROPOSED RULES
Metal and nonmetallic mine safety:
    Ionizing radiation standards, 26352

Mine Safety and Health Federal Review Commission
See Federal Mine Safety and Health Review Commission

National Aeronautics and Space Administration
PROPOSED RULES
Federal Acquisition Regulation (FAR):
    Contracting by negotiation; Truth in Negotiations Act
    amendments, 26446

National Archives and Records Administration
NOTICES
Agency records schedules; availability, 26381

National Institutes of Health
NOTICES
Committees; establishment, renewals, terminations, etc.:
    Epidemiology and Disease Control Study Section et al.,
    26372

National Park Service
NOTICES
Concession contract negotiations:
    Bryce-Zion Trail Rides, Inc., 26373
    Oberlitner, Carl F., 26374
National Register of Historic Places:
    Pending nominations—
        Colorado et al., 26374
        District of Columbia et al., 26374

Navy Department
NOTICES
Meetings:
    Chief of Naval Operations Executive Panel Advisory
    Committee, 26368
    (2 documents)

Nuclear Regulatory Commission
NOTICES
Meetings:
    Reactor Safeguards Advisory Committee, 26382, 26383
    (2 documents)
Meetings; Sunshine Act, 26399
Applications, hearings, determinations, etc.:
    Texas Utilities Electric Co. et al., 26383
    Texas Utilities Generating Co. et al., 26383

Parole Commission
NOTICES
Meetings; Sunshine Act, 26399
    (2 documents)

</td><td>

Public Health Service
See Food and Drug Administration; National Institutes of
    Health

Research and Special Programs Administration
NOTICES
Hazardous materials:
    Applications; exemptions, renewals, etc., 26387, 26389
    (2 documents)

Securities and Exchange Commission
NOTICES
Self-regulatory organizations; proposed rule changes:
    Chicago Board Options Exchange, Inc., 26383
Self-regulatory organizations; unlisted trading privileges:
    Philadelphia Stock Exchange, Inc., 26384
    (2 documents)

Small Business Administration
NOTICES
Agency information collection activities under OMB review,
    26385
Disaster loan areas:
    New Jersey, 26384
Applications, hearings, determinations, etc.:
    Mezzanine Capital Corp., 26385
    Wilber Venture Capital Corp., 26385

Surface Mining Reclamation and Enforcement Office
RULES
Permanent program submission:
    Kentucky, 26299
    Pennsylvania, 26300

Transportation Department
See Coast Guard; Federal Aviation Administration; Federal
    Highway Administration; Research and Special
    Programs Administration; Urban Mass Transportation
    Administration

Treasury Department
See also Customs Service
RULES
Freedom of Information Act and Privacy Act;
    implementation, 26302

United States Information Agency
NOTICES
Art objects, importation for exhibition:
    Berthe Morisot—impressionist, 26394
Grants; availability, etc.:
    Private non-profit organizations in support of
    international educational and cultural activities,
    26395

Urban Mass Transportation Administration
NOTICES
Environmental statements; availability, etc.:
    Los Angeles Metro Rail Project, CA, 26393
Grants; UMTA sections 3 and 9 obligations:
    Bay Area Rapid Transit District, CA, et al., 26390

Veterans Administration
RULES
Loan guaranty:
    Securities released without prior approval; increase in
    value, 26342

</td></tr>
</table>

Federal Register / Vol. 52, No. 134 / Tuesday, July 14, 1987 / Notices   **26463**

DEPARTMENT OF EDUCATION

Office of Special Education and Rehabilitative Services

Research in Education of the Handicapped; Final Annual Funding Priority

AGENCY: Department of Education.

ACTION: Notice of Final Annual Funding Priority.

SUMMARY: The Secretary announces an annual funding priority for the Research in Education of the Handicapped program. This priority supports an early childhood research institute on policy.

EFFECTIVE DATE: This final annual funding priority takes effect either 45 days after publication in the **Federal Register** or later if Congress takes certain adjournments. If you want to know the effective date of this final annual funding priority, call or write the Department of Education contact person.

FOR FURTHER INFORMATION CONTACT: Linda Glidewell, Division of Innovation and Development, Office of Special Education Programs, Department of Education, 300 "C" Street SW. (Switzer Building, Room 3094—M/S 2313), Washington, DC 20202. Telephone: (202) 732–1099.

SUPPLEMENTARY INFORMATION: The Research in Education of the Handicapped program, authorized by sections 641–644 of Part E of the Education of the Handicapped Act (20 U.S.C. 1441–1444), supports research, surveys, and demonstration projects relating to the educational needs of children and youth with handicaps; and, as amended by the 1986 Amendments, authorizes funding for research related to early intervention services for infants and toddlers with handicaps. Under this program, the Secretary makes awards to eligible parties for research and related activities to assist special education personnel, related services personnel, and other appropriate persons, including parents, in improving the education and related services for infants, toddlers, children, and youth; and to conduct research, surveys, or demonstrations relating to the education of infants, toddlers, children, and youth with handicaps. Research and related activities supported under this program must be designed to increase knowledge and understanding of handicapping conditions and services for infants, toddlers, children, and youth with handicaps, including physical education or recreation.

Summary of Comments and Responses

A notice of proposed annual funding priority was published in the **Federal Register** on May 5, 1987 at 52 FR 16766. The public was given thirty days in which to comment. One comment was received in response to the notice of proposed annual funding priority. The comment was in support of the priority. Therefore, no changes have been made in the final priority.

Priority

In accordance with the Education Department General Administrative Regulations at 34 CFR 75.105(c)(3), and subject to available funds, the Secretary gives an absolute preference to each application submitted in response to the following priority. Each application must provide satisfactory assurance that the recipient will use funds made available to conduct the following activity:

Early Childhood Research Institute—Policy

This priority will establish an Early Childhood Research Institute to conduct a program of research related to policy development and implementation for providing early intervention and services for infants and toddlers with handicaps and their families. The research program must consist of two major areas of inquiry.

First, the institute must conduct descriptive studies that would identify, document, and analyze existing policies and policy development activities related to establishing comprehensive services for infants and toddlers with handicaps and their families. These studies must be conducted on an annual basis and must provide a State-by-State description of the status of States' efforts to implement comprehensive services. In conducting the studies, the institute must analyze data made available by the States and the Federal Government. The institute's research must include, but need not be limited to, studies that provide information about funding patterns for services, the numbers and kinds of infants and toddlers and their families receiving services, the numbers and kinds of services and service delivery agencies involved, the numbers and kinds of personnel involved in service delivery, and the status of personnel preparation, certification, and employment within each State.

Second, the institute must conduct explanatory research that includes, but is not limited to, studies that determine: (1) The positive and negative consequences of different State policies and funding patterns in providing comprehensive services; (2) State factors that account for variations in service availability; (3) State and local policies and practices that serve as incentives and disincentives for establishing comprehensive services; (4) policy development procedures and models that will assist State and local entities to develop comprehensive services; and (5) alternative statutory and/or regulatory changes that might be made at State levels to facilitate the development of comprehensive services.

In carrying out its research activities, the institute must provide research training and experience for at least 10 graduate students annually.

Period of Award

The Secretary will approve one cooperative agreement with a project period of 60 months subject to the requirements of 34 CFR 75.253(a) for continuation awards. In determining whether to continue the institute for the last two years of the project period, in addition to considering the factors in 34 CFR 75.253(a), the Secretary will also consider the recommendation of a review team consisting of three external experts selected by the Secretary and designated Federal program officials. The services of the review team are to be performed during the last half of the institute's second year, and will replace that year's annual evaluation which the recipient is required to perform under 34 CFR 75.590. During all other years of the project, the recipient must comply with 34 CFR 75.590. Costs associated with the services to be performed by the three external members of the review team are to be incorporated into the applicant's proposed budget. In developing its recommendation, the review team will consider, among other factors, the following:

(1) The timeliness and the effectiveness with which all requirements of the negotiated cooperative agreement have been or are being met by the recipient of the cooperative agreement and its subgrantees; and

(2) The degree to which the institute's research design and methodological procedures demonstrate the potential for producing significant new knowledge and products.

(20 U.S.C. 1441–1444)

(Catalog of Federal Domestic Assistance Number 84:023; Research in Education of the Handicapped Program)

Dated: July 1, 1987.

William J. Bennett,
Secretary of Education.

[FR Doc. 87–15909 Filed 7–13–87; 8:45 am]

BILLING CODE 4000-01-M

FIGURE 10.2.   *(continued)*

26466   Federal Register / Vol. 52, No. 134 / Tuesday, July 14, 1987 / Rules and Regulations

DEPARTMENT OF EDUCATION

34 CFR Part 237

Christa McAuliffe Fellowship Program

AGENCY: Department of Education.

ACTION: Final regulations.

SUMMARY: The Secretary issues regulations governing the Christa McAuliffe Fellowship Program for outstanding teachers currently authorized by Title V, Part D, Subpart 2 of the Higher Education Act of 1965, as amended by the Higher Education Amendments of 1986. These regulations specify the responsibilities of the Secretary in administering the program, the duties of State panels in selecting fellows, and the terms and conditions that apply to recipients of the fellowship awards.

EFFECTIVE DATE: These regulations take effect either 45 days after publication in the Federal Register or later if the Congress takes certain adjournments. If you want to know the effective date of these regulations, call or write the Department of Education contact person.

FOR FURTHER INFORMATION CONTACT: Ms. Willi Webb, Director, Policy, Planning, and Executive Operations, Office of Elementary and Secondary Education, U.S. Department of Education, 400 Maryland Avenue SW., Room 2189, Washington, DC 20202. Telephone (202) 732–5104.

SUPPLEMENTARY INFORMATION: The Christa McAuliffe Fellowship Program is authorized by Title V, Part D, Subpart 2 of the Higher Education Act of 1965, as amended by the Higher Education Amendments of 1986. It establishes a national fellowship program for outstanding full-time public and private school teachers. These teachers may use awards for projects approved by the Secretary to improve their knowledge or skills and the education of their students, including (1) sabbaticals for study or research directly associated with the objectives of the statute, or their own academic improvement, (2) consultation with or assistance to other school districts or private school systems, (3) development of special innovative programs, or (4) model teacher programs and staff development.

On May 13, 1987 the Secretary published a notice of proposed rulemaking (NPRM) for the Christa McAuliffe Fellowship Program in the Federal Register (52 FR 18184).

There are no significant changes or differences between the NPRM and

these final regulations. No comments were received regarding the NPRM.

Executive Order 12291

These regulations have been reviewed in accordance with Executive Order 12291. They are not classified as major because they do not meet the criteria for major regulations established in the order.

Paperwork Reduction Act of 1980

These regulations have been examined under the Paperwork Reduction Act of 1980 and have been found to contain no information collection requirements.

Assessment of Educational Impact

In the notice of proposed rulemaking, the Secretary requested comments on whether the proposed regulations would require transmission of information that is being gathered by or is available from any other agency of authority of the United States.

Based on the response to the proposed rules and on its own review, the Department has determined that the regulations in this document do not require transmission of information that is being gathered by or is available from any other agency or authority of the United States.

List of Subjects in 34 CFR Part 237

College and universities, Education, Elementary and secondary education, Scholarships and fellowships, Teachers.

(Catalog of Federal Domestic Assistance Number 84.196, Christa McAuliffe Fellowship Program)

Dated: June 30, 1987.

William J. Bennett,

Secretary of Education.

The Secretary amends Title 34 of the Code of Federal Regulations by adding a new Part 237 to read as follows:

PART 237—CHRISTA MCAULIFFE FELLOWSHIP PROGRAM

Subpart A—General

Sec.

237.1   What is the Christa McAuliffe Fellowship Program?
237.2   Who is eligible to apply under the Christa McAuliffe Fellowship Program?
237.3   How are awards distributed?
237.4   In what amount are fellowships awarded?
237.5   For what purposes may a fellow use an award?
237.6   What priorities may the Secretary establish?
237.7   What regulations apply?
237.8   What definitions apply?

Subpart B—How Does One Apply For An Award?

237.10   How does an individual apply for a fellowship?

Subpart C—How Are Fellows Selected?

237.20   What are statewide panels?
237.21   What are the responsibilities of a statewide panel?

Subpart D—What Conditions Must Be Met By Fellows?

237.30   What is the duration of a fellowship?
237.31   May a fellowship be awarded for two consecutive years?
237.32   What records and reports are required from fellows?
237.33   What is the service requirement for a fellowship?
237.34   What are the requirements for repayment of the fellowship?

Authority: 20 U.S.C. 1113–1113e, unless otherwise noted.

Subpart A—General

§ 237.1   What is the Christa McAuliffe Fellowship Program?

The Christa McAuliffe Fellowship Program (CMFP) is designed to reward excellence in teaching by encouraging outstanding teachers to continue their education, to develop innovative programs, to consult with or assist LEAs, private schools, or private school systems, and to engage in other educational activities that will improve the knowledge and skills of teachers and the education of students.

(Authority: 20 U.S.C. 1113, 1113b)

§ 237.2   Who is eligible to apply under the Christa McAuliffe Fellowship Program?

An individuals is eligible to apply for a Christa McAuliffe Fellowship if the individuals at the time of application—

(a)(1) Is a citizen or national of the United States;

(2) Is a permanent resident of the United States;

(3) Provides evidence from the Immigration and Naturalization Service that the individuals is in the Unites Stated for other than a temporary purpose with the intention of becoming a citizen or permanent resident; or

(4) Is a permanent resident of the Commonwealth of Puerto Rico, Guam, the Virgin Islands, American Samoa, the Trust Territory of the Pacific Islands, or the Northern Mariana Islands; and

(b) Is a full-time teacher in a public or private elementary or secondary school.

(Authority: 20 U.S.C. 1113b, 1113d(a))

§ 237.3   How are awards distributed?

(a) Except as provided in section 563(a)(3) of the Act, the Secretary awards one national teacher fellowship

Federal Register / Vol. 52, No. 134 / Tuesday, July 14, 1987 / Rules and Regulations   **26467**

under this part to an eligible teacher in each of the following:

(1) Each congressional district in each of the fifty States.

(2) The District of Columbia.

(3) The Commonwealth of Puerto Rico.

(4) Guam.

(5) The Virgin Islands.

(6) American Samoa.

(7) The Northern Mariana Islands.

(8) The Trust Territory of the Pacific Islands.

(b)(1) If the conditions stated in section 563(a)(3) of the Act apply, the Secretary publishes an alternative distribution of fellowship under this part that—

(i) Will permit fellowship awards at the level stated in § 237.4; and

(ii) Is geographically equitable as determined by the Secretary.

(2) The Secretary sends a notice of this distribution to each of the statewide panels established under § 237.20.

(Authority: 20 U.S.C. 1113b(a))

§ 237.4 In what amount are fellowships awarded?

A fellowship awarded under this part may not exceed the average national salary of public school teachers in the most recent year for which satisfactory data are available, as determined by the Secretary.

(Authority: 20 U.S.C. 1113b(a)(2))

§ 237.5 For what purposes may a fellow use an award?

Christa McAuliffe fellows may use fellowships awarded under this part for projects to improve education including:

(a) Sabbaticals for study or research directly associated with objectives of this part, or academic improvement of the fellows.

(b) Consultation with or assistance to LEAs, private schools, or private school systems other than those with which the fellow is employed or associated.

(c) Development of special innovative programs.

(d) Model teacher programs and staff development.

(Authority: 20 U.S.C. 1113b(b))

§ 237.6 What priorities may the Secretary establish?

(a) The Secretary may annually establish, as a priority, one or more of the projects listed in § 237.5.

(b) The Secretary announces any annual priorities in a notice published in the Federal Register.

(Authority: 20 U.S.C. 1113d(a))

§ 237.7 What regulations apply?

The following regulations apply to the Christa McAuliffe Fellowship Program:

(a) The Education Department General Administrative Regulations (EDGAR) in 34 CFR Part 77 (Definitions That Apply to Department Regulations).

(b) The regulations in this Part 237.

(Authority: 20 U.S.C. 1113d(a))

§ 237.8 What definitions apply?

(a) The following definitions apply to terms used in this part:

"Act" means the Higher Education Act of 1965, as amended.

"Fellow" means a fellowship recipient under this part.

"Fellowship" means an award made to a person under this part.

(b) *Definitions in EDGAR.* The following terms used in this part are defined in 34 CFR 77.1:

Department

EDGAR

Elementary school

Local educational agency

Private

Public

Secondary school

Secretary

State educational agency

(Authority: 20 U.S.C. 1113d(a))

Subpart B—How Does One Apply For An Award?

§ 237.10 How does an individual apply for a fellowship?

(a) To apply for a fellowship under this part, an individual must submit an application containing a proposal for a fellowship project as described in § 237.5, indicating the extent to which the applicant wishes to continue current teaching duties.

(b) The application shall provide this application to the appropriate LEA for comment prior to submission to the statewide panel for the State within which the proposal project is to be conducted as described in § 237.20.

(c) The applicant shall submit the application to the statewide panel within the deadline established by the panel.

(Authority: 20 U.S.C. 1113c, 1113d(a))

Subpart C—How Are Fellows Selected?

§ 237.20 What are the statewide panels?

(a) Recipients of Christa McAuliffe Fellowships in each State are selected by a seven-member statewide panel appointed by the chief State elected official, acting in consultation with the State educational agency (SEA), or by an existing panel designated by the chief State elected official and approved by the Secretary.

(b) The statewide panel must be representative of school administrators,

teachers, parents, and institutions of higher education.

(Authority: 20 U.S.C. 1113c)

§ 237.21 What are the responsibilities of a statewide panel?

(a) Each statewide panel has the responsibility for—

(1) Establishing its own operating procedures regarding the fellowship selection process; and

(2) Disseminating information and application materials to the LEAs, private schools, and private school systems regarding the fellowship competition.

(b) Each panel may impose reasonable administrative requirements for the submission, handling, and processing of applications.

(c) Each statewide panel must consult with the appropriate LEA in evaluating proposals from applicants.

(d) In their applications to the statewide panel, individuals must include—

(1) Two recommendations from teaching peers;

(2) A recommendation from the principal; and

(3) A recommendation from the superintendent on the quality of the proposal and its educational benefit.

(e) A statewide panel may establish additional criteria, consistent with the Act, for the award of fellowships in its area as it considers appropriate.

(f) A statewide panel shall submit to the Secretary its selections for recipients of fellowships under this part within the schedule established by the Secretary.

(Authority: 20 U.S.C. 1113d)

Subpart D—What Conditions Must Be Met By Fellows?

§ 237.30 What is the duration of a fellowship?

An individual may receive a Christa McAuliffe Fellowship under this program for up to 12 months.

(Authority: 20 U.S.C. 1113d(a))

§ 237.31 May a fellowship be awarded for two consecutive years?

A Christa McAuliffe fellow may not receive an award for any two consecutive years.

(Authority: 20 U.S.C. 1113b(a)(2))

§ 237.32 What records and reports are required from fellows?

Each fellow shall keep any records and submit any reports that are required by the Secretary.

(Authority: 20 U.S.C. 1113d(a))

FIGURE 10.2. *(continued)*

i

Reader Aids

Federal Register

Vol. 52, No. 134

Tuesday, July 14, 1987

INFORMATION AND ASSISTANCE

SUBSCRIPTIONS AND ORDERS

Subscriptions (public)	202-783-3238
Problems with subscriptions	275-3054
Subscriptions (Federal agencies)	523-5240
Single copies, back copies of FR	783-3238
Magnetic tapes of FR, CFR volumes	275-1184
Public laws (Slip laws)	275-3030

PUBLICATIONS AND SERVICES

Daily Federal Register

General information, index, and finding aids	523-5227
Public inspection desk	523-5215
Corrections	523-5237
Document drafting information	523-5237
Legal staff	523-4534
Machine readable documents, specifications	523-3408

Code of Federal Regulations

General information, index, and finding aids	523-5227
Printing schedules and pricing information	523-3419

Laws   523-5230

Presidential Documents

Executive orders and proclamations	523-5230
Public Papers of the President	523-5230
Weekly Compilation of Presidential Documents	523-5230

United States Government Manual   523-5230

Other Services

Library	523-5240
Privacy Act Compilation	523-4534
TDD for the deaf	523-5229

FEDERAL REGISTER PAGES AND DATES, JULY

24443–24970	1
24971–25192	2
25193–25344	6
25345–25578	7
25579–25860	8
25861–25962	9
25963–26126	10
26127–26292	13
26293–26468	14

CFR PARTS AFFECTED DURING JULY

At the end of each month, the Office of the Federal Register publishes separately a List of CFR Sections Affected (LSA), which lists parts and sections affected by documents published since the revision date of each title.

3 CFR

Proclamations:

5674	25345
5675	25347
5676	25963

Administrative Orders

Memorandums:

June 30, 1987	24971

Proposed Rules:

102	25124

5 CFR

213	25193
315	25193
841	25195
842	25197
870	25197
890	25197
1620	26293
2411	26127

Proposed Rules:

723	25124
1207	25124
1262	25124
2416	25124

7 CFR

29	25199
246	25182
250	24973
252	24973
301	25579
330	25861
340	25861
400	24978
418	25585
419	25585
427	25585
429	25585
453	25349
713	25353
795	26294
910	25200, 25965
925	24443
929	25201
967	25202
985	25202
1065	25203
1427	25354
1807	26130
1863	26130
1864	26130
1866	26130
1900	26130
1910	25585
1924	26130, 26139
1941	26130
1950	26130
1951	26130
1955	26130
1956	26130
1965	26130

1980	25586

Proposed Rules:

29	25235
418	25381
419	25382
427	25383
429	25384
439	25015
945	25016
1065	26016
1076	25020

8 CFR

3	24980
244	24982
·292	24980

Proposed Rules:

103	24475

9 CFR

114	26140

Proposed Rules:

92	25606
94	25020
317	24475
381	24475

10 CFR

4	25355

12 CFR

571	26295

Proposed Rules:

211	26153
225	26153
262	26153
350	25021
501	25870
543	25870
544	25870
545	25870
546	25870
551	25870
564	26017

13 CFR

Proposed Rules:

144	26019

14 CFR

39	24982, 24984, 25204, 25206, 25361, 25589, 25591, 25965, 26296
71	26141
97	24985

Proposed Rules:

Ch. I	25886, 26020
39	25022–25028, 25236–25239, 25606, 26021, 26022, 26, 348, 26349
71	25029, 25240, 26023, 26153, 26350, 26351

Other Publications

Another publication that will help you locate information on government sources is the *Federal Yellow Book* (see Fig. 10.3). 10.3).

If you are an experienced grant seeker, you may wish to become involved in the government contracts marketplace, and in this case will utilize the *Commerce Business Daily* (Fig. 10.4). For the purposes of this book, however, only the grants area is treated in depth—the contracts business requires a special effort on your part.

FIGURE 10.3.   A sample of the *Federal Yellow Book.*

| Fall 1987 | ▮▮▮▮▮▮▮▮▮▮▮ | Vol. XXII, No. 2 |

Federal

YELLOW
BOOK

a directory of the federal departments and agencies

A Publication of Monitor Publishing Co.

New York Office	**Washington, D.C. Office**
104 Fifth Avenue	**1301 Pennsylvania Avenue, N.W.**
New York, NY 10011	**Washington, DC 20004**
(212) 627-4140	**(202) 347-7757**

FIGURE 10.3.   *(continued)*

NATIONAL SCIENCE FOUNDATION
1800 G Street, N.W.
Washington, DC 20550

(Area Code 202)

Personnel Locator 357-9859
Procurement Info 357-7922
Grants Info 357-9498
Public Inquiries 357-9498
Freedom of Info 357-9492
Privacy Act 357-7335

OFFICE OF THE DIRECTOR

(Area Code 202)

Director Erich Bloch (Aug 29, 1990) 520 357-7748
Dep Director John H Moore 520 357-9427
  Sr Science Advisor Mary Clutter 518 357-9443
  Sr Staff Assoc Harvey A Averch 518 357-9433
  Special Asst Bertha R Salsburg 518 357-9419
Assistant Directors:
  Administration Jeff Fenstermacher 525 357-9482
  Biological, Behavioral, & Social Sciences David T Kingsbury 506 . . . 357-9854
  Computer & Info Science & Engr'g C Gordon Bell 306 357-7936
  Engineering Nam Pyo Suh 537 357-9832
  Geosciences William J Merrell Jr 510 357-9715
  Mathematical & Physical Sciences Richard S Nicholson 512 357-9742
  Science & Engineering Education Bassam Z Shakhashiri 516 357-7557
  Scientific, Technological, & Internatl Affairs Richard J Green 538 . . . 357-7631

NATIONAL SCIENCE BOARD

*Chairman Roland W Schmitt 545 357-9582
*Vice Chairman Charles E Hess 545 357-9582

Staff
Executive Officer Thomas Ubois 545 357-9582
Staff Assistants:
  Catherine M Flynn 545 357-9763
  Lois Hamaty 545 357-7512
Administrative Asst Dorothy Higgins 545 357-9585

*Members serve in these positions for a period of two years. The next election of officers will be held in May 1988.

OFFICE OF BUDGET, AUDIT AND CONTROL

Controller Sandra D Toye 425 357-9418
  Special Asst David E Gould 425 357-9418
  Administrative Asst Louise J McIntire 425 357-9418
Program Eval Staff Dir James M McCullough 425 357-9531

Audit and Oversight Division
Director Jerome H Fregeau 1241 357-9457
External Audit Sec Hd Clifford L Bennett 1241 357-7798
Internal Audit Sec Hd Chelton T Givens 1241 357-7833
Oversight Sec Hd James J Zwolenik 1241 357-9458

Budget Division
Director Joseph L Kull 425 357-7835
Budget Execution Sec Hd Edward L Blansitt III 425 357-7835
Program Analysis Sec Hd Jane T Stutsman 425 357-7835

OFFICE OF THE GENERAL COUNSEL

General Counsel Charles H Herz 501 357-9435
Dep General Counsel Robert M Andersen 501 357-9435
  Special Asst (Vacant) 501 357-9435
Assistant General Counsel:
  John C Chester 501 357-9435
  Lewis E Grotke 501 357-9435
  Arthur J Kusinski 501 357-9435
  Jesse E Lasken 501 357-9435

a

OFFICE OF INFORMATION SYSTEMS

(Area Code 202)

Note: A reorganization plan for this office has been proposed. Reorganization details and information regarding approval and/or implementation schedule were not available at press time.

Director Constance K McLindon 403 357-9760
  Special Asst Elizabeth A VanderPutten 403 357-7448
  Administrative Ofcr Annetta V Jeter 403 357-7448
Information Mgmt Dir Albert A Muhlbauer 403 357-7448

Central Applications Branch
Chief Robert L Adams Jr 401 357-9423
Financial Systems Sec Hd (Vacant) 401 357-9423
Office Systems Sec Hd Ruth Y Himes 401 357-9423
Proposal Systems Sec Hd Doris Hudnall 401 357-9423

Computer Center Branch
Chief Frederic J Wendling 401 357-7684
Central Systems Mgmt Sec Hd Lloyd E Douglas 401 357-7684
Technology Assessment Sec Hd Michael Morse 401 357-7684

Distributed Systems Branch
Chief Gerald B Stuck 401 357-9767
Distributed Software Sec Hd David P Krasnow 401 357-9767
Equipment Mgmt Sec Hd David H Hurley 220 357-7573
Network Sec Hd Richard V Langguth 401 357-9767
User Assistance Sec Hd Joanne G Hazlett 220 357-9646

OFFICE OF LEGISLATIVE AND PUBLIC AFFAIRS

Director Raymond E Bye Jr 527 357-9838
Dep Director Allen M Shinn Jr 527 357-9838
NSF Historian George Mazuzan 527 357-9838
Resource Ctr Dir Darla Clark 527 357-9838

Issues Group
Director Allen M Shinn Jr 527 357-9838
Issues Analyst (Vacant) 527 357-9720
Policy Analyst Marta Cehelsky 527 357-9730

Legislative Affairs Group
Director Raymond E Bye Jr 527 357-9838
Legislative Assistants:
  Shirley Y Day 527 357-9730
  Denise Michel 527 357-9730
Legislative Specialists:
  Joyce M Hamaty 527 357-9730
  Joel Widder 527 357-9730

Public Affairs Group
Director Karen Sloan Lebovich 527 357-9498
Public Info Chf Jack Renirie 527 357-9498
Public Affairs Specialists:
  Joyce Latham 527 357-9494
  Jeffrey Norris 527 357-9498
  Patrick Olmert 527 357-9498
  Elizabeth Tate 527 357-9498
  (Audio-Visuals) Susan Bartlett 527 357-9498
  (Freedom of Info) Maryellen Schoolmaster 527 357-9498
Natl Science-Technology Week Coord Mary Keeney 527 357-9838
Mosaic Editor Warren Kornberg 527 357-9498

DIRECTORATE FOR ADMINISTRATION

Assistant Director Jeff Fenstermacher 525 357-9482
Sr Assoc Marjorie MacFarlane 525 357-9524
Health Svc Dir Robert Smith 439 357-7775

b

7/10/87

FIGURE 10.4. A sample of *Commerce Business Daily*.

Commerce Business Daily

WEDNESDAY, July 15, 1987

Issue No. PSA-9381

A daily list of U.S. Government procurement invitations, contract awards, subcontracting leads, sales of surplus property and foreign business opportunities

U.S. GOVERNMENT PROCUREMENTS

Services

A Experimental, Developmental, Test and Research Work (research includes both basic and applied research)

Kirtland Contracting Center, Attn: AFCMD/BCW, 505/844-3819, Kirtland AFB NM 87117-5320

A – FUSED SILICA SURFACE FINISHING AND COATING INTERACTIONS STUDY Program Research and Development Announcement (PRDA) ADCMD 87-03. The Air Force Weapons Lab is interested in receiving proposals on the research effort described below. Proposals in response to this PRDA are desired by COB (1600 hours), 30 days after date of pub to AFCMD/PKRC, Kirtland AFB NM 87117-5320. Addtl proposals may be submitted at a later date if deemed necessary and required by the Govt. If sufficient proposals are selected to satisfy the PRDA ojectives as a result of the first submission, subsequent opportunities for proposed submission would not be made avail. Responders should consider instructions contained in the "Proprietary Info" and "When and How to Submit" sections of the AFSC Unsolicited Proposal Guide, AFSC Pamphlet 70-5; copies of which are avail from AFCMC/PKR, AFB, NM 87117-5320, 505/844-4565 on req. AFSC Form 91 Policy Agreements do not apply to PRDAS. The selection of one or more sources for contract award will be based on a scientific and engineering evaluation of your proposal to determine the relative merit of the approach taken in response to the announcement. New and creative solutions are of primary interest and will be ranked as number one in the evaluation process. Cost is ranked as the second order of priority. No further evaluation criteria will be used in source selection. The cost and technical proposals will be evaluted at the same time. Proposals must provide new or unique concepts, ideas, or approaches in order to qualify for evaluation and consideration for award. Proposals should ref PRDA No. 87-03. This annoucement is an expression of interest only and does not commit the govt to pay any proposal costs. The cost of proposal preparation in response to a PRDA is not considered an allowable direct charge to the resulting contract or any other contract. It is, however, an allowable expense to the normal bid and proposal indirect cost specified in FAR 31.205-16. The Air Force reserves the right to select for award any, all, or none of the proposals received in response to this announcement. It is est that 300,000 dollars/year for 1.5 years involving 2 manyears/year divided among two or more projects will be required for this effort. Multiyear awards are possible. Work should be scheduled to begin on 1 Sep 87. Questions on technical issues may be referred to the Project Officer, Lt David J. Doryland, AFWL/ARDB, 505/844-1776. Contractural issued should be referred to Ms Marlene Thacker, Hq AFCMD/PKRC, KAFB NM 505/844-8696. Cost proposal format and questions should be referred to Roger Shinnick, Hq AFCMD/PKF, 505/844-3720. Only Govt contracting officers are legally authorized to commit the Govt. Firms responding should indicate whether they are, or are not, a socially and economically disadvantaged business and whether or not they are a woman owned business. Foreign firms should be aware that restrictions may be imposed which could preclude their participation in this contract. The purposed of this effort is to study both the finishing of fused silica, and the interactions between the surface and any coating that might be deposited. The eventual goal is to develop a unique process that will be able to take finising techniques for small pieces and apply them to polishing a one meter diameter fused silica blank, producing a surface which has a finish that exceeds the state-of-the art and is compatible for applying an optical thin film. The process used should be cost effective and capable of polishing fused silica at high rates, while still addressing the following areas. In the area of finishing; unique and creative ideas are solicted for polishing large syrface areas. The following issued are considered to be critical: reduction of subsurface damage, surface impurities and surface roughness all of which correspond to surface absorption and scatter; the ability to maint uniformity on surface figure over large areas; and how the finishing technique affects laser damage thresholds. In the area of coating interaction, unique and creative ideas are solicited for studying the interface between the surface and an antireflection coating. The following issues are considered to be critical: the effect of polishing techniques on film adhesion; the introduction of impurites into the coating due to finishing; non destructive techniques used to study the film/surface interface; and how the finishing technique may alter the damage threshold of the coating. The contractor will document his ideas and demonstrate his tecnique. On Govt satisfaction of the two deliverables (a process report and studied samples) two options may be envoked to verify the process. The first option shzsll be to demonstrate the process on two 60 centimeter diameter Govt furnished pieces over a 1.5 year period. The second option shall be to further demonstate the process on one 100 centimeter diameter govt furnished piece over a 9 mo period. Teaming between different organizations is acceptable due to the thrusts in both finishing and coatings interactions. Submit only unclassified info for consideration and evaluation. In connection with this proposed acquisition, info is required as to whether your firm is considered a small business. For this R&D action a small business is: a concern, including its affiliates, whose annual receipts for its preceding three fiscal years do not exceed $13,500,000. (192)

CBD ELECTRONIC EDITION

An electronic edition of the COMMERCE BUSINESS DAILY is available from the following. Interested parties may contact them for full details. Mercury Computer Services CBD Electronic Data Files on P/C Diskette (in PA) 1-800/372-7368 or 1-800/522-2441. NATIONAL BID GUIDE, Inc. 6860 N. Kenanna, Tucson, AZ 85704, 602/575-1856. BIDNET, 5 Choke Cherry Rd, Rockville, MD 02850, 301/330-7000 or toll free 1-800/325-6871. CBD SEARCH SERVICES, INC., 13316 Rowles Pl. Herndon, VA 22070. 703/481-6644 or toll free 1-800/CBD-4750. UNITED COMMUNICATIONS GROUP, 4550 Montgomery Ave, Suite 700, North Bethesda, MD 20814 301/656-6666; SOFTSHARE, a Div. of MCR Technology Inc., 55 Depot Rd., Goleta, CA 93117, Sue Ernst 805/683-3841 (Collect); McGRAW HILL/DATA RESOURCES INC. (DRI), 24 Hartwell Ave., Lexington, MA 02173, 617/863-5100; DIALOG INFORMATION SERVICES, INC., 3460 Hillview Ave., Palo Alto, CA 94304, toll free 1-800/334-2564.

BUSINESS NEWS

FEDERAL PROCUREMENT CONFERENCE - ATLANTA, GA

U. S. Senator Sam Nunn and the other members of the Georgia Congressional Delegation and the U. S. Small Business Administration are sponsoring a Federal Procurement Conference on August 11, 12 and 13, 1987 at the Westin Peachtree Plaza Hotel, Atlanta, Georgia. The purpose of the conference is to assist the business community in doing business with federal, state agencies and federal prime contractors. There will be training sessions on various procurement topics in addition to one-on-one counseling in the marketplace. For further information contact: James Parker, Small Business Administration, 1375 Peachtree Street, N.E., 5th Floor, Atlanta, Georgia. 30367 or call 404/347-7587.

FEDERAL PROCUREMENT CONFERENCE, ANCHORAGE, AK

Senator Ted Stevens, in cooperation with the US Depts of Commerce and Defense, is sponsoring a Federal Procurement Conference on 20 Aug 87 at the Hotel Captain Cooke, Anchorage, AK. The purpose of the conference is to provide the business community with an opportunity to meet on a person-to-person basis with procurement specialists from Federal military and civilian agencies and Federal prime contractors. Attendees will be counseled on sales opportunities to the Federal Govt. Federal procurement and contracting procedures, and export opportunities. For further info contact: Barbara Andrews c/o Senator Stevens, Box #2 701 C St. Anchorage, AK 99513. Tel: 907/221-5915.

HQ Electronic Systems Div, Directorate of R&D Contrs, Deputy Contracting (PKR), Hanscom AFB, MA 01731-5000

A – ON-ORBIN EFFECTS OF SPACECRAFT CONTAMINATION. Contracting Officer, John L' Nunziato, 617/377-2689. Program Research and Development Announcement (PRDA) AFGL 87-1. The Air Force Geophysics Lab is interested in receiving responses on the research effort described below. Responses to PRDA due 45 days after publ of this notice to Dr E Murad, AFGL/PHK, Bldg 1102C, Rm 314A, Hanscom AFB, MA. Responses received after that date will not be considered. Responses must be IAW the Air Force Systems Command Pgm Research and Development Announcement guide. Copies of this document (AFSCP 70-4) can be obtained from the Small and Disadvantged Business Utilization Office (ESD/BC, Hanscom AFB, MA, 617/377-4973) upon req. The selection of one or more sources for contr award will be based on a scientific and engineering evaluation of the responses (cost and tech) to determine the relative merit of the approach taken in response to the announcement. Cost is ranked as the second order of priority. Responses must provide new and unique concepts, ideas or approaches and an associated technology development pgm to establish the reliability of these concepts, ideas or approaches, in order to qualify for evaluation and consideration for award. Responses should ref PRDA No. The cost of preparing proposals in response to this announcement is not considered an allowable direct charge to any resulting contr or any other contr. It is, however, an allowable expense to the normal bid and proposal indirect cost specified in FAR 31.205.18. The Air Force reserves the right to select for award any, all, or none of the responses received to this announcement. The period of performance for any contr award will not exceed 36 mos. It is anticipated that multiple awards will be made and the govt funding est for any given contr is between 36 man-mos and 72 man-mos. Proposals greater than the recommended man-mos will be considered, but the govt prefers proposals responsive to the stated est. Contractors should not propose the purchase of any eqpt as a direct charge to any contemplated contr. All tech data and computer software delivered under any resultant contr will be furnished to the govt w/unlimited rights. Tech proposals should not exceed 30 pages of double-spaced typewritten matls. Innovative concepts for partial solutions will be considered for smaller awards. Work should be scheduled to commence in 1st qtr FY88. Questions on tech issues may be referred to Dr Edmond Murad, AFGL/PHK, 617/377-3176. Contractural and cost response format questions should be referred to Lt Ron Ortiz, ESD/PKR, 617/377-4784. Offerors are cautioned that only Contracting Officers are legally authorized to commit the govt. The intent of this effort is to establish tech baseline for the effects on spacecraft in earth orbit of contamination. Responses are sought for the development of a predictive code which will provide info as to the sources and signatures of molecular contaminants, particulates and optical contamination and their effects on systems. Included in the pgm wil be a phase for the validation of the codes by comparison w/experimental results. Specific areas of interest are: (1) optical contamination in the space shuttle vicinity; (2) measurements of particulates in the space shuttle vicinity; (3) experiments to test the critical velocity theory; (4) experiments to image the molecular contaminant cloud surrounding spacecraft in low earth orbit; (5) codes for predicting contamination effects, especially by the inclusion of ionization phenomena; (6) analysis of the composition of spacecraft gaseous contaminants. (192)

Aeronautical Systems Div, Wright-Patterson AFB OH 45433-6503

A – HIGHLY SPECIALIZED SCIENTIFIC AND TECHNICAL INTELLIGENCE ANALYSIS TO SUPPORT AND COMPLEMENT, ANALYSIS BEING CONDUCTED BY FTD'S COMMAND, CONTROL AND COMMUNICATIONS (C3) DIVISION. The specialized, in-depth analysis would focus on the performance and effectiveness, in the environment and context of C3 in modern conventional and nuclear warfare, of a foreign country's: A) C3 processes, B) Communications media, C) Signals, D) Equipments, E) Subsystems, F) Systems, G) Networks, H) Technologies, I) Implications of the man-in-the-loop. The specialized, in-depth analysis would include exploitation of all-source intelligence data, engineering analysis, and operational analysis of the proceses by which a given foreign country organizes, equips, communicates with, controls and operates ea of its military forces and civil defense forces. The offeror would be required to provide evidence of expertise and experience in approaching and solving tech and analytical problems in the intelligence analysis environment. FTD is considering a fixed price, indefinite qty

Content

FIGURE 10.4. *(continued)*

Page 2 — COMMERCE BUSINESS DAILY — Issue No. PSA-9381; Wednesday, July 15, 1987

(FPIQ) person-hour rate order type contract, with a 36 month period of performance. Teaming between contractors is encouraged. The successful bidder would be required to accomplish a min of 50% of the work within his own organizaton and to subcontract out work to his team member(s) or subcontractors, as the need arises. Since the prime contractor may not know which special expertise will be required to perform a task levied upon him until he receives the task, the prime contractor would not be required to have his entire subcontracting team organized and specified when the proposal is submitted. In the course of a contract of this type, the prime contractor may gain access to proprietary info of other companies in performing advisory services for the govt. Thus, in accepting an award, the prime contractor would be required to agree 1) to protect othedr company(ies)'s info from unauthorized use or disclosure for as long as it is considered proprietary by other company(ies) and 2) to refrain from using the info for any purpose other than that for which it was furnished for a period of 3 yrs following the period of performance under contract. Upon accepting an award, it is anticipated that the contractor will be required to have an office, furnished by the contractor, and a Sensitive Compartmented Information Facility (SCIF) external to HQ FTD, located within a 25 mile radius of HQ FTD. All contractor personnel proposed for this effort will be, from time to time, working within the FTD SCIF: hence, all personnel proposed for this effort must be both eligible for Top Secret clearance IAW the Industrial Security Manual (DoD 5220.22-M) and meet Sensitive Compartmented Information (SCI) eligibility requirements. The offeror would be required to provide a cadre of personnel holding Top Secret clearances at the time of contract award. Those failing to demonstrate proper evidence may not be provided an RFP. Sources are requested to submit their responses within 15 days after publication of this notice. Contact Attn: ASD/PMWB, Deanna Hall. (194)

U.S. Army Aviation Systems Command, Directorate for Procurement & Production, 4300 Goodfellow Blvd., St. Louis, MO 63120

A -- INTEGRATION AND INSTALLATION OF THE AIRBORNE TARGET HANDOVER SYS/AVIONICS INTEGRATION (ATHS/AI) ONTO THE APACHE AH-64A ACFT The procurement will encompass the design, development qualification and productionof hardware and software required to provide the AH 64A with an integrated ATHS and communications navigation and identification control and display sys. The procurement will result in providing the AH 64A with a secure jam resistant digital communication capability fully integrated into the existing acft avionics system. It will facilitate intelligent automatic digital data processing for missiles weapons and related info transfer between other AH-64A's scout acft and ground units via tacfire compatible digital waveforms. This procurement will be a three phase end to end competitive buy. The first phase of the ATHS/AI acquisition is the design integration and validation of the ATHS processor and a Cockpit Managmenet Sys (CMS) in the AH-64A, the procurement of a technical data pkg with level III dwgs, and the low rate production of initial modification work orders (MWO) kits to satisfy fielding requirements. Integration of the ATHS processor will provide for the reliable transfer of target data in digital form between the scout acft and tha AH-64A attach helicopter, between AH-64A helicopters, or between a ground statiin and the AH-64A. Integration of the CMS will provide for interface with the fire control computer, control of the ATHS, UHF-AM radio, VHF-FM/AM radios or sincgars, doppler, and identification-fire or foe (IFF) via a control display unit. Additionally, a data transfrer sys will be integrated to allow for rapid loading of info into the CMS and ATHS. The second phase is to execute a contr option IAW FAR 17.207 to procure MWO kits for follow-on yr requirements. The third and final phase is the installation of the MWO kits via execution of a contr option IAW FAR 17.207 for installation. It is anticipated that a total of 653 MWO kits will be required. In view of the mangitude of the software integration requirement and the lack of comprehensive validated Govt doc, it is expected that offerors will possess extensive prior knowledge of both the AH-64A acft or acft of similar complexity as well as all of the types of sys being integrated, with particular emphasis on the ATHS sys, a digital burst data transfer sys operated by a control and display unit. RFP DAAJ09-87-R-A215, BOD o/a 22 Jul 87, closing o/a 7 Sep 87. All responsible sources may submit a proposal which shall be considered by the agency. For info contact Yvonne Watson, Contr Officer, 618/452-4331, AMSAV-PRR-AI, US Army St Louis Area Support Center, Bldg 331, Granite City IL 62040-1801. (192)

US Army Belvoir Research, Development and Engineering Center, AMSTR-PB, Belvoir Procurement Division, Fort Belvoir, VA 22060-5606

A – BROAD AGENCY ANNOUNCEMENT Sol No. DAAK70-87-Q-BAA1. Response date: 1 Aug 87 thru 8 Jan 88. POC: Michele Reichelt, Contract Specialist, AMSTR-PBLL, 703/664-5148. Broad Agency Announcement (BAA) describing research and development opportunities at the US Army Belvoir Research, Development and Engineering Center. The BAA is general in nature and identifies current research and development projects and areas of research interest in current and projected near term capabilities. Research Areas of Interest include Mobility, i.e., Bridging and Countermine; Survivability, Countersurveillance and Tactical Deception; Energy, i.e., Electric Power, Fuels and Lubricants and Environmental Control; Logistics, i.e., Water Supply, Fuels Handling, Supply Distribution, Marine Craft and Support Equipment; Mat'ls Technology Base, i.e., Corrosion Prevention and Coatings Systems, Composite mat'ls, Adhesives and Packaging; and fLow Intensity Conflict, o.e., LIC Tactical Forces Protection and LIC Countermine. Potential sources are encouraged to request copies of the BAA. After review of the BAA, Potential Sources are encouraged to have technical discussions with Center Technical Contacts. If a Potential Source has a novel research approach, a BAA proposal should be prepared. The proposal should address (1) the major research thrust; (2) the technical apporoach; and (3) the research goals and military relevancy. This BAA expires 3:30 EDT, 8 Jan 88. Successor Broad Agency Announcements are contemplated. Sol No. for this Broad Agency Announcement is DAAK70-88-Q-BAA1. Industrial Liason Office is M Harrisson, Advanced Systems Concepts Directorate, 703/664-1068, STRBE-HPPD. Responsible sources may submit a proposal which will be considered by Belvoir Research, Development and Engineering Center. All requests shall be in writing. No telephone requests will be honored. See Notes 57 and 80. (191)

The **Commerce Business Daily** (USPS 966-360) is published daily, except Saturdays, Sundays and holidays, for $243 a year (1st Class mailing) or $173 a year (2nd Class mailing) by the U.S. Government Printing Office, Washington, DC 20402. Second Class postage paid at Washington, DC and additional mailing offices. POSTMASTER: Send address changes to Superintendent of Documents, U.S. Government Printing Office, Washington, DC 20402-9373, with entire mailing label from last issue received.

The Secretary of Commerce has determined that the publication of this periodical is necessary in the transaction of the public business required by law of this Department. Use of funds for printing this periodical has been approved by the Director of the Office of Management and Budget through 30 September 1987.

US Dept of Energy, Idaho Operations Office, 785 DOE Pl, Idaho Falls, ID 83402, Attn: Trudy A Thorne, Contrs Mgmt Div, 208/526-9519

A – AUTOMOBILE SHREDDER RESIDUE COMBUSTION. Research and development culminating in proof-of-principle tests for the combustion of automobile shredder residue. Shredder residue consists primarily of the nonmetallic portions (plastics, etc.) of discarded automobiles and to a lesser extent, household and commercial appliances. At present, the matl is landfilled although nationally it represents an energy resource of about $3x10^{13}$ Btu ea yr. Recovery and utilization of shredder residue through combustion and generation of useful energy has been studied and general feasibility is indicated. This Pgm Research and Development Announcement (PRDA) req proposals for development and testing of integrated systems which encompass shredder residue handling and processing, combustion and energy conversion, emissions and ash mgmt, and energy utilization. The concepts proposed must be innovative, economical, and broadly appl throughout the nation. Concept research and development work will include system design and evaluation culminating in proof-of-principle testing at significant scale such that private sector implementation and commercialization may subsequently take place. The DOE seeks industrial participation in the development and testing effort; as a min, this participation shall include a combustion systems mfgr and a shredding operations firm. A cost share contr(s) is anticipated; cost sharing by the private sector participants is a requirement, and its extend will be part of the evaluation criteria. DOE ests $450,000 will be avail as the Fedl share of the initial phase of the projects selected for award (multi-phase projects are anticipated). Sol document, PRDA No. DE-PR07-87ID12704, expected to be avail in early Aug. Firms, individuals, or organizations interested in performing research and development on combustion of shredder residue must req the PRDA in writing from the above address. (192)

Robert Mueller, NASA Lyndon B Johnson Space Center, BG2/STS Operations Procurement Officed, Attn: Cindy Lynn, Houston, TX; 713/483-4165

A -- FLIGHT PREPARATION SUPPORT SERVICES. NASA/JSC is planning to modify an existing contract to extend the period of performance for the ongoing engineering development support for the ground-based hardware and software data systems in the Mission Control Center (MCC) and other ground-based data systems managed by JSC. These data systems support the Shuttle flights of the Space Transportation System (STS) and advanced systems planning for future NASA projects. The primary engineering development support will be associated with the MCC upgrade activities and follow-on development completion and implementation of the Digital Voice Intercom System (DVIS). These data systems support a wide variety of activities such as real-time and postmission spaceflight operations, flight controller training and simulations, medical laboratory and clinical systems, Program Office management support, and general scientific and engineering data reduction. The work will consist of: (a) management support services, (b) systems definition and design, (c) hardware and software engineering analysis, design, fabrication, implementation and testig, (d) product management, and (e) technical publications and documentation. Respondents must demonstrate experience, expertise and be knowledgeable of all of the above. The basis period of performance for this extension is 15 months commencing Jan 1, 88. Also two firm options are planned: the first will be for an additional 3-months performance following the basic extension period, and the second will be for continued work on certain DVIS requirements only, thru approx Dec 31, 90. Interested firms capable of meeting these requirements are invited to submit their specific qualifications to the above address within 20 days of this publication. This announcement is not a RFP and only responses providing adequate info will be considered. See Notes 11 and 68. (194)

Naval Weapons Support Ctr., Crane, IN 47522-5011

A -- EVALUATE COMPLIANT SUBSTRATES N00164-87-R-0275, due 083187, contact Lorene Trusty, Mr. Lee Sullivan, Contracting Officer, 812/854-1803. The contractor shall conduct and doc an industry search to determine component replacement techniques currently being employed or developed by the printed wiring board (PWB) manufacturing assembly community. Replacement techniques should be applicable to standard electronic modules (SEMS) in all formats specified in MIL-STD-1378B, printed wiring boards, thick-film multi-layer boards and leaded components. The search shall address ea of the following: soldering techniques employed, history of use, test and evaluation of replacement techniques, adaptability of techniques to Navy activities, and future trends in replacement techniques. The contractor shall conduct and doc an industry search to determine solder inspection techniques currently being employed or develnped by the PWB manufacturing/assembly community. Techniques should be applicable to SEMS in Formats B, C, and D as specified MIL-STD-1378B and thick-film mulit-layer boards to include copper ceramic, ceramic noble metal, and compliant boards. The search shall address ea of the following: Soldering processes, process controls, quality assurance parameters, disadvantages, and limitations, and future trends. The contractor shall provide a program status report to the government describing work accomplished, problems encountered, problems solved and est completion date. The contractor shall develop a program mgmt plan for executing all tasks required by this statement of work. The contractor shall develop and maintain a data mgmt program for addressing all facets of the generation, preparation, and del of all contructual mgmt, financial, administrative, and tech data, including software, del to Navwpnsuppcen Crane, IN. Period of performance shall be 1 Oct 87 through 30 Sept 88. All responsible sources may submit an offer which will be considered. (192)

NASA, George C Marshall Space Flight Center, Procurement Office, Code: AP29-K, Mellina Hudgins, Marshall Space Flight Center, AL 35812

A -- RESEARCH STUDY ENTITLED "ESSENTIAL EDUCATIONAL ENGINEERING R&D CAPABILITY" RFP 8-1-7-EM-70653. RFP will be released o/a 31 Jul 87. Contact Mellina Hudgins, 205/544-0309. FOB Destn. Period of performance 5 years. Est to require 190,000 direct labor hours. The proposed contract is intended to be awarded to the University of Alabama in Huntsville, Huntsville, AL 35899. This requirement is for maintenance of an essential educational engineering, research and development capability of an ongoing program which has been maintained by the University of Alabama in Huntsville for several years. This requirement will include a broad range of scientific and engineering activities which requires an essential capability for performing thecretical analyses; exploratory and analytical studies and experimentation in earth science dynamics; magnetospheric plasma and solar physics and aeronomy research. Also, general and specialized instrumentation experimentation and development; broad mat'ls processing in space experimentation and development; mat'ls research, evaluation, and data base development, evaluation and analyses; mission/flight operations analyses, and evaluation and integration research. See Note 22. All responsible sources may submit a proposal which shall be considered. RFP release date will be 15 days after this publication. (192)

US Army Belvoir Research, Development and Engineering Center, Belvoir Procurement Div, Fort Belvoir, VA 22060-5606

★ **A -- SYSTEM/HARDWARE INTEGRATION AND MANAGEMENT SCIENCE SUPPORT** Contact Nancy Boyd, contr specialist, Attn: AMSTR-PBCE, 703/664-4176. Contr officer, James LeViner, 703/664-5040. Contr No. DAAK70-84-D-0052. Award date: 7/30/87. McLean Research Center Inc. Perform System Hardware Integration and Management Science Support for the Directorate of Combat Engineering for an additional six month period to enable issuance of sol and award of new contr. This is a time and material contr and negotiations will be conducted with McLean Research Center Inc, Contr No. DAAK70-84-D-0052. See Note 46.

★ **A -- SYSTEM/HARDWARE INTEGRATION AND MANAGEMENT SCIENCE SUPPORT** Contact Nancy Boyd, contr specialist, Attn: AMSTR-PBCE, 703/664-4176. Contr Officer, James LeViner, 703/664-5040. Contr No. DAAK70-84-D-0053. Award date: 7/30/87. Science Applications International Corp. Perform System Hardware Integration and Management Science Support for Directorate of Logistics Support for an additional six months to enable sol and award of a new contr. This is a time and material contr and negotiations will be conducted with Science Applications International Corp, Contr No. DAAK70-84-D-0053. See Note 46. (192)

Commander, US Army Armament Munitions and Chemical Command, Procurement Directorate (Edgewood Area), Attn: AMSMC-PCB (A)/Price, Aberdeen Proving Ground (EA), MD 21010-5423

A -- TECHNICAL SUPPORT TO DEVELOP PERFORMANCE ESTIMATES AND DEGRADATION CAUSED BY ELECTRONIC WARFARE ENVIRONMENTS ON EXISTING AND DEVELOPMENAL ARMY MATL ITEMS AND SYS The contractor's effort under this sol shall be to provide technical support in the areas of electronic countermeasures (ECM), electronic counter-countermeasures (ECCM), infra-red countermeasures (IRCM) and infra-red counter-countermeasures (IRCCM) to assist AMSAA in evaluating selected Army sys. The support shall include technical expertise and resources to assist AMSAA in planning ECM/ECCM and/or IRCM/IRCCM test programs, evaluating the resulting test data, and preparing verbal and written reports and comand-level briefings. Support may also include conduct of comprehensive countermeasure susceptibility/vulnerability assessments (tactical and technical) of conceptual developmental, and fielded sys. DAAA15-87-R-0113, issued o/a 23 Sep 87. George Rittle, Contr Officer, 301/671-3821; Sarah Price, Contr Specialist, 301/671-2541. (192)

Headquarters Contracts Branch, Div of Contracts & Grants Management, HFA-512, 5600 Fishers Lane, Park Bldg, Room 3-30, Rockville, MD 20857

A – DRUG PRODUCT PROBLEM REPORTING PROGRAM. Sol 223-88-6061. BOD 31 Aug 87. Contact, Debbie Powell, 301/443-4420. Contracting Officer, Cynthia Hawley, 301/443-4460. Drug Product Problem Reporting Program (DPRP). In general, the Program involves mailing reporting forms to potential respondents, providing feedback to reporters and promoting participation in the program. This work can be categorized into 2 Modules as follows: (1) Program Operations - Maintaining the established activities of the problems including: mailing Problem Reporting Program (PRP) report forms, processing of Medical Device Reporting (MDR) Regulation, PRP and other adverse experience info received by FDA, editing, coding and data entry. (2) Program Development - This consists of promotional activities that are intended to increase the amount of info submitted to the PRP program by identifying new sources of info; explaining the program, encouraging participation, and disseminating data about the programs activities. (192)

Commander, US Army Armament Munitions and Chemical Command, Procurement Directorate (Edgewood), Attn: AMSMC-PCB (A)/Hash, Aberdeen Proving Ground (Edgewood Area), MD 21010-5423

A – MODELLING SUPPORT FOR DESIGN OF ADVANCED SOLID-PROPELLANT CHARGES. The Ballistic Research Laboratory is seeking qualified sources for a proposed task order contract. The proposed 3 yr contract will require tech support in the development of an advanced propelling charge by using, developing and modifying state-of-the-art modeling capabilities in the area of propelling charge phenomenology and/or the area of the use of advanced graphics displays to aid a charge design engineer in visualization of interior ballistic phenomena predicted by state-of-the-art interior ballistic codes. Individual tasks will be negotiated and approved as needed. A security clearance of Secret will be required for performance. The sol to be issued o/a 1 Aug 87. DAAA15-87-R-0114. POC Tandee Hash, Contract Specialist, Ernest D Henry, Contracting Officer. Notes 42 and 48 apply. (194)

NASA-Ames Research Ctr., Mail Stop 241-1, Moffett Field, CA 94035

CHAPTER 11

Characteristics of Government Grants

Many nonprofit agencies exhibit great fear and trepidation over concerns about strings attached to federal monies. While some of these fears are warranted, they are the concern of organizations that don't have adequate fiscal accountability. The restrictions governing usage of federal funds are understandable and in most cases reasonable. Yes, there are instances of disallowed expenditures many years after the grant has terminated, but they are avoidable and most people remember the exception rather than the rule. There are 30 billion dollars in federal grant funds and not everyone will have their expenditures disallowed.

The use of the Federal Grants-Requirements Worksheet (pp. 99–100) will help you comply with federal details.

Another important factor with federal funds is *time*. See Figure 11.1 for several considerations involved in this area.

Raising Matching Funds

One of the usual characteristics of a federal grant is the requirement for matching funds (also known as cost sharing). An

FIGURE 11.1. The time factor in federal funding.

Developing federal funds through the grants mechanism takes considerable lead time to generate. State funds have the same cycle constraints.

° You develop a proposal idea and redefine your project and start a search.

° You find through research that a federal program accepts proposals twice a year -- sometimes only once a year. In these cases your lead time may be more than one year.

Idea Generation Redefinition	Source & Deadline Research	Pre-proposal Contract	Deadline Date & Submit	Peer and Staff Review	Answer on Grant	1 year for generation of funds from grant proposal
			(months)			
1	3	5	7	9	12	

Meanwhile the federal bureaucracy has had a similar time constraint.

Draft Announcement in Federal Register	Announcement Comments	Publish Comments	Publish Final Grant Rules or Interim Rules	Publish Guidelines	Due Date	Review		Award Hardly Possible in 12 months from start of process
			(months)					
1	3	5	7	9	10	11	12	

The federal and state bureaucracies have to have six months to one year to get their mechanism to follow prescribed rules and produce applications. They do extremely well to get funds out of the system in twelve months of the federal year. Remember, federal year starts October 1 and ends September 30.

The federal system will not respond to your funding needs. They do have funds that can be used to fund unsolicited proposals. These monies are reserved funds or leftover funds (funds given back by inconsiderate grantees who didn't develop an accurate cash flow). If you know enough to inquire about the use of these funds, the federal bureaucrats may respond to a unique project that meets a need of the category or type of area they deal with. You may not always be successful, however, the program director will at least be aware that you know how to "play the game."

FEDERAL GRANTS -- REQUIREMENTS WORKSHEET

Project Title _____

Funding Sources _____

____   Periodic Progress Reports (see Project Planner)

____   Final Completion Reports   Date Due: _____

        Individual Responsible: _____

        Delivered to Whom: _____

____   OMB Circulars Applicable -- List Them: _____

        In Grants Library: _____ Ordered and Received: _____

____   Rules on Continuation of Funding -- How Many Years: _____

        Is there a progression in awards (first consulting grant, then

demonstration, then evaluation, etc.)? If so, what is best progression?

_____

_____

____   Cost Sharing Requirement -- How Much Matching Funds Do You Have To

        Contribute

        _____% -- $_____

____   Rules Governing Materials Produced on

            Grants:

            Copyrights:

            Patents:

____   On-site Visits by Feds.

                        Announced Yes____   No____

____   Review OMB and FMC guidelines governing procedures requirements and

        rules for this grant. (Find rules listed in CFDA Appendix.) This

        is not an impossible task to accommodate.

                                                        (Cont.)

FEDERAL GRANTS -- REQUIREMENTS WORKSHEET (Cont.)

____   Can We Provide Human Subjects Review?

        Do We Need A Committee?

        These are just a few eye-opening concerns to be raised at this point

in our search for federal funds. These concerns are only a few of the many

assurances you will be required to sign. This page is meant to get you

thinking. Federal funds do have their "strings."

---

organization can be asked to supply either cash, services, or facilities to match a percentage of the grant.

The worksheet on Sources of Matching Funds (p. 101) can help you plan a successful matching-funds campaign, even before you begin to approach federal agencies; it contains several standard methods for cost sharing and provides you with an evaluation system for each method.

Federal Grants-Management Circulars

Perhaps the most imposing characteristics of federal grants are the highly regulated, detailed rules about grant management: allowable costs, indirect cost rates, accounting requirements, and the like.

Before getting involved in government grants, you and/or your accounting department should review the appropriate grants management circulars.

The Office of Management and Budget produces OMB circulars that outline uniform standards for financial dealings with government granting agencies. These circulars are described in Table 11.1 and Figure 11.2.

The circulars can be ordered free from the Office of Management and Budget, 17th and Pennsylvania Avenue, N.W., Washington, D.C. 20503, or directly at your federal regional office.

SOURCES OF MATCHING FUNDS

Project Title: _____

TYPE	HOW IS THIS APPLICABLE TO THE PROJECT	LIST SUGGESTIONS THAT CAN BE USED	HOW MUCH MONEY COULD BE ATTRIBUTED TO THIS METHOD
In-kind contributions, donated services, space, equipment			
If training is involved, how much more will trainees be paid after training is completed			
Fund Raising Techniques			
Direct Mail			
Dance			
Raffles			
Wills & Bequest			
Sales – Products			
Can you donate indirect costs?			
Matching Grants – can you get a grant to match this grant? Example – Community Foundation to match federal or state grant			

TABLE 11.1. A Brief Description of the Major OMB Circulars

NAME	WHAT IT DOES	AREAS COVERED	SPECIAL RAMIFICATIONS
OMB Circular A-21	Defines cost principles for federal research and development grants to educational institutions	Cost definition, allowable costs, unallowable costs	Long and complex circulars; wide range of allowable costs
OMB Circular A-95	Designates a procedure of review by local government before dispursing Federal funds	Any grant area covered is listed in *CFDA* by program number	Get on the local committee or develop a "friend" who is on it; call your county planning department for information
OMB Circular A-102	Sets administrative standards for federal agencies in management of grants to state and local governments	Application forms, grant payments, eligibility, matching share, financial management system, property management procurement standards	Although different federal agencies may set their own guidelines, they are usually in harmony with the standard set down in this circular

OMB Circular A-110	Set administrative standards for federal agencies in the management of grants to nonprofit organizations	Application forms, grant payment, matching shares, procurement standards	No federal agency may set more rigid standards than those outlined in the circular; exceptions to this rule are allowed when grantee has weak financial history
OMB Circular A-111	Sets out guidelines for joint funding of grant programs		Tells how to get funding from more than one agency for your project
Federal Management Circular 74-4	Establishes principles and standards for determining costs applicable to grants and contracts to state and local government	Outlines what costs are allowable under grants and contracts	Tells what rules apply to lease and rental of equipment, etc.

Note: You don't have to be an expert on OMB circulars; these government publications were researched to provide information for matrixes for regulations on purchase/lease applicability.

FIGURE 11.2.   A description of OMB circulars.

Appendix I: Programs Requiring Circular Coordination

This appendix lists programs requiring Circular and or other types of management coordination. The Circulars and management directives represented are OMB Circular No. A-87; OMB Circular No. A-102; Environmental Impact Statement; OMB Circular A-110; and Executive Order 12372.

A-87

OMB Circular No. A-87 establishes principles and standards for determining costs applicable to grants and contracts with State and local governments. They are designed to provide the basis for a uniform approach to the problem of determining costs and to promote efficiency and better relationships between grantees and the Federal Government.

When State and local governments are recipients, the following programs listed in the Catalog of Federal Domestic Assistance are subject to the provision of A-87, except where restricted or prohibited by law.

Included also in the list are programs falling under the purview of A-87 because the Federal grantor agencies have elected to use the A-87 standards for recipients and programs not otherwise covered by the circular.

A-102

OMB Circular No. A-102, establishes uniform administrative standards for the administration of grants and contracts to State and local governments.

When State and local governments are recipients, the following programs listed in the Catalog of Federal Domestic Assistance are subject to the provisions of OMB Circular No. A-102.

Included also in the list are programs falling under the purview of OMB Circular No. A-102 because the Federal grantor agencies have elected to use the OMB Circular No. A-102 standards for recipients and programs not otherwise covered by the circular.

Environmental Impact Statement

Specific programs listed in the Catalog of Federal Domestic Assistance have been determined to have a significant effect on the environment and require an environmental assessment or an Environmental Impact Statement (EIS) under Section 102(2)(C) of the National Environmental Policy Act of 1969 (Public Law 90-190; 42 U.S.C. 4332(2)(C), and Executive Order 11514 (34 FR 4247) of March 4, 1970, (Significant effects include actions that may have both beneficial and detrimental effects.)

In the early stages of project application, and in all cases prior to agency decisions concerning major action, the applicant should be ad-

vised by the Federal agency from which assistance is being sought that he will be required to submit environmental impact information (to be submitted under agency guidelines) in connection with the proposed project for an environmental assessment (to be made by the Federal agency), or an Environmental Impact Statement (to be supplied by the Federal agency) concerning the proposed project.

Although the list below is not inclusive, it contains programs normally requiring either an environmental assessment or an Environmental Impact Statement.

For EIS coordination requirements, refer to the Preapplication Coordination section of each program description.

A-110

OMB Circular No. A-110 sets forth administrative requirements for the administration of grants and other agreements to include money or property in lieu of money; does not include technical assistance programs providing services, loans, loan guarantees, insurance, or direct payments to individuals. Reference to this circular appears in the Application Procedure section of programs that apply.

Applicants are public and private institutions of higher education, hospitals, and other quasi-public and private nonprofit organizations.

Executive Order 12372

Executive Order 12372 "Intergovernmental Review of Federal Programs," structures the Federal government's system of consultation with State and local governments on its decisions involving grants, other forms of financial assistance, and direct development. Under E.O. 12372, States, in consultation with their local governments, design their own review processes and select those Federal financial assistance and direct development activities they wish to review.

Since October 1, 1983 most States have acted to establish a review and comment system in response to E.O. 12372. In such cases, applicants for grants will need to meet the requirements of the intergovernmental consultation process established by a particular State and its local governments before Federal agencies take action on an application.

For more information on the process a particular State requires to be followed, an applicant should contact the office or official designated as the single point of contact in his or her State. Consult the individual program description in the Catalog to determine whether the programs under which he/she plans to apply is subject to E.O. 12372. Consult the Federal agency's application package for instructions on State notification.

The State Single Point of Contact List is printed at the end of the listing of programs.

PROGRAM DESCRIPTION	A-87	A-102	EIS	A-110	E.O.12372
DEPARTMENT OF AGRICULTURE					
10.001 Agricultural Research—Basic and Applied Research		X		X	
10.025 Plant and Animal Disease and Pest Control	X	X		X	X
10.028 Animal Damage Control	X	X		X	
10.069 Conservation Reserve Program			X		
10.140 Minority Research and Teaching Grants				X	
10.153 Market News	X				
10.156 Federal-State Marketing Improvement Program	X	X			X
10.164 Wholesale Market Development	X	X		X	X
10.200 Grants for Agricultural Research, Special Research Grants				X	
10.202 Cooperative Forestry Research		X		X	
10.203 Payments to Agricultural Experiment Stations Under Hatch Act				X	
10.205 Payments to 1890 Land-Grant Colleges and Tuskegee University				X	
10.206 Grants for Agricultural Research—Competitive Research Grants				X	
10.207 Animal Health and Disease Research				X	
10.209 1890 Research Facilities				X	
10.210 Food and Agricultural Sciences National Needs Graduate Fellowship Grants				X	
10.211 Higher Education Strengthening Grants				X	
10.213 Competitive Research Grants for Forest and Rangeland Renewable Resources				X	
10.214 Morrill-Nelson Funds for Food and Agricultural Higher Education		X			
10.350 Technical Assistance to Cooperatives	X	X		X	
10.405 Farm Labor Housing Loans and Grants	X	X	X	X	X
10.411 Rural Housing Site Loans			X		X
10.414 Resource Conservation and Development Loans		X	X	X	X
10.415 Rural Rental Housing Loans			X		X
10.416 Soil and Water Loans					X
10.418 Water and Waste Disposal Systems for Rural Communities	X	X	X		X
10.419 Watershed Protection and Flood Prevention Loans		X	X	X	X
10.420 Rural Self-Help Housing Technical Assistance		X	X	X	X
10.421 Indian Tribes and Tribal Corporation Loans		X			
10.422 Business and Industrial Loans			X		X
10.423 Community Facilities Loans		X	X	X	X
10.427 Rural Rental Assistance Payments					X
10.433 Rural Housing Preservation Grants	X	X	X	X	X
10.434 Nonprofit National Corporations Loan and Grant Program			X		X
10.475 Cooperative Agreements with States for Intrastate Meat and Poultry Inspection	X	X			X
10.500 Cooperative Extension Service				X	
10.550 Food Distribution		X			X
10.553 School Breakfast Program	X	X		X	X
10.555 National School Lunch Program	X	X		X	X
10.556 Special Milk Program for Children		X		X	X
10.557 Special Supplemental Food Program for Women, Infants, and Children	X	X			X
10.558 Child Care Food Program	X	X		X	X
10.559 Summer Food Service Program for Children	X	X		X	X
10.560 State Administrative Expenses for Child Nutrition	X	X			X
10.561 State Administrative Matching Grants for Food Stamp Program	X	X			X
10.564 Nutrition Education and Training Program	X	X			X
10.565 Commodity Supplemental Food Program	X	X			X
10.566 Nutrition Assistance For Puerto Rico					X
10.567 Needy Family Program	X	X			X
10.568 Temporary Emergency Food Assistance (Administrative Costs)		X			X
10.652 Forestry Research	X	X		X	
10.664 Cooperative Forestry Assistance	X	X	X		X
10.665 Schools and Roads—Grants to States		X			
10.666 Schools and Roads—Grants to Counties		X			
10.668 Additional Lands—Grants to Minnesota		X			
10.669 Accelerated Cooperative Assistance for Forest Programs on Certain Lands Adjacent to the Boundary Waters Canoe Area	X	X			X
10.850 Rural Electrification Loans and Loan Guarantees			X		
10.851 Rural Telephone Loans and Loan Guarantees			X		
10.852 Rural Telephone Bank Loans			X		
10.901 Resource Conservation and Development	X	X	X		X
10.904 Watershed Protection and Flood Prevention	X	X	X		X
10.906 River Basin Surveys and Investigations					X

CHAPTER 12

How to Contact Government Funding Sources

The importance of pre-proposal contact with government funding sources cannot be overemphasized. In a study of 10,000 federal proposals, the only variable that was statistically significant in separating the funded and rejected proposals was *pre-proposal contact with the funding source.*

It is estimated that chances for success go up 300 percent when contact with the funding source before the proposal is written. Up to this point in our book, we have not discussed the writing of the proposal; instead we have discussed the organization of the funding effort or project. You cannot write a proposal accurately until you know about the funding source. Who will read your application? What should you say? What should you avoid saying?

Contact is encouraged by letter (see sample on p. 111), phone, and when possible, in person. One way to force yourself to follow this systematic approach to funding sources is to set up a schedule of preproposal contact as follows:

106

SAMPLE LETTER TO A FEDERAL AGENCY

(REQUEST FOR MAILING LIST AND PAST GRANTEES)

Date:

Name
Title
Address

Dear _____ :

　　Our organization is developing a project we would like to have funded under your program _____ .

　　Please add me to your mailing list to receive the necessary application forms, program guidelines, and any other information you feel would be helpful to me in this endeavor. A list of last year's grant recipients under this program would be very much appreciated.

　　I have enclosed a self-addressed stamped envelope for your convenience in returning the list of successful grantees. Thank you for your cooperation and assistance in this matter.

　　　　　　　　　　　　　　　　Sincerely,

　　　　　　　　　　　　　　　　Name/Title
　　　　　　　　　　　　　　　　Phone Number

Note to the Letter Writer: You will receive the agency's publications as a result of this letter (see, e.g., Fig. 12.1).

- *Week 1:*　Write to two funding sources.

- *Week 2:*　Write to two more funding sources.

- *Week 3:*　Call the first two funding sources from Week 1 and ask for appointments.

- *Week 4:*　Call the second two funding sources from Week 2 and ask for appointments.

- *Week 5:*　Follow up on appointments from phone conversations.

- *Week 5:* Follow up on appointments from phone conversations.

The worksheets in this chapter will help you organize your approach. Follow these suggestions and your chances of winning a grant and developing a positive relationship with the funding source will increase.

First, evaluate each funding source by utilizing the federal grants Prospect Analysis Form (pp. 109–110). Then move on to contacting those sources with the highest probability of funding your proposal.

Prospect Analysis Form

This worksheet will help you draw conclusions from your interviews and grant research. Use it to determine how well matched your project is with the funding agencies you have investigated. Fill out one analysis form for each prospective grant source.

Evaluate each of the criteria on the basis of the information you have gathered. Circle a number in the "Match" column corresponding to the amount of similarity between what you have and what they want. Multiply this figure by the "Weight" of each criterion and place that number in the "Total" column, then add up the totals and interpret your score. A higher score means a higher probability of winning grant support from a funding source.

The top or highest score will become the first funding source you will approach by personal contact.

Questions for Past Grantees

You have requested a list of previous grantees by letter (see sample on p. 107) and enclosed a self-addressed stamped envelope for their convenience. You may have to request the list again by phoning the funding source. (It is wise to keep a checklist of requested materials, and a summary sheet of each contact with the funding source—see pp. 113 and 114.) Let the funding source know that you are aware that you are entitled to a list under the "Sunshine Law" (or Freedom of Information

PROSPECT ANALYSIS FORM

Fill out this sheet if you are within the funder's:

° geographic scope of giving (has this funding source given in your

   geographic vicinity?)

° type of funding (does funding source buy what you have to sell -- bricks

   and mortar, equipment?)

° restrictions (do they give to your type of organization, 501 C-3 Tax

   Exempt?)

	CRITERION	MATCH	WEIGHT	TOTAL
A.	Your staff, expertise advocates -- will they appeal to this funding source	0 1 2 3 4 5	X2	
B.	Interest Area -- how important is the need in this area to the funding source -- have they given to the need you represent	0 1 2 3 4 5	X2	
C.	Financial Giving Patterns -- average grant size -- can they afford you	0 1 2 3 4 5	X1	
D.	Contact/Friends -- can you link yourself to funding source	0 1 2 3 4 5	X3	
		TOTAL SCORE		

(Cont.)

Act). If all else fails, you may ask your congressperson to get the list for you. By law, federal bureaucrats have to respond to a congressperson's request. He or she *will* get the list! Once your list is in hand:

1. Select a grantee that is not in close proximity to you.
2. Call grantee and tell them where you got their name.

PROSPECT ANALYSIS FORM (Cont.)

0 = NO MATCH BETWEEN YOUR PROJECT AND FUNDING SOURCE

1 = POOR MATCH

2 = FAIR MATCH

3 = GOOD MATCH

4 = EXCELLENT MATCH

5 = PERFECT MATCH

<u>Interpreting Your Score</u>

Below 20:   buy a lottery ticket

20-25:   borderline

25-40:   good matches

Adapted from "Matching Your Proposal With Foundations Not All Luck," by Robert F. Semple, in <u>Fund Raising Management</u>, September-October 1971, pp. 29-32.

---

3. Ask to speak to the director or person who worked on the proposal. (They will generally feel flattered you called.)
4. Prioritize or select from the following list of questions, or ask any of your own that will assist you in learning about the funding source.

   - Did you call or go see the funding source before writing the proposal?

   - Whom did you find most helpful on funding source staff?

   - How did you use your advocates or congresspeople?

   - Did you utilize a review by the funding source before submission?

   - Did you use consultants to help you on the proposal?

SAMPLE LETTER TO A GOVERNMENT AGENCY

(REQUEST FOR APPOINTMENT)

Date:

Name
Title
Address

Dear _____ :

My research on your funding program indicates that a project we have developed would be appropriate for consideration by your agency for funding under _____ .

I would appreciate five to ten minutes of your time to discuss my project. Your insights, knowledge, and information on any grants that have been funded using a similar approach would be invaluable. My travel plans call for me to be in your area on _____ .

I will phone to confirm the possibility of a brief meeting to discuss this important proposal.

Sincerely,

Name/Title
Phone Number

Note to the Letter Writer: You will not get a response back from this letter. Its intent is to show protocol and that you mean business.

- Was there a hidden agenda to the program's guidelines?

- When did you begin the process of developing your application – contacting the funding source?

- What materials did you find the most helpful in developing your proposal?

- Did the funding source come to see you (site visit) before the proposals were awarded? After awarded? Who came?

FIGURE 12.1.   A sample of the National Science Foundation *Bulletin*.

Ecosystem Studies Program

The following guidelines should be followed for the preparation of multi-investigator/multi-disciplinary proposals for the Ecosystem Studies Program, Division of Biotic Systems and Resources. Proposals should be limited to 60 doublespaced pages for the body of the research proposition (i.e., introduction, literature, review, hypothesis exposition, methods, project execution, and management plan). Appendices of supporting materials (e.g., bibliographies, budgets, professional resumes, catalogs of extant information and related research efforts) should be limited to 40 single-spaced pages. Proposals should be printed on one side only, numbered at the bottom, and secured only in the top left corner.

Proposals for studies involving only one or two investigators/disciplines must comply with the limitations expressed in **Grants for Research and Education in Science and Engineering** (NSF 83-57). For this class of proposals, the total pages for appendices must not exceed 15 single-spaced pages.

General format requirements (NSF 83-57) apply to all proposals. Proposals not adhering to these guidelines will be returned.

Contact Dr. James Callahan, Associate Program Director for Ecosystem Studies, for further information (357-9596).

Elementary School Science Instruction Programs

NSF announces the second of two program solicitations intended to encourage partnerships among publishers, school systems, and scientists/science educators for the purpose of providing a number of competitive, high quality, alternative science programs for use in typical elementary schools. Proposals are sought for projects that will improve the content, increase the role of the child as an active agent in the learning process, and lead to an increase in the time allotted to science instruction in elementary schools.

Preliminary proposals, which are required, must be received by June 1, 1987. The deadline for formal proposals is Aug. 3, 1987. Request Brochure NSF 87-13. For further information, contact Mr. Jerry Theise, Ms. Mary Kohlerman, or Ms. Alice Moses, Instructional Materials Development Program (357-7066).

Advisory Committee for Science and Engineering Education

The Science and Engineering Education Advisory Committee will meet May 18-19, 1987, in Rm. 540, NSF. For further information, contact Dr. Truman Schwartz, Executive Secretary (357-7074).

Computer and Information Science and Engineering Reorganized

Effective Mar. 1, 1987, the networking and communications research activities of the Division of Advanced Scientific Computing (ASC) in the CISE directorate were moved into a new Division of Networking and Communications Research and Infrastructure (NCRI). The affected programs are NSFNET, EXPRES, and Networking and Communications Research.

The Supercomputer Center and New Technologies programs remain in ASC, and other CISE activities are unchanged.

Dr. Stephen Wolff is Acting Division Director of NSRI (357-9717). Dr. John Connolly is Division Director of ASC (357-7558), and Dr. Melvin Ciment is Deputy Division Director (357-9776).

Organizational Changes in Grants and Contracts

The following listing reflects recent personnel and organizational changes in the Division of Grants and Contracts (DGC).

Policy Office
Head, William Kirby (357-7880)

Institutional Activities and Data Management Office
Acting Head, Leonard Redecke (357-9496)

BBS/MPS Branch
Branch Chief, George Lynch (357-9662)
Head, Section I, Joanna Rom (357-9653)
Head, Section II, Aaron Asrael (357-9843)

ENG/STIA/SEE Branch
Branch Chief, Richard Hastings (357-9626)
Head, Section I, Karen Sandberg (357-9626)
Head, Section II, Herbert Wolff (357-9602)

GEO/ADM/CISE
Branch Chief, Michael Kenefick (357-9784)
Head, Section I, Stephen Williams (357-9621)
Head, Section II, William Bruning (357-7544)

For a more detailed listing, contact Debra Poczik, DGC Administrative Officer, Rm. 1140, (357-7880).

Changes in the Directorate for Engineering

The Division of Fundamental Research in Emerging and Critical Engineering Systems (ECES) has been organized as follows:

Division of Fundamental Research in Emerging Engineering Technologies
Frank L. Huband, Acting Division Director (357-9618)
T. Kenneth Gustafson, Deputy Director (357-9545)

Division of Fundamental Research in Critical Engineering Systems
Arthur A. Ezra, Division Director (357-9545)
Michael P. Gaus, Deputy Division Director (357-9500).

New Pay Rate for Consultants Under NSF Awards

Effective Feb. 15, 1987, the maximum daily rate of pay for consultants under NSF awards is increased from $263 to $277. This new rate is equivalent to the current maximum rate paid to a GS18 Federal employee and is exclusive of indirect costs, travel, per diem, clerical services, vacation, fringe benefits, and supplies. Contact the Division of Grants and Contracts (357-7880) for further information.

Brochure Revision and Update

A major revision and updating of the former Grants for Scientific and Engineering Research, renamed **Grants for Research and Education in Science and Engineering**, was published in March. For consistency, the former identification number, NSF 83-57, has been retained, with the addition of "rev. 1/87" to indicate that the material is current.

The new brochure covers, for the first time, proposals to the Science and Engineering Education (SEE) directorate.

NATIONAL SCIENCE FOUNDATION,
WASHINGTON, D.C. 20550

Erich Bloch, Director
John Moore, Deputy Director

The **NSF Bulletin** is issued monthly (except July and August). Use of funds for printing this periodical has been approved by the Office of Management and Budget through March 31, 1991.

Editor: Mary Wilson, Office of Legislative and Public Affairs (357-9498).

CHECKLIST OF MATERIALS FROM PUBLIC FUNDING SOURCES

Directions: Check those materials sent for. Put the date requested in column A and the date received in column B.

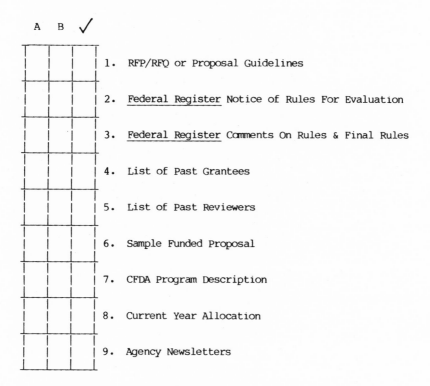

A   B   ✓

			1. RFP/RFQ or Proposal Guidelines
			2. <u>Federal Register</u> Notice of Rules For Evaluation
			3. <u>Federal Register</u> Comments On Rules & Final Rules
			4. List of Past Grantees
			5. List of Past Reviewers
			6. Sample Funded Proposal
			7. CFDA Program Description
			8. Current Year Allocation
			9. Agency Newsletters

on the visit? What did they wear? How old were they? Would you characterize them as conservative, moderate, liberal? Did anything in the process surprise you?

• How close was your initial budget to the awarded amount? (You can check honesty here by taking a look at their proposal when you visit the funding source. The Freedom of Information Act allows you to see any proposal funded by government money.)

• Who on the funding source's staff negotiated the budget?

• What would you do differently next time?

PUBLIC FUNDING SOURCE CONTACT

SUMMARY SHEET

Project Title: _____

This sheet should be added to each time you contact a public funding source:

AGENCY NAME: _____

PROGRAM OFFICER: _____

Contacted on (date): _____

By Whom: _____

Contacted by: LETTER _____   PHONE _____

                PERSONAL CONTACT _____

Staff or Advocates Present: _____

DISCUSSED: _____

_____

_____

_____

_____

RESULTS: _____

_____

_____

_____

_____

Questions for Past Reviewers

You have requested a list of reviewers (see sample on p. 115) Under the Sunshine Law, you *can* demand one, but don't. Tell the funding source you are concerned about the make-up or background of their reviewers. If they are reluctant to give names, try to get general information on the reviewers, their

SAMPLE LETTER TO A FEDERAL AGENCY

(for a list of reviewers)

Date:

Name
Title
Address

Dear _____:

    I am presently developing a proposal under your _____
program. I would find it very helpful to have a list of last year's
reviewers. Such a list would assist me in developing my approach
and the appropriate writing style. Please advise me if the make-up
or background of the review committee will change significantly in
the next grant year.

    My proposal is based upon the level, expertise and diversity of
the reviewers. Information on the composition of the review committee
will be used to prepare a quality proposal based upon the reviewers'
background.

    I have enclosed a self-addressed stamped envelope for your
convenience in responding to this request. I will utilize the
materials you send and I thank you for your consideration in
providing them.

                     Sincerely,

                     Name
                     Title
                     Phone Number

Note to the Letter Writer: You want a list of last year's reviewers
so you can write a proposal based on their expertise, reading level,
biases, etc. Once you have the list, you can contact the reviewers
themselves to discuss the points they look for when reviewing proposals. (See "Questions for Past Reviewers.")

---

selection process, and the process of reviewing and allocating
points to a proposal.

    You can utilize your congressperson or his or her administra-
tive assistant to procure your list. If you use this method, ask your

congressperson not to use your name in describing who wants the material.

When you get the list, examine it for bias and make-up (where they are from, background, etc.), call a reviewer and explain that you understand that he or she was a reviewer for _____ program. Then ask:

- How did you get to be a reviewer?
- Did you review proposals at a funding source location or at home?
- What training or instruction did the funding sources give you?
- Did you follow a point system? What and how?
- What were you told to look for?
- How would you write a proposal differently now that you have been a reviewer?
- What were the most common mistakes that you saw?
- Did you meet other reviewers?
- How many proposals were you given to read?
- How much time did you have to read them?
- How did the funding source handle discrepancies in point assignments?
- What did the funding source wear, say, and do during the review process?
- Did you know about a staff review to follow your review?

Using the Phone with Federal and State Funding Sources

Calling public funding sources on the phone is best described as an experience in itself. The informational contact you develop from your research seldom yield the correct name and phone number of the best individual to handle your request. Ask who else could help you or where the person listed in your research has moved to. There is usually a person in your congressperson's office assigned to help people in your district with grants. These techniques should enable you to locate the office that administers the funds for the program your research has uncovered.

The best approach is to go see the funding source. If this is the approach you choose, use the techniques outlined in "Making an Appointment with a Public Funding Source Official."

If you cannot go to visit the funding source, you will want to gather the same information over the phone that you would if you were face to face with the funding source. Although it is harder to "read" what the funding source is really saying through voice inflection as opposed to watching the nonverbal behavior visible in personal contact, you need to uncover his or her hidden agenda so that you can meet the needs of the funding source and increase your chances of success.

Review the suggestions under "Questions to Ask a Program Officer," below.

Making an Appointment with a Public Funding Source Official

The objective of seeking an appointment is to get an interview with a decision maker in the program.

- Step 1: Call and ask for the program officer or information contact.

- Step 2: Get the secretary's name and ask when his or her boss can be reached. (Some federal employees are on flex-time or come in and leave at odd hours to cope with the D.C. traffic.)

- Step 3: Call back; try person-to-person, and if that fails, ask the secretary for help.

An alternative plan might involve any of the following:
a. Try to get an advocate to set up your appointment.
b. Try getting congressional help with appointment.

c. Try going in "cold" early in the week to get an appointment for later in the week. They prefer to get you out of the way *now*!

- Step 4: Ask the secretary if anyone else can answer technical questions on the program. You may get an appointment with a screen (they're better than talking to yourself).

- Step 5: When you get to the program person on the phone, introduce yourself and give a brief (ten words) description of your organization. Say:
  a. The need for _____ in our area is extreme.
  b. We are uniquely suited to deal with the problem, the research, etc.
  c. You understand that their programs deal with these needs and you would like to make an appointment to talk to them about their program priorities and your approaches.
  When you get an appointment, stop and hang up. If no appointment is possible, refer to "Questions to Ask a Program Officer." Tell them you have some questions; can you set up a ten-minute call or would they prefer to answer your questions now? (*Note:* fill in any information you get—names, phone numbers, etc.—on the research sheet.)

The Visit and Questions to Ask

PRE-PROPOSAL CONTACT WITH PUBLIC FUNDING OFFICIALS

This initial meeting is vital to getting the input you need to prepare a proposal that is tailored to the funding source (see p. 119). This visit will allow you to review and update any information you have.

The object of such a visit is to find out as much as possible about the funding source and how they perceive their role in the awarding of these grants. With your newly acquired information you can produce a proposal that reflects a sensitivity to their needs

TAILORING WORKSHEET

A. From your background on the funding source, what approach to meeting the needs would be preferred by them? How will you tailor your approach?

_____

_____

B. How many points has the funding source assigned to each of the following grant components?

POINTS

_____ THE TITLE: _____

_____

_____ THE NEEDS: _____

_____

_____ THE OBJECTIVES: _____

_____

_____ THE METHODOLOGY: _____

_____

_____ THE BUDGET: _____

_____

_____ THE EVALUATION: _____

_____

_____ OTHER: _____

_____

_____ TOTAL POINTS: _____

_____

These points will determine importance and time appropriated to each section of the proposal.

and their perception of their mission. In *A Theory of Cognitive Dissonance,* Festinger states that the more different we are perceived to be from what the funding source expects, the greater the problems with communication, agreement, and acceptance. We want the funder to *love us,* so we need to produce less dissonance and more agreement by looking and talking as the funder "thinks" we should. Dress is critical. If you don't know the funding source's expectations on dress, play it safe and read *Dress for Success* by John T. Molloy (New York: Warner Books, 1976).

PLAN FOR YOUR VISIT

In a personal visit, two people are better than one. An advocate or graduate of your program has more credibility than a paid staff member. Try to match up age, interests, and other characteristics of your people with funding executive (see p. 121). Before the visit, it will be helpful to role-play your presentation with your team member and to decide who will take responsibility for the various parts of the presentation.

WHAT TO TAKE

1. Materials that help demonstrate the *need.*
2. Your Proposal Development Workbook (Swiss Cheese Book).
3. Audio-visual aids—short filmstrip, videotape, film-loop, slide presentation, pictures, cassette tape, or the like—that document the need. Visual aids should be short (three to five minutes long). Avoid talking about your methods and solution. Be sure you can work machines with ease and replace bulbs, etc. Bring extension cords, three-prong to two-prong plug adapter, and whatever other peripheral equipment you will need.
4. Information on your organization that you can leave, but *never leave a proposal.*

QUESTIONS TO ASK A PROGRAM OFFICER

Check over these questions you will ask:

• Do you agree that the need addressed by our project is important?

FUNDING SOURCE STAFF PROFILE

Before each visit to a funding source, review this sheet to be sure you are taking the correct materials, advocates, and staff.

AGENCY DIRECTOR: _____

PROGAM DIRECTOR: _____

CONTACT PERSON: _____ TITLE: _____

PROFILE: Birthdate: _____ Birthplace: _____

Education: College _____

          Postgraduate _____

Work Experience: _____

_____

Military Service: _____

Service Clubs: _____

Religious Affiliations: _____

Interests/Hobbies: _____

Publications: _____

_____

Comments: _____

_____

- Your average award in this area last year was X dollars; do you expect that to change?

- How will successful grantees from last year affect people putting in new or first applications? Will last year's grantees be in competition with me or have their funds been set aside? If so, how much is left for new awards?

- Are there any unannounced programs or unsolicited proposal funds in your agency to fund an important project like ours?

- What is the most common mistake or flaw in proposals you receive?

- Are there any areas you would like to see addressed in a proposal that may have been overlooked by the other grantees or applicants?

- We have developed several approaches to this needs area. You may know whether or not one of our approaches has been tried. Could you review our concept paper and give us any guidance?

- Would you review or critique our proposal if we got it to you early?

- Would you recommend a previously funded proposal for us to read for format and style? (Remember—you are entitled to read funded proposal, but be cool!)

- What changes do you expect in types or number of awards this year (fewer new awards versus continuing awards, etc.)?

- Is there a relationship between the type of grant programs and awards? Is there a progression (consultant grant—demonstration—evaluation)?

- The guidelines call for _____ copies of the proposal. Could you use more? If I provided all copies, may I bind them in an inexpensive binder? What type do you prefer?

- Will I create any problems by using tabs or dividers in my proposal?

CHAPTER 13

The Project Planner

How To Control the Proposal-Preparation Process

The Project Planner (see pp. 124–125) is arranged in the order in which you approach each phase of the proposal-preparation process. You must take each part separately and control the process or it can overwhelm even experienced grant seekers.

The end result is a proposal that is tailored to the funding source by using the information you have obtained and recorded on the preceding worksheets.

The *order* that a typical proposal follows when it is to be read *is not* the same order used to construct the proposal.

The "How To" Grants Manual is designed in a step-by-step process that follows the sequence involved in proposal preparation. The sequence that most proposal outlines follow is misleading to the beginning grant writer. The order of the parts of the proposal and the sequence designated by the funder have been designed for accuracy and understanding while reading the proposal, and are *counterproductive when applied to the writing of the proposal.*

PROJECT PLANNER™

PROJECT TITLE: _____

A. List Project objectives or outcomes A. B. B. List Methods to accomplish each objective as A-1, A-2, A-3 . . . B-1, B-2 . . .	MONTH		TIME	PROJECT PERSONNEL	PERSONNEL COSTS		
	BEGIN	END			SALARIES & WAGES	FRINGE BENEFITS	TOTAL
	C / D		E	F	G	H	I

TOTAL DIRECT COSTS OR COSTS REQUESTED FROM FUNDER ▶

MATCHING FUNDS, IN-KIND CONTRIBUTIONS, OR DONATED COSTS ▶

TOTAL COSTS ▶

Sheet _____ of _____

Proposal Developed for _____

PROJECT DIRECTOR: _____ Proposed starting date _____ Proposal Year _____

CONSULTANTS • CONTRACT SERVICES			NON-PERSONNEL RESOURCES NEEDED SUPPLIES • EQUIPMENT • MATERIALS				SUB-TOTAL COST FOR ACTIVITY	MILESTONES PROGRESS INDICATORS	
TIME	COST/WEEK	TOTAL	ITEM	COST/ITEM	QUANTITY	TOT. COST	TOTAL I. L. P	ITEM	DATE
J	K	L	M	N	O	P	Q	R	S
							T	◄ % OF TOTAL	
								◄	
							100%	◄	

TYPICAL PROPOSAL SEQUENCE	PROJECT PLANNER SEQUENCE	
		Page
A. Cover Letter	1. Needs Statement	000
B. Title Page	2. Objectives	000
C. Summary	3. Methods	000
D. Introduction	4. Evaluation	000
E. Problem/Need	5. Future Funding	000
F. Objectives	6. Dissemination	000
G. Methods	7. Budget	000
H. Evaluation	8. Title Page	000
I. Future Funding	9. Summary	000
J. Dissemination	10. Attachments	000
K. Budget	11. Cover Letter	000
L. Attachments		

The Project Planner can be used to develop a variety of proposals and projects. Each part of the process has the corresponding page numbers and the forms and worksheets that will help the beginning grant seeker to write the section, while the veteran may use the forms as a checklist to insure that he or she has included all he or she can under each section.

Needs Statement

Most grant seekers feel very strongly about the need for their project or research. Too many grant seekers assume that the funding source shares the same feelings of concern and the urgency of addressing the need as soon as possible. This wishful thinking is rarely correct. The funding source has to choose from among many interesting proposals, and you must *create* the feeling of *immediacy* or *urgency* so that the funding source cannot put you off until next year.

Record any of the following types of data that can demonstrate the need. Keep the data in this section of your Proposal Development Workbook (Swiss Cheese Book). Later, when you write a tailored proposal to each funding source, you can select the data that you think will be best used to convince the particular funding source of the need. Why document the need? The documented

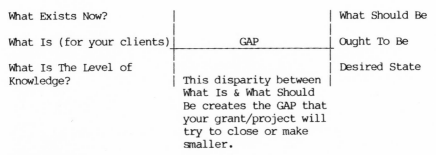

FIGURE 13.1

existence of a problem or need that is viewed by the funding source as a state of affairs that could be better, improved, or different, is the reason they give away their money. Funding sources are *"buying"* a better state of affairs. From pure research to model or demonstration projects, the funding source is supporting a change or improvement in what exists now. This can be represented by the diagram in Figure 13.1.

The urgency is created by how well you document the need and make the funding source feel that the movement toward the desired state cannot wait any longer. Since not all proposals can be funded, reality says that some will have to wait. Those that do not get funded did not do as good a job at:

- documenting a real need (perceived as important)
- demonstrating what ought to be (for clients)
- creating the urgent need to close the gap

DOCUMENTING WHAT IS

1. Review the section on "Ways to Perform Needs Surveys" to assess whether any of these will help document the need.
2. Use statistics from articles and research: e.g., 70 percent of children have . . .
3. Use quotes from leaders or experts in the field: Dr. Flockmeister said—
4. Use case statements: e.g., John Quek, a typical client who lives in a . . .
5. Describe national need and reduce it to a local number that

is more understandable: e.g., 90 percent of the elderly have . . . This means that at the West Side Senior Center, 215 elderly . . .

6. State need in terms of one person: e.g., the average veteran has had . . .

7. Use statements of community people: police, politicians, clergy, and others.

To establish what "Ought To Be," proven statistics may be difficult or impossible to find. The use of experts' statements and quotes to document what ought to be is much more credible than your opinion. (*Note:* You do not put your opinion in the needs statement. You are demonstrating your knowledge of the field; you have surveyed the literature; you know the situation.)

The needs section is written to be motivating. One way to motivate a funding source is to use their own studies, surveys, or statistics. The same basic proposal can be tailored to two different funding sources by quoting different studies that appeal to their own view of the need. You can "appear" at the end of the needs statement as the logical choice to attack the gap and move toward reducing the problem. If the proposal format required by the funding source does not have a section that deals with your capability, the best place to put in your credentials is at the end of the needs statement.

HERE IS A COMPELLING NEED $\longrightarrow$ Here is the "right" organization to fund to reduce the gap.

This transition from the need to your credibility can come from a simple sentence that states: It is the mission of our organization to address this need. For example, you develop a gap between what is and what ought to be. This is the basis for need and urgency to move to close the gap.

After the case is made for the need in a factual way, you add that:

- It is the mission of our institution to deal with this problem.

- Your unique qualities make you best suited for the job. You have the staff or facilities for this project to work or use your "sameness" to others: "Our project will serve as a model to the many other similar agencies that face this dilemma each day." (This results in a multiple effect from funding this project; the results potentially have effect on many.)

• The needs are here and now; each day they go unmet and the problem grows.

Objectives

The objectives are measurable steps you will take to narrow or close the gap created in the needs statement (see Figure 13.2).

When you have accomplished Objectives A and B, you will move toward closing the gap. You will have less gap left than you had before.

Objectives follow the needs statement since you cannot write the objectives unless you document the need and what is to be reduced.

Since the accomplishment or attainment of each objective will close the gap, you must write objectives that are measurable and can be evaluated for the degree to which they have been attained, and thus, the amount of the gap that has been closed.

Note for researchers: The search or review of relevant research in the field is analagous to "what is" and what ought to be. The objective of a research proposal is different from a model project in that you seek to disprove the null hypothesis. When this is ac-

FIGURE 13.2

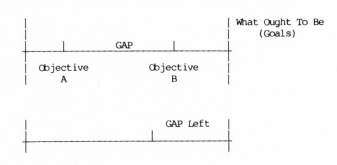

complished at a level of statistical significance, it acts to close the gap on what knowledge we have that is predictable and proven.

There has been increasing pressure by various groups (Proxmire's Golden Fleece Awards, "Reaganism") to make all researchers relate their research in a practical way to what (exactly) can be done with it. Philosophical arguments aside, there are conservative elements that want a component of research grants to deal with such issues as dissemination of results and how the findings can be used by the general public.

WRITING OBJECTIVES

Objectives tell the grant seeker and funding source "what it is" that will be accomplished at the end of the grant—how much or how little change will occur or what will be different at the end of this expenditure of funds from what was there before.

The *methods* tell *how* you will accomplish this change. The objective tells what will be accomplished and *how much* will be accomplished. Objectives state the measurable end for which you will be held accountable.

Methods state the means to that end. The first rule-of-thumb is: If there is only one way to accomplish the objective, you have probably written a method. Accomplishing the objective involves a good choice of methods or activities. For example, one seminar participant stated his objective as: "To build a visitors' center for our museum." Ask yourself how many ways you can build a visitors' center. (Yes, you can build it below ground or above, two stories or three.) Building the visitors' center is not the objective; it is a method—*how you will do it* ("it" being the actual objective).

When asked why he wanted to build a visitors' center, his response was: "To understand the relationship between the museum buildings so visitors can more effectively use the museum." The *"what"* that this man wanted to accomplish could be done in a variety of ways (*methods*). The visitors' center is a means to an end—effective utilization of the museum. Why go through all of this? Because the reason a funding source will give you money relates to helping people use and appreciate the museum, not to the bricks and mortar of a visitors' center. The bricks and mortar do not lend themselves to the kind of measurement that the issue of effective utilization does.

A TECHNIQUE FOR WRITING OBJECTIVES

Step 1: Determine result areas. Result areas are the key places you will look at to see improvements or changes in the client population. Examples include "Health of people over 65 years of age in St. Louis"; "Better-educated minority students"; or "More efficient use of our museum."

Step 2: Determine measurement indicators. Measurement indicators are quantifiable parts of your result area. By measuring your performance with these indicators, you are able to see how well you are doing. Examples include: "Number of hospital readmissions of people over 65 years old"; "Scores on standardized tests"; or "Number of people who understand relationship of museum buildings." Brainstorm a number of measurement indicators for each result area, then select the one that reflects your intent and is the least difficult to deal with.

Step 3: Determine performance standards. Performance standards answer the question, "How much [or how little] of the measurement indicators do we need to consider ourselves successful?" (closing the gap). Using our above examples, we might determine the following performance standards: "10 percent drop in hospital readmissions"; "Scores rising from 80th to 90th percentile on the Flockmeister reading scale"; or "50 percent reduction in direction giving by staff."

Step 4: Determine the time frame. The time frame is the amount of time in which you want to reach your performance standards. It's *your* deadline. You might decide you want to see a 10 percent drop in hospital readmissions within six or eighteen months. Usually, this time frame is determined for you by the funding source. Most grants are for twelve months. Use months one through twelve, instead of January, February, etc., because you seldom get to start the grant when you expect to.

Step 5: Determine cost frame. This is the amount of money that represents the cost of the methods or activities you have selected as your approach to meet this objective. The cost estimate is obtained from the planning document you will fill out next. You may leave this blank until you complete your project planner and then come back and fill it in. *Remember:* a funding source could take the number of clients to benefit and divide the amount requested to complete this objective. The end result could be embarrassing.

Step 6: Write the objectives. This step combines the data you have generated in the previous five steps. The standard format for an objective is: "To [action verb and statement reflecting your *measurement indicator*] by [*performance standard*] by [*deadline*] at a cost of no more than [*cost frame*]." The example concerning reading scores could look like this: "To increase the reading scores of freshmen at Flockmann University minority skills program by 20% on the Flockmann reading scale in 12 months at a cost of $50,000."

Step 7: Evaluate the objective. Review your objective and answer the question: "Does this objective reflect the amount of change we want in the result area?" If your answer is "yes," you probably have a workable objective. If not, the chances are that your measurement indicator is wrong or your performance standards are too low. Go back to those steps and repeat the process.

When writing program objectives, you should go through the same seven steps. Again, remember to emphasize end results, not tasks or methods. Do not say what you are going to do; instead, try to emphasize the ultimate benefit of your program's work.

Methods

The methods, or activities, section is the detailed description of what you will actually do to accomplish or meet the objectives. The methods tell:

- What you will have to do.
- Who will be needed.
- How long they will work.
- The materials and equipment you will need.

These are all a function of what you set out to accomplish. The best order to proceed in is to develop your methods to meet the objectives. Rather than inflating your budget or price for this project, add several methods that would insure the meeting of your objectives. When you negotiate the final award, you will gain much more credibility with the funding source by eliminating methods, instead of lowering the price for the same amount of work.

The methods section will:

- *describe program activities* in detail: How do they fulfill objectives?

- describe the *sequence, flow, and interrelationship* of activities.

- describe planned *staffing of program:* Who is responsible for what?

- describe the *client population* and method of determining client selection.

- present a *reasonable scope of activities* that can be accomplished within the stated time frame and with the resources of your agency.

It should also:

- make reference to the cost/benefit ratio of your project.

- state specific time frames.

- include a discussion of risk (why your success is probable).

- describe the uniqueness of your methods and overall project design.

- assign responsibility to specific individuals for each part of the project.

The Project Planner will provide a form that will insure that your methods section reflects a well-conceived and well-laid-out plan for the accomplishment of your objectives.

Project Planner

The Project Planner we present here is the result of ten years of work with grant and contract preparation. Use these explanations as you look at the form on pp. 124–125.

1. List your objectives or tasks under A. Give them what they want; some contracts may require tasks or enabling objectives.

2. Under B, list the method necessary to meet the objective. These are the tasks you have decided upon and are *your approach* to meeting the need. (Note that this newest form of the Project Planner has combined what were two columns: A and B. This was done to promote more efficient utilization of space. State your Objective A, B, C,... and list your method as A-1, A-2, A-3...B-1, B-2....)

3. In Column C/D, place the date you will begin and end each activity.

4. In Column E designate the number of person-weeks (you can use hours or months) needed to accomplish that task.

5. Column F is used for designating the key personnel that will use measurable or significant amounts of time on this activity and the accomplishment of this objective. The designation of key personnel is critical for developing the job description for each individual. If you list the activities for which the key personnel are responsible and the minimum qualifications or background required, you will have a rough job description. Call a placement agency to get an estimate of the salary needed to fill the position. The number of weeks or months will determine full- or part-time classification. (*Note:* This provides the opportunity to look at how many hours of work you are providing in a given time span. If you have your key personnel working more than 160 hours per month, it may be necessary to adjust the number of weeks in Column E to fit a more reasonable time frame. You may have to reschedule activities or shift responsibility to another staff member.)

6. *Personnel costs:* special care should be placed on analyzing staff who will be donated from your organization. This may be a

requirement for your grant (refer back to the section on matching funds). You may want to use this donated contribution to show your good faith and appear as a better investment to the funding source. (*Note:* Put an asterisk by each person you donate to the project. Be sure to include your donation of fringes, as well as wages. As you complete the remaining columns, put an asterisk by anything else you donate.)

7. *Consultants and contract services:* these three columns are for the individuals and services that are most cost-efficiently supplied by individuals who are not in your normal employ. They may be experts at a skill you need that does not warrant your training a staff member or hiring an additional staff person for (evaluation, computers, commercial art, etc.). There are no fringes paid to consultants and contract services.

8. *Nonpersonnel resources needed:* this is where you list the components that are necessary to complete each activity and achieve your objective. Many a grant seeker has gone wrong by underestimating the materials and supplies necessary for successful completion of the project. Most grant seekers lose out on the many donated or matching items because they did not sit down and ask themselves, "What do I need to have to complete this activity?" Notice in the sample that travel, supplies, and telephone communication have been donated.

9. This column can be completed in two ways:

- Each activity can be subtotaled.

- You may wish to subtotal several activities into the subtotal for objectives.

10. *Milestones:* Column R is necessary to record what the funding source will receive as indicators of your working toward the accomplishment of your objectives. Column S lists the date on which the funding source will receive the milestone or progress indicator.

11. *Indirect costs:* federal grants contain a concept that is critically important and poorly understood by *most* grant seekers and *everyone not connected* with grants. The concept involves repaying the recipient of a federal grant for costs that are difficult to break

down individually, but are indirectly attributable to performing the federal grant. These costs include such things as:

- the heat and lights for those individuals on the grant:
- the cost for upkeep on the building:
- the maintenance staff: or
- the payroll department.

Indirect costs are calculated by using a formula that is provided by the Federal Regional Controller's Office. It is expressed as a percentage of the total amount requested from the funding source (represented by the Total in Column Q), or as a percentage of the people on the grant (represented by Total of Column I).

Evaluation

Federal and state funding sources place a much heavier emphasize on evaluation than most private sources do. While there are many books written on evaluation, the best advice on how to handle it is to get an expert. I suggest seeking out a qualified individual at a college or university who has experience in dealing with this area. College professors generally enjoy the involvement and the extra pay. Professors also lead you to a storehouse of inexpensive labor—undergraduate and graduate students. A graduate student in statistics can help you deal with the problem of quantifying your results inexpensively, while he or she gathers valuable insight and experience.

Writing your objectives properly makes the process of evaluation much simpler. Using the sections in this chapter on how to write objectives (pp. 130–132) will provide you with a valuable resource for developing objectives that can be measured. Many grant seekers proceed smoothly with objectives that deal with cognitive areas or areas that provide for results that can be easily qualified. The problems start when they move into the area known as the *affective domain*—values, feelings, and appreciation are difficult to measure.

If you use the form for writing objectives and ask yourself: "What will these people do differently after the grant that they don't do now?," you will help keep yourself on the road to evaluation that will pass the federal and state tests. For example, a grant to increase appreciation for opera could be measured by seeing how many of the subjects attend an inexpensive performance after the free ones are completed.

Future Funding

Most funding sources are buying a piece of the future. It is in their best interest to see the project live on. This way, they are able to take credit for it and its benefits over a greater length of time. Many of us grant seekers begin to show our "tunnel vision" by forgetting the funding sources' needs concerning the future and neglect to plan to keep their investment alive by outlining a future finance plan.

You will continue the project through:

- Service fees
- Membership fees
- Other granting agencies (United Way)
- Big-gift campaigns aimed at wealthy individuals
- Starting an endowment program
- Getting other grants
- Starting a direct-mail campaign
- Other fund-raising mechanisms

Include the cost of one or more of these activities in your expenses and budget for them in the grant. You are not automatically considered an ingrate for doing this, but rather you may come across as a good executor of the funding source's estate. You are planning for continuation.

Dissemination

In addition to the good that will come from meeting the objectives and closing the gap established in the needs statement, much good can come from letting others know what you and the funding source have accomplished in this grant.

The funding source may pay for your dissemination of the results of the grant through one or more of the following mechanisms. Request funds for:

- A final report mailed to others in your field

- A quarterly journal mailed to others

- A newsletter mailed to others in your field

- Sponsoring a seminar or conference on the topic

- Attending a national (try international) conference to deliver results of the project (Many government funding officials cannot travel to conferences, but they can fund you to go and disseminate the results.)

- Production of a film or slide/tape presentation on the project

This type of thinking is viewed by most funding sources as positive and creative. They want their name up in lights too.

The end result is that others in your field will know your name. They will call you to enter consortiums, and other funding sources will ask you to apply for funding.

The Budget

While the budget may produce trauma for most unorganized grant seekers, you can see that the project planner has all the information you need to forecast your financial needs accurately. The Project Planner is not the budget; it is the analysis of what will have to be done and the estimated costs and time frame for each activity.

In most government proposal formats the budget area is not in close proximity to the methodology. Government funders do not understand why you want to talk about your methods when they talk about money. As you know, the budget is a result of what you plan to do. If you cut or reduce the money requested, you have to cut the methods. If you must cut so many methods that you can no longer be sure of accomplishing the objective, consider refusing the funds or reducing the amount of change (reduction of the need) outlined in the objective when you are asked to negotiate the amount of your award.

Draw the public funding source back into your Project Planner so that you both understand what will be missing as a result of a 10 percent budget cut.

The sample budget in Table 13.1 is provided for your review. The format may change, but the information you will need usually lies in your project planner. (If you are required to provide a quarterly cash forecast, list your activities/methods on the Proposed Time Frame and Cash Forecast (p. 142), and place the estimated cost in the far-right column. Total the costs by the quarter and you will develop your cash forecast.)

Title Page

The title of your proposal is very important. It is often hastily conceived as the proposal is "flying" out of the typewriter. *The title of a proposal gets read first,* and sometimes it is the last part that is read. The effect of the title on encouraging the reviewer or staff reader to continue to read the proposal is not known. What must a title do to insure that your proposal gets attention?

The proposal title must:

- Be descriptive of your project.

- Express the end result of the project, not the methods.

- Describe benefits to clients.

- Be short and easy to remember.

T A B L E 13.1. A Sample Project Budget

PROJECT NAME: NUTRITION EDUCATION FOR DISADVANTAGED MOTHERS THROUGH TELE CONFERENCING.	EXPEN-DITURE TOTAL	DONATED/IN-KIND	REQUESTED FROM THIS SOURCE
	$60,157	*$29,956*	*$30,201*
I. *PERSONNEL*			
A. *Salaries, Wages*			
Project Director @ $1,200/mo × 12 mos × 50% time	7,200	7,200	
Administrative Assistant @ $800/mo × 12 mos × 100% time	9,600		9,600
Secretary @ $800/mo × 12 mos × 100% time	9,600		9,600
Volunteer Time @ $3.50 × 10 mos × 400 hours	14,000	14,000	
B. *Fringe Benefits*			
Unemployment Insurance (3.6% of first $6,000 of each salary)	648	216	432
FICA (6.65% of first 22,900 of each employee salary)	1,756	479	1,277
Health Insurance ($30/mo per employee × 12 mos) Work-	1,080	360	720
men's Compensation (1% of salaries paid—$26,400)	264	72	192
C. *Consultants/Contracted Service*			
Copy Editor ($80/day × 5)	400		400
PR Advisor ($100/day × 10)	1,000		1,000
Accounting Services ($100/day × 12)	1,200	1,200	
Legal Services ($125/day × 6)	750	750	
Personnel Subtotal	*$47,498*	*$24,277*	*$23,221*
II. *NONPERSONNEL*			
A. *Space Costs*			
Rent (.50 square feet × 400 square feet office × 12 mos)	2,400	2,400	
Utilities ($30/mo × 12 mos)	360	360	
B. *Equipment*			
Desk ($175 × 1)	175		175
Typewriters (3 @ rental rate of $50/mo × 12 mos)	1,800		1,800
Office chairs (3 × $50/ea)	150		150

T A B L E 13.1. (Cont.)

PROJECT NAME: NUTRITION EDUCATION FOR DISADVANTAGED MOTHERS THROUGH TELE CONFERENCING.	EXPEN-DITURE TOTAL	DONATED/ IN-KIND	REQUESTED FROM THIS SOURCE
	$60,157	*$29,956*	*$30,201*
Slide Projectors (2 @ $150/each)	300	300	
File Cabinets (3 @ $95/ea)	285	285	
C. *Supplies (Consumables)* 3 employees × $85/ each/year	255	255	
D. *Travel*			
Local			
Project Director ($.20 mile × 500 miles/mo × 12 mos)	1,200		1,200
Administrative Asst. ($.20/mile × 750 miles/mo × 12)	1,800		1,800
Out-Of-Time Project Director to American Institute of Nutrition Conference 12/3–5/81 in St. Louis (1 round trip economy @ $275) Per Diem—$75/day × 3	275		275
E. *Telephone* Installation ($15 + $4/line × 3 lines)	27	27	
Monthly Charges ($7/line × 3 lines × 12 mos)	252	252	
Long Distance ($40/mo × 12)	480		480
F. *Other Nonpersonnel Costs* Printing (25,000 brochures × $35/Thousand)	875		875
Postage ($125/mo × 12 mos)	1,500	1,500	
Insurance ($25/mo × 12 mos)	300	300	
Personnel Subtotal:	$12,659	$ 5,679	$ 6,980
Personnel Subtotal:	$47,498	$24,277	$23,221
Project Total:	$60,157	$29,956	$30,201
Percentage:	100%	49.8%	50.2%

PROPOSED TIME FRAME
and CASH FORECAST

For _____Proposal

Methods	1	2	3	4	5	6	7	8	9	10	11	12	Cost/ Method

Quarterly													
Cash Forecast for Project													Total Cost Requested from Funder
	1		2		3		4						

The best titles are the "newspaper-type" titles that are descriptive and to the point, for example, "Women Stabbed at Hilton Hotel."

Titles that try to entice the reader by giving only part of the story seldom work. Remember, the reader usually has a pile of grant proposals that are crying out to be read. The same newspaper title, rewritten to "entice" a reader, may turn out to be: "Bloody End in Hotel Lobby while Hundreds Watch." Although some grant seekers have told me that an enticing title got their proposal read, I believe they are in the minority.

Titles can vary in length. Ask funding officials what they prefer. Since you have a list of titles used by past grantees, examine it for clues that may give you an idea of what the funding source wants. Some federal programs have rules on the number of characters or spaces that a title may use. Check the rules.

Titles can be up to ten to thirteen words. The best person to write or select the title may not be you. Have friends read the proposal and ask them what to call it.

Since you have written the proposal, you develop "tunnel vision" and attribute more meaning to the words than a person reading the title for the first time. One good technique is to read your title to other people who know little or nothing about your proposal and then ask them what they think the proposal is about, based on the title.

You must be careful not to assume that the funding source is familiar with references you may make to biblical characters or Greek gods in your proposal title. Calling your solar energy project, "Apollo's Flame," is not a good idea if the reviewer does not know who Apollo is or fails to make the connection.

Acronyms should be used only if the funding source has a preference for them. Trying to develop a title that describes the benefits of your project is difficult enough without adding the additional task of attempting to use specific words to develop an acronym.

The key to checking out your title is to look at the titles of past grants and ask the funding source what they prefer.

TITLE PAGE

Most federal forms and many state granting programs have standard formats for the title page. The key to the title page is to design it like a well-addressed envelope. Insure its delivery to the correct place by including all required information and more. Remember, you are dealing with a bureaucracy, a grants-logging office, a mail dissemination and delivery service, and relogging as your proposal gets to the final destination. You must be sure that the title page allows for anyone to pick it up and:

- Know what program you are applying to.

- See a clear address for the office that will handle the program.

- See the federal contact person.

- Know your return address, phone number, and contact person.

The Summary (or Abstract)

The summary (or abstract) is written after the proposal is completed. It is a summary of each part of the proposal, not a repetition of what you have written. The summary should:

- Summarize the objectives, not list them.

- Summarize the approach, not list methods.

- Summarize the evaluation, not detail every pre-post test.

The summary or abstract is the most important part of the proposal after the title, because the summary is the next most often read part of the proposal. If the summary is not succinct and motivating, you have lost the reader, which you cannot afford to do. Make an outline of each of the preceding sections. Using the points or evaluation system printed or discussed with funding sources or past grantees or reviewers, you may evaluate the space and time spent on developing your abstract to fit the funding source. Show them that they will find what they want in this proposal.

Many forms have explicit directions on the summary and even designate the space and number of words or characters you can use. Some federal forms ask you to underline a certain number of key words or phrases—*do it!*

Attachments (Appendix)

This section can provide the "winning edge" when your proposal is compared to a competitor's for final analysis. Throughout the proposal-development process, collect the materials that will make up the attachments and set them aside. Your task is to present materials in the attachments that will back up your proposal. The funding source may skim over the attachments or look to them for:

- Studies/research and tables or graphs.
- Vitae of key personnel.
- Minutes of Advisory Committee Meetings.
- List of board members.
- Credibility builders—auditor's report/statement.
- Letters of recommendation/endorsement.
- Copy of your tax-exempt designation by the IRS.
- Pictures, architect's drawings.
- Copies of your agency publications.
- List of other funding sources you will approach for funding.

For the appropriate *length* of your attachments section, check funding source rules. Guidelines may state that the attachments can be up to twice as long as the proposal.

Also check funding source rules for the appropriate appendix format. Provide a separate Contents page. Many grant writers number the pages sequentially with the proposal to provide ease in referral to the attachments.

Cover Letter

The cover letter is the last part of the proposal to be written, although it may be the first one read by the funding source. The purpose of the cover letter is to provide the funding source with a reintroduction to you. You may want to remind the funding source of your contact with them and the changes you have made in your proposal on the basis of their input. (You want to remind them that you did what they said: "I did what you told me to do—now fund it!")

If you have had contact with a particular individual on the funding organization's staff and you remind them of it, be sure to note it on *one* of the funding official's or your contact person's copy. Telling *everyone* who reads the proposal that you received special attention is not a good idea.

In public funding, the cover letter is seldom read unless they know you and it is written to a contact person at the funding agency.

If you include a cover letter on each copy of the proposal, it must:

- be short (half a page),
- be motivating,
- say something different, and
- show dramatic need or uniqueness.

In today's world of board-member liability insurance, you may want to use the cover letter to show board commitment. Have the president of the board sign, along with your top-ranking administrator. (It is acceptable to have two signatures on the cover letter.)

Writing Your Federal/State Proposal

WRITING TIPS

- Follow the guidelines exactly (even when they seem senseless).
- Fill in all the blanks.
- Doublecheck all computations.

- Repeat anything they ask for (do not refer them back to what you consider a similar question and answer).

WRITING STYLE

Your writing style must reflect what the funding source wants and what the reviewers will be looking for. Since you have contacted a past reviewer, you know his or her level of expertise and familiarity with your proposal area. You also know the amount of time that a proposal reviewer spends with a proposal. The proposal must be readable and skimmable. Follow these suggestions:

- Begin each section with a strong motivating "lead" sentence.

- Use an active voice and describe emotions and feelings.

- Cite dialogue.

- Use humor (in a nonoffensive way).

- Ask the funding source a question and answer it.

In developing your writing style and preparing your proposal, be sure to check on the aspects of the proposal that follow.

VOCABULARY

Do you use the words they expect? (Your research has given you insight into vocabulary.) Shorter words are generally better than long, complex words.

STYLE

To produce an easily skimmable proposal:

- Use short sentences (no more than two commas).

- Use contractions.

- Use short paragraphs (from five to seven lines).

VISUAL ATTRACTIVENESS

To enhance the "skimmability" of the project, use:

- Underlining.

- Bullets (lower case "o," filled in, "●").
- Use different **type** faces.
- Change margins and s p a c i n g .
- Use **BOLD HEADINGS.**
- Use pictures.
- Use charts and graphs.
- Use *Handwriting* .

CHAPTER 14

Checklist for Government Proposal Preparation

CHECKLIST FOR GOVERNMENT PROPOSAL PREPARATION

_____ Read guidelines again; many have a forms checklist that must be signed and included.

_____ Have you checked the submission date for postmark and/or receipt by funding source?

_____ Correct address and logging center.

_____ Have you included all sections that will be given points by the reviewers?

_____ Check required assurances:

    _____ A-95 Review   _____ Other

    _____ Protection of Human Subjects   _____

    _____ Equal Employment   _____

_____ Check all purchases for equipment:

     _____ Is purchase allowable?

     _____ Can you lease with option to buy?

     _____ Rent?

     _____ Any forms or sign off's for purchases over $ _____

_____ Required number of copies.

_____ Signatures of appropriate officials.

_____ Matching or cost sharing rules.

_____ Indirect costs used appropriately.

Additional Comments: _____

_____

_____

_____

_____

_____

_____

CHAPTER 15

Submission

WHAT TO DO AND WHAT NOT TO DO

Submission of grants to public funding sources requires a very different and more complex procedure from submissions to private funding sources. Because you are dealing with public funds, the procedure for submission and the deadline dates must comply with public-information laws and give equal voice and opportunity to everyone.

Government officials cannot give you any leeway on deadlines. (*Note:* at the federal level, any change in the deadline date must be announced in the *Federal Register* thirty days before the change.) *Deadlines are exactly that.*

The normal submission procedure is to have a federal proposal stamped in at the post office by a post office employee. Most federal proposals also have a grants-logging center in Washington that can receive the proposal. *Call the funding source regardless of whether you are submitting your proposal by mail or in person,* just to be sure your grant made the trip from the logging center or post office to the correct federal office.

Most public agencies will refuse to talk to you when you have an application under consideration. There are other actions you can take:

1. Send your abstract or summary to your congressperson. Do not ask him or her to contact the government agency; simply state that you have applied and would like any help he or she can offer. State that you know that any assistance he or she could give would be *informal;* you do not want letters to funding officials.
2. Call any "friends" you found in your linkages and webbing and ask them to put in a good word where possible.

Proposal Review

PUBLIC FUNDING SOURCES

The best way to critique your proposal is to use a proposal review committee. The committee may be comprised of your peers, or better yet, individuals whose backgrounds are similar to those of the review committee members. Give your committee as much information as you can concerning the review process, especially the actual length of time spent by the reviewers reading the proposal.

The reviewers can get the proposal in advance and bring it to a review session after careful analysis with the points criteria.

If the funding source reviewers get the proposal to work on for only thirty minutes, pass the proposal out at your review session, ask your reviewers to spend thirty minutes for review, give them the points criteria and let them go to work. (Why spend more time than will be used at the actual review session?)

After they distribute the criteria points, ask them to list the points. Discuss what they think is positive concerning the proposal and what needs improvement.

Some federal programs utilize a review process whereby the reviewers receive, evaluate, and return the proposals by mail. This type of committee may never meet as a group. Many funding sources use a system like this to avoid the reviewers' travel expenses.

CHAPTER 16

Dealing with the Decision of Public Funding Sources

You will receive a response to your proposal in several months. The response will be one of the following:

- Accepted.

- Accepted with budget modifications. (Let's talk about the budget.)

- Approved but not funded. Supportable but not fundable.

- Rejected.

Accepted

If your proposal is accepted, observe the following procedure:
1. Send them a warm personal thank-you letter.
2. Request a critique of your proposal to learn what the funding source liked. Include a mailing label or stamped, self-addressed envelope.

3. Ask the funding source to visit you or arrange for you to visit them.
4. Request any completion forms and learn what records you need to keep.
5. Ask the funding source what the common problems with grants like yours are and how to avoid them.

Accepted with Budget Modifications

Should your proposal receive this response, do the following:
1. Send them a warm personal thank-you letter.
2. Call funding source (they may call you) and refer the funding source to your project planner to negotiate the budget items.
3. Take out some of the methods.
4. Drop the accomplishment of an objective.
5. Be prepared to turn down the funds before you enter into an agreement that will cause you to lose credibility later.

Approved But Not Funded

Observe the following guidelines if your proposal is approved but not offered funding by this source:
1. Send them a warm personal thank-you letter.
2. Call the funding source and ask them how far your proposal was from the funding cut-off point.
3. Ask what you could have done better.
4. Request the reviewers' comments.
5. Try to get additional appropriations.
6. Ask them if they may have discretionary money left over (for unsolicited proposals).

Rejected

If your proposal is rejected, take the following actions:
1. Send them a warm personal thank-you letter.

2. Request the reviewers' comments (enclose self-addressed stamped envelope for their convenience).
3. Ask the funding official for his or her suggestions.
4. Ask if the proposal could be funded as a pilot project, needs assessment, or in some other way.
5. Are there any ways the funding source would assist you in getting ready for the next submission?
6. Should you bother? What are your chances for another try? What would you have to change?
7. Could you become a reviewer to learn and become more familiar with the review process?

CHAPTER 17

Follow-up with Government Funding Sources

The object of follow-up is to make yourself appear as an asset to the funding source and not as a pest. Send the funding source:

- notes on special articles or books in your area;

- an invitation for them to visit you;

- a request for them to review an article you're writing;

- an invitation for one of their representatives to speak at a conference or seminar;

- an invitation to speak at a special grant conference; or

- a request for information about what you could do to impact legislation affecting their funding levels or decisions affecting their allocations.

By remaining on their mailing list and reviewing the *Federal Register,* you will have knowledge of the next opportunity with this funding source.

Do not wait until next year's deadline to begin thinking about your application; start right after the decision. The aggressive grant seeker does not shelve the project for eleven months. The best way to get to know what's going on is to visit the funding source personally. Keep in touch. Watch for meetings announced in the *Federal Register*. Testify at committee hearings that have impact on the agency and its funding level. Send the agency blind carbon copies of your efforts to impact legislation for them (and yourself). Use your association memberships and legislative committees to write and push for changes that benefit the particular agency.

Developing Continued Grant Support

The key to success is to continue the steps that have brought you to this point. If you have put into place the concepts presented in this manual, you have a system that alerts you to changes in program rules, deadlines, and the like, through the mailing lists and personal contacts and webbing linkages you have established.

Although the public funding officials may change, they seem to reappear again and again. This systematic approach to recording research on funding sources and officials will prove its usefulness time and time again.

Once in place, you can keep the funding source on your mailing list and make repeat contacts. By maintaining your relationship, whether you have received funding or not, you demonstrate to the funding source that you plan to be around for a while and that you will not forget them as soon as you receive a check.

One of the best outgrowths of your grants efforts can be your grants library. If you invite others to use your grants resources and demonstrate your systematic grant-seeking abilities, you will be invited into consortiums and end up in other people's proposals.

PART THREE

Private Funding Sources

CHAPTER 18

The Difference between Private and Public Funding

The private marketplace consists of 2.3 million corporations and 24,859 foundations. Estimates are that only 30% to 40% of corporations are contributors. Therefore, the total number of potential private grantors is approximately 800,000 corporations and 24,859 foundations. In 1986 private grantors awarded 10 billion dollars in grants, and each grantor had its own priorities, values, and needs to satisfy in the awarding of its grants.

In comparison to the federal government, which has many bureaucrats involved in the awarding and monitoring of its 30 billion dollars, the private sector is characterized by having a small, part-time, or shared staff. Consider the following facts.

- Fewer than 1,000 foundations have an office.

- There are only 1,500 professionals and 1,700 support staff in all 24,859 foundations.

In the corporate grants area, the executives who meet to review proposals and make grants are often taken away from their important functions in the corporation (making money) to become involved in *giving away* profits.

With all of these differences taken into consideration, it is not surprising that the private marketplace is not characterized by the many forms and rules that are common in the federal marketplace. Many grant seekers interpret this lack of restrictions as a great advantage and apply to foundations and corporations to avoid government regulations. However, private funding sources are sensitive to this issue, and some require that you must show why you have not been able to obtain government funding.

Private funding sources view their role in the grants marketplace very differently from public funding sources. In addition to having few standard forms, guidelines, and requirements, only the largest private funding sources employ experts or utilize outside reviewers. Most private funders rely on the board members to read proposals and evaluate them.

While the government has an abundance of public information, newsletters, application forms, etc., the private sector requires a little more research and work in the initial stages. However, writing the proposal is an easier process (see Chapter 23). Obtaining grants from the private sector is like a treasure hunt. Try to involve your staff, volunteers, and board members in the "hunt." The incorporation of a webbing and linkage system will prove a valuable tool in your search for "gold."

Note: Visit your local college or university grants office to find out what resources they have available and may share with you. Since a working knowledge of the grants mechanism is often a requirement for many degree programs, you may want to consider offering a student an internship or assistantship to assist you in your grant seeking. Since many of the resources for corporate and foundation grants are part of a university library, the relationship you develop will save you money on the duplication of resources.

CHAPTER 19

How to Record Research and Information

Research Worksheet

Another key to successful grant seeking is gathering complete and accurate information on each funding source you approach. The Corporate and Foundation Research Form (pp. 164–165) will help you to do this. Fill in one worksheet for each granting agency you research; try to fill in as much of the form as possible, but remember, even a partially completed worksheet will help you make a more intelligent decision on whether you should solicit grant support from a funding source. If you do apply, it will serve as a guide to solicitation strategy and proposal development.

Try to enlist the help of volunteers to ferret out this information. (*Note:* The use of data-processing equipment for storing this information has been very successful for many of Bauer Associates' clients.)

CORPORATE AND FOUNDATION RESEARCH FORM

Source & Date

1. Name of Corp./Fdn.: _____

    Address: _____

    _____

    Phone: _____

2. Contacts: _____

    (title) _____

    _____

3. Areas of Interest:

    _____   _____

    _____   _____

    _____   _____

    _____   _____

4. Eligibility Requirements/Restrictions:

    Activities: _____

    _____

    _____

    Organizations: _____

    _____

    Geographic: _____

    _____

5. Policy:

    Guidelines Available?   Sent for: _____

                            Received: _____

    Committee Members/Board of Directors

    _____   _____

    _____   _____

CORPORATE AND FOUNDATION RESEARCH FORM (Cont.)

Source & Date

6. Financial Information: Fiscal Year, 19___

    <u>Corporations</u>:   Asset Base   _____

    Net Earnings Before Taxes   _____

    Total Contributions   _____

    Contributions as % NEBT   _____

    <u>Foundations</u>:   Asset Base   _____

    Total Contributions   _____

    BOTH: High Grant   _____

            Low Grant   _____

            Average Range   _____

            Number of Proposals
            Received   _____

            Number of Proposals
            Funded   _____
                                          (amount)
7. Sample Grants in 19___

    _____ $ _____

    _____ $ _____

    _____ $ _____

    _____ $ _____

    _____ $ _____

8. Application Process:

    Deadlines:

    Application Form? Sent for: _____

                      Received: _____

    Send letter included:

    Phone inquiry required:

    Submit full proposal:

    Other:

    _____

    RESEACHER: DATE:

    SOURCES:

Funding-Executive Research Worksheet

In addition to the research you conduct on grant-making organizations, you should also uncover and record as much data as possible on the decision makers in those organizations. The following worksheet is designed to help you do this.

FUNDING EXECUTIVE RESEARCH WORKSHEET

                                                                    Source & Date
                                                                    _____

1. Funding Source Name: _____

2. Name of Contributions Officer: _____

3. Title: _____ Birthdate: _____

4. Business Address: _____

5. Home Address: _____

6. Education: Secondary: _____
                College: _____
                Post-Graduate: _____

7. Military Service: _____
    _____

8. Clubs/Affiliations: _____
    _____

9. Corporate Board Memberships:_____
    _____

10. Business History (Promotions, other firms, etc.)
    _____
    _____

11. Religious Affiliation: _____

12. Other Philanthropic Activities of Note: _____
    _____

13. Newspaper/Magazine Clippings Attached:
    Yes: _____ No: _____

14. Contacts in Our Organization: _____
    _____

15. Recent Articles/Publications: _____
    _____

16. Awards/Honors: _____
    _____

You can find information on private funding officials in books such as *Trustees of Wealth, Dun & Bradstreet's Directory of Corporate Managements* and *Who's Who* publications. You should also check periodical indexes, libraries, and newspapers.

The data you record here can help you in two ways:

1. It can help you determine, in advance, likely preferences and biases you will encounter at an in-person grant interview.
2. It makes it easier to locate "linkages" between your organization and a funding source.

Note: You do not have to have this information in order to consider a source for a proposal, but it helps. Each step you include will increase your chances of success.

CHAPTER 20

Foundation Funding Source Research Tools

This chapter contains sample entries from selected grants' research tools commonly used in the foundation and corporate grant areas (see pp. 169, 170, 171). The samples have been changed slightly to assist you in understanding the way the research is indexed and what an entry looks like.

To make research on foundations easier for prospective grant seekers, the foundations formed the Foundation Center. National in scope, with cooperating regional libraries, the Foundation Center provides the best possible sources of free information about foundations (who and what they fund).

Locate the Foundation Center's nearest library on the accompanying list (pp. 172–175) and visit it. The national collections have many more resources than mentioned here. The Foundation Center will be happy to sell you a membership program where you become an "associate" for $325.00 and receive:

- Toll-free telephone reference service (10 free calls or 2½ hours of information/month). $28.00 for each additional multiple of 10 calls.

THE FOUNDATION DIRECTORY

THE FLORA FLUBOCKER FOUNDATION
20 Money Place
New York, NY 10005 (212) 234-1234
Incorporated in 1952 in New York

Donor(s): Members of Flubocker Family

Purpose and Activities: Special emphasis
on education for the developmentally
disabled, health care for the aged, and
research on eye diseases. No grants to
individuals. Report published annually.

Financial Data: (yr. ended 12/31/86):
Assets, $27,137,892 (m); gifts received
$8,396,000; expenditures, $936,152;
including $756,300 for 32 grants
(high: $37,000; low: $1,500)

Officers: Melvin J. Flubocker, Pres.
Mary J. Flubocker, Sylvia Skim, Vice
President; Jonathan S. Bills, Treas.

Trustees: Orving Flood, Laurel Lisez,
Maxwell Litesky, Luch Maddox, William
Martin, C. Pape, A. Rankin, Anna Slide,
Arthur Flubocker, M. Stillwater, IV.

Write: Mary J. Flubocker, Vice President

Grant Application Information: Board
meets quarterly. IRS Employment
Identification No.: 410896132

The Foundation Directory

(Edition 11), Foundation
Center, 79 Fifth Avenue,
New York, NY 10003

The Foundation Directory,

Edition 11 is the best
place to find general
data on the largest
private foundations. It
includes the following
information on foundations
with assets of over $1
million, or that made over
$100,000 in grants:

- Name & Address
- Donors
- Financial Data
  (including assets,
  number of grants, &
  size of high & low
  grants)
- Officers & Trustees

The Directory is indexed by:

- Field of Interest
- Foundations by State &
  City
- Donors, Trustees &
  Administrators
- Foundaitons in
  Alphabetical Order

A supplement to the
Foundation Directory will be
published in mid-year.
It will include updated
addresses, indexes of
grant-making foundations
and other bibliographical
data.

- Computerized foundation files ($75.00 for up to 75 records).

- Copy services (associates can get copies of foundation profiles from Source Book Profiles and other information such as foundation assets, officers, etc. for $1.00 for the first page and $.50 for each additional page).

- Complimentary *Foundation Fundamentals* and one Comsearch print-out.

THE FOUNDATION GRANTS INDEX

THE FLUBOCKER FOUNDATION

$30,000 to ZAP UNIVERSITY, Ithaca, NY.
1986. For center to rehabilitate
developmentally disabled in Ithaca area.
SD: 1/20/87   (3147)

$8,000 to HARLEM HOSPITAL, New York, NY.
1986. For general support.
SD: 1/20/87   (3149)

$8,500 to COMMUNITY DEVELOPMENT LEAGUE
1986. For programs to find employment
for the developmentally disabled.
SD: 1/20/87   (3150)

$10,000 to SUNY AT BAYSHORE, Bayshore, NY.
1986. For research into development
disabilities.
SD: 1/20/87   (3151)

$10,750 to YENTALTA EYE CLINIC. For
research on retina detachment. 1986.
SD: 1/20/87   (3152)

$5,000 to ZOLA CENTER. General operating
expenses.
SD: 1/20/87   (3153)

(This is a hypothetical entry)

THE FOUNDATION GRANTS INDEX

Foundation Center
79 Fifth Avenue
New York, NY 10003

The Foundation Grants Index
is a good place to turn
when you begin searching
for a foundation's
"granting pattern." It
includes listings of grants
over $5,000, some given by
foundations not large
enough to be listed in
The Foundation Directory.

The Foundation Grants Index
lists grants by state and
foundation. It also
indexes them by:

- recipients
- key words & phrases
- subject categories
- foundation names

The information you gather
here, along with that you
find in foundaiton annual
reports and IRS returns,
will give you a good idea
of whether your project
fits into the funding
priorities of a foundation.

You can buy a copy of this
valuable tool from the
Foundaiton Center, or find
it (along with The
Foundation Directory) in
Foundation Center Regional
Collections.

IRS Forms—990-PF and 990-AR Returns

Foundations are required to submit income tax returns. These returns are public record and can be purchased from the Internal Revenue Service for a minimal fee. (See Figure 20.1.) They are available for the entire United States at the national Foundation Center and on a geographically limited basis at the regional libraries. You can use them in the library on a "no charge" basis.

FIGURE 20.1 Sample IRS form

Form **990-PF**
Department of the Treasury
Internal Revenue Service

Return of Private Foundation
or Section 4947(a)(1) Trust Treated as a Private Foundation
Note: *You may be able to use a copy of this return to satisfy State reporting requirements.*

OMB No. 1545-0052

1983

For the calendar year 1983, or tax year beginning _____, 1983, and ending _____, 19___

Please type, print, or attach label. See Specific Instructions.

NAME

ADDRESS

ASSETS*

PHONE

GIFTS RECEIVED

GRANTS PAID

previously mentioned receive their information on a voluntary basis and it is always at least one year old. It is estimated that about 50 percent of the grants for more than $5,000 are reported voluntarily. In order to find the other 50 percent of grants awarded, you must search out the foundations, by looking them up through their income tax returns.

You will notice that many foundation research books give the

REFERENCE COLLECTIONS OPERATED BY
THE FOUNDATION CENTER

• The Foundation Center
79 Fifth Avenue
New York, New York 10003
212-620-4230

• The Foundation Center
1001 Connecticut Avenue, NW
Washington, D.C. 20036
202-331-1400

• The Foundation Center
Kent H. Smith Library
1442 Hanna Building
1422 Euclid Avenue
Cleveland, Ohio 44115
216-861-1933

• The Foundation Center
312 Sutter Street
San Francisco, California
94108
415-397-0902

COOPERATING COLLECTIONS

Those collections marked with a bullet (•) have sets of private foundation information returns (IRS Form 990-PF) for their states or regions, available for public reference.

ALABAMA

• Birmingham Public Library
2020 Park Place
Birmingham 35203
205-226-3600

Huntsville–Madison County
Public Library
108 Fountain Circle
P.O. Box 443
Huntsville 35804
205-536-0021

• Auburn University at
Montgomery Library
Montgomery 36193 - 0401
205-271-9649

ALASKA

• University of Alaska,
Anchorage Library
3211 Providence Drive
Anchorage 99508
907-786-1848

ARIZONA

• Phoenix Public Library
Business and Sciences
Department
12 East McDowell Road
Phoenix 85004
602-262-4636

• Tucson Public Library
Main Library
200 South Sixth Avenue
Tucson 85701
607-791-4393

ARKANSAS

• Westark Community College
Library
Grand Avenue at Waldron Road
Fort Smith 72913
501-785-4241

• Little Rock Public Library
Reference Department
700 Louisiana Street
Little Rock 72201
501-370-5950

CALIFORNIA

• California Community
Foundation Funding
Information Center
3580 Wilshire Blvd., Suite
1660
Los Angeles 90010
213-413-4042

• Community Foundation for
Monterey County
420 Pacific Street
Monterey 93940
408-375-9712

California Community
Foundation
4050 Metropolitan Drive #300
Orange 92668
714-937-9077

Riverside Public Library
3581 7th Street
Riverside 92501
714-787-7201

California State Library
Reference Services, Rm. 309
914 Capital Mall
Sacramento 95814
916-322-4570

• San Diego Community
Foundation
625 Broadway, Suite 1015
San Diego 92101
619-239-8815

• The Foundation Center
312 Sutter Street
San Francisco, California
94108
415-397-0902

• Grantsmanship Resource Center
Junior League of San Jose, Inc.
Community Foundation of Santa
Clara County
960 West Hedding, Suite 220
San Jose 95126
408-244-5280

• Orange County Community
Developmental Council
1440 East First Street, 4th Floor
Santa Ana 92701
714-547-6801

• Peninsula Community
Foundation
1204 Burlingame Avenue
Burlingame, 94011-0627
415-342-2505

• Santa Barbara Public Library
Reference Section
40 East Anapamu
P.O. Box 1019
Santa Barbara 93102
805-962-7653

Santa Monica Public Library
1343 Sixth Street
Santa Monica 90401-1603
213-458-8603

Tuolomne County Library
465 S. Washington Street
Sonora 95370
209-533-5707

COLORADO

Pikes Peak Library District
20 North Cascade Avenue
Colorado Springs 80901
303-473-2080

• Denver Public Library
Sociology Division
1357 Broadway
Denver 80203
303-571-2190

CONNECTICUT

Danbury Public Library
155 Deer Hill Avenue
Danbury 06810
203-797-4505

• Hartford Public Library
Reference Department
500 Main Street
Hartford 06103
203-525-9121

D.A.T.A.
880 Asylum Avenue
Hartford 06105
203-278-2477

D.A.T.A.
25 Science Park
Suite 502
New Haven 06513
203-786-5225

DELAWARE

• Hugh Morris Library
University of Delaware
Newark 19717-5267
302-451-2965

DISTRICT OF COLUMBIA

• The Foundation Center
1001 Connecticut Avenue, NW
Washington, D.C. 20036
202-331-1400

FLORIDA

Volusia County Public
Library
City Island
Daytona Beach 32014
904-252-8374

• Jacksonville Public Library
Business, Science, and
Industry Department
122 North Ocean Street
Jacksonville 32202
904-633-3926

- Miami–Dade Public Library
  Humanities Dept.
  101 W. Flagler St.
  Miami 33132
  305-375-2665

- Orlando Public Library
  10 North Rosalind
  Orlando 32801
  305-425-4694

- University of West Florida
  John C. Pace Library
  Pensacola 32514
  904-474-2412

  Selby Public Library
  1001 Boulevard of the Arts
  Sarasota 33577
  813-366-7303

- Leon County Public Library
  Community Funding
  Resources Center
  1940 North Monroe Street
  Tallahassee 32303
  904-478-2665

  Palm Beach County
  Community Foundation
  324 Datura Street, Suite 340
  West Palm Beach 33401
  305-659-6800

GEORGIA

- Atlanta–Fulton Public Library
  Ivan Allen Department
  1 Margaret Mitchell Square
  Atlanta 30303
  404-688-4636

HAWAII

- Thomas Hale Hamilton Library
  General Reference
  University of Hawaii
  2550 The Mall
  Honolulu 96822
  808-948-7214

  Community Resource Center
  The Hawaiian Foundation
  Financial Plaza of the Pacific
  111 South King Street
  Honolulu 96813
  808-525-8548

IDAHO

- Caldwell Public Library
  1010 Dearborn Street
  Caldwell 83605
  208-459-3242

ILLINOIS

- Belleville Public Library
  121 East Washington Street
  Belleville 62220
  618-234-0441

  DuPage Township
  300 Briarcliff Road
  Bolingbrook 60439
  312-759-1317

- Donors Forum of Chicago
  53 W. Jackson Blvd. Rm. 430
  Chicago 60604
  312-726-4882

- Evanston Public Library
  1703 Orrington Avenue
  Evanston 60201
  312-866-0305

- Sangamon State University
  Library
  Shepherd Road
  Springfield 62708
  217-786-6633

INDIANA

Allen County Public Library
900 Webster Street
Fort Wayne 46802
219-424-7241

Indiana University Northwest
Library
3400 Broadway
Gary 46408
219-980-6580

- Indianapolis–Marion County
  Public Library
  40 East St. Clair Street
  Indianapolis 46204
  317-269-1733

IOWA

- Public Library of Des Moines
  100 Locust Street
  Des Moines 50308
  515-283-4259

KANSAS

- Topeka Public Library
  Adult Services Department
  1515 West Tenth Street
  Topeka 66604
  913-233-2040

- Wichita Public Library
  223 South Main
  Wichita 67202
  316-262-0611

KENTUCKY

Western Kentucky University
Division of Library Services
Helm-Cravens Library
Bowling Green 42101
502-745-3951

- Louisville Free Public Library
  Fourth and York Streets
  Louisville 40203
  503-223-7201

LOUISIANA

- East Baton Rouge Parish Library
  Centroplex Library
  120 St. Louis Street
  Baton Rouge 70821
  504-389-4960

- New Orleans Public Library
  Business and Science Division
  219 Loyola Avenue
  New Orleans 70140
  504-596-2583

- Shreve Memorial Library
  424 Texas Street
  Shreveport 71101
  318-226-5894

MAINE

- University of Southern Maine
  Center for Research and
  Advanced Study
  246 Deering Avenue
  Portland 04102
  207-780-4411

MARYLAND

- Enoch Pratt Free Library
  Social Science and History
  Department
  400 Cathedral Street
  Baltimore 21201
  301-396-5320

MASSACHUSETTS

- Associated Grantmakers of
  Massachusetts
  294 Washington Street
  Suite 501
  Boston 02108
  617-426-2608

- Boston Public Library
  Copley Square
  Boston 02117
  617-536-5400

  Walpole Public Library
  Common Street
  Walpole 02081
  617-668-5497 ext.340

  Western Massachusetts Funding
  Resource Center
  Campaign for Human
  Development
  Chancery Annex
  73 Chestnut Street
  Springfield 01103
  413-732-3175 ext.67

- Grants Resource Center
  Worcester Public Library
  Salem Square
  Worcester 01608
  617-799-1655

MICHIGAN

- Alpena County Library
  211 North First Avenue
  Alpena 49707
  517-356-6188

  University of Michigan–Ann
  Arbor
  Reference Department
  209 Hatcher Graduate Library
  Ann Arbor 48109-1205
  313-764-1149

- Henry Ford Centennial Library
  16301 Michigan Avenue
  Dearborn 48126
  313-943-2337

- Purdy Library
  Wayne State University
  Detroit 48202
  313-577-4040

- Michigan State University
  Libraries
  Reference Library
  East Lansing 48824
  517-353-9184

- Farmington Community Library
  32737 West 12 Mile Road
  Farmington Hills 48018
  313-553-0300

- University of Michigan–Flint
  Library
  Reference Department
  Flint 48503
  313-762-3408

- Grand Rapids Public Library
  Sociology and Education Dept.
  Library Plaza
  Grand Rapids 49502
  616-456-4411

- Michigan Technological
  University Library
  Highway U.S. 41
  Houghton 49931
  906-487-2507

MINNESOTA

- Duluth Public Library
  520 Superior Street
  Duluth 55802
  218-723-3802

- Southwest State University
  Library
  Marshall 56258
  507-537-7278

- Minneapolis Public Library
  Sociology Department
  300 Nicollet Mall
  Minneapolis 55401
  612-372-6555

  Rochester Public Library
  Broadway at First Street, SE
  Rochester 55901
  507-285-8002

  Saint Paul Public Library
  90 West Fourth Street
  Saint Paul 55102
  612-292-6311

MISSISSIPPI

Jackson Metropolitan Library
301 North State Street
Jackson 39201
601-944-1120

MISSOURI

- Clearinghouse for Midcontinent
  Foundations P.O. Box 22680
  Univ. of Missouri, Kansas City
  Law School, Suite 1-300
  52nd Street and Oak
  Kansas City 64113
  816-276-1176

- Kansas City Public Library
  311 East 12th Street
  Kansas City 64106
  816-221-2685

- Metropolitan Association for
  Philanthropy, Inc.
  5585 Pershing Avenue
  Suite 150
  St. Louis 63112
  314-361-3900

- Springfield–Greene County
  Library
  397 East Central Street
  Springfield 65801
  417-866-4636

MONTANA

- Eastern Montana College Library
  Reference Department
  1500 N. 30th Street
  Billings 59101-0298
  406-657-2262

- Montana State Library
  Reference Department
  1515 E. 6th Avenue
  Helena 59620
  406-444-3004

NEBRASKA

University of Nebraska, Lincoln
106 Love Library
Lincoln 68588-0410
402-472-2526

* W. Dale Clark Library
Social Sciences Department
215 South 15th Street
Omaha 68102
402-444-4826

NEVADA

* Las Vegas—Clark County
Library District
1401 East Flamingo Road
Las Vegas 89109
702-733-7810

* Washoe County Library
301 South Center Street
Reno 89505
702-785-4190

NEW HAMPSHIRE

* The New Hampshire
Charitable Fund
One South Street
Concord 03301
603-225-6641

Littleton Public Library
109 Main Street
Littleton 03561
603-444-5741

NEW JERSEY

Cumberland County Library
800 E. Commerce Street
Bridgeton 08302
609-455-0080

The Support Center
17 Academy Street, Suite 1101
Newark 07102
201-643-5774

County College of Morris
Masten Learning Resource
Center
Route 10 and Center Grove
Road
Randolph 07869
201-361-5000 x470

* New Jersey State Library
Governmental Reference
185 West State Street
Trenton 08625
609-292-6220

NEW MEXICO

Albuquerque Community
Foundation
6400 Uptown Boulevard N.E.
Suite 500-W
Albuquerque 87110
505-883-6240

* New Mexico State Library
325 Don Gaspar Street
Santa Fe 87503
505-827-3824

NEW YORK

* New York State Library
Cultural Education Center
Humanities Section
Empire State Plaza
Albany 12230
518-474-7645

Bronx Reference Center
New York Public Library
2556 Bainbridge Avenue
Bronx 10458
212-220-6575

Brooklyn in Touch
101 Willoughby Street
Room 1508
Brooklyn 11201
718-237-9300

* Buffalo and Erie County
Public Library
Lafayette Square
Buffalo 14203
716-856-7525

Huntington Public Library
338 Main Street
Huntington 11743
516-427-5165

* Levittown Public Library
Reference Department
One Bluegrass Lane
Levittown 11756
516-731-5728

* The Foundation Center
79 Fifth Avenue
New York, New York 10003
212-620-4230

SUNY/College at Old
Westbury Library
223 Store Hill Road
Old Westbury 11568
516-876-3201

* Plattsburgh Public Library
Reference Department
15 Oak Street
Plattsburgh 12901
518-563-0921

Adriance Memorial Library
93 Market Street
Poughkeepsie 12601
914-485-4790

Queens Borough Public Library
89-11 Merrick Boulevard
Jamaica 11432
718-990-0700

* Rochester Public Library
Business and Social Sciences
Division
115 South Avenue
Rochester 14604
716-428-7328

Staten Island Council on the Arts
One Edgewater Plaza Rm. 311
Staten Island 10305
718-447-4485

* Onondaga County Public Library
335 Montgomery Street
Syracuse 13202
315-473-4491

* White Plains Public Library
100 Martine Avenue
White Plains 10601
914-682-4488

* Suffolk Cooperative Library
System
627 North Sunrise Service Road
Bellport 11713
516-286-1600

NORTH CAROLINA

* The Duke Endowment
200 S. Tryon Street, Ste. 1100
Charlotte 28202
704-376-0291

Durham County Library
300 N. Roxboro Street
Durham 27701
919-683-2626

* North Carolina State Library
109 East Jones Street
Raleigh 27611
919-733-3270

* The Winston-Salem Foundation
229 First Union National Bank
Building
Winston-Salem 27101
919-725-2382

NORTH DAKOTA

Western Dakota Grants Resource
Center
Bismarck Junior College Library
Bismarck 58501
701-224-5450

* The Library
North Dakota State University
Fargo 58105
701-237-8876

OHIO

Public Library of Cincinnati
and Hamilton County
Education Department
800 Vine Street
Cincinnati 45202
513-369-6940

* The Foundation Center
Kent H. Smith Library
1442 Hanna Building
1422 Euclid Avenue
Cleveland, Ohio 44115
216-861-1933

* The Public Library
of Columbus and
Franklin County
Main Library
96 S. Grant Ave.
Columbus OH 43215
614-222-7151

* Dayton and Montgomery County
Public Library
Social Sciences Division
215 E. Third Street
Dayton 45402-2103
513-224-1651

* Toledo—Lucas County Public
Library
Social Science Department
325 Michigan Street
Toledo 43624
419-255-7055 ext.221

Ohio University–Zanesville
Community Education and
Development
1425 Newark Road
Zanesville 43701
614-453-0762

* Stark County District Library
715 Market Avenue North
Canton 44702-1080
216-452-0665

OKLAHOMA

* Oklahoma City University
Library
NW 23rd at North Blackwelder
Oklahoma City 73106
405-521-5072

* Tulsa City–County Library
System
400 Civic Center
Tulsa 74103
918-592-7944

* OREGON

* Library Association of Portland
Government Documents Room
801 S.W. Tenth Avenue
Portland 97205
503-223-7201

Oregon State Library
State Library Building
Salem 97310
503-378-4243

PENNSYLVANIA

Northampton County Area
Community College
Learning Resources Center
3835 Green Pond Road
Bethlehem 18017
215-865-5358

* Erie County Public Library
3 South Perry Square
Erie 16501
814-452-2333 ext.54

* Dauphin County Library System
Central Library
101 Walnut Street
Harrisburg 17101
717-234-4961

Lancaster County Public Library
125 North Duke Street
Lancaster 17602
717-394-2651

* The Free Library of Philadelphia
Logan Square
Philadelphia 19103
215-686-5423

* Hillman Library
University of Pittsburgh
Pittsburgh 15260's
412-624-4423

* Economic Development Council
of Northeastern Pennsylvania
1151 Oak Street
Pittston 18640
717-655-5581

James V. Brown Library
12 E. 4th Street
Williamsport 17701
717-326-0536

RHODE ISLAND

* Providence Public Library
Reference Department
150 Empire Street
Providence 02903
401-521-7722

SOUTH CAROLINA

* Charleston County Public Library
404 King Street
Charleston 29403
803-723-1645

- South Carolina State Library
  Reader Services Department
  1500 Senate Street
  Columbia 29201
  803-734-8666

SOUTH DAKOTA

- South Dakota State Library
  State Library Building
  800 North Illinois Street
  Pierre 57501
  605-773-3131

  Sioux Falls Area Foundation
  404 Boyce Greeley Building
  321 South Phillips Avenue
  Sioux Falls 57102-0781
  605-336-7055

TENNESSEE

- Knoxville–Knox County
  Public Library
  500 West Church Avenue
  Knoxville 37902
  615-523-0781

- Memphis Shelby County
  Public Library
  1850 Peabody Avenue
  Memphis 38104
  901-725-8876

- Public Library of Nashville and
  Davidson County
  8th Avenue, North and Union
  Street
  Nashville 37203
  615-244-4700

TEXAS

  Amarillo Area Foundation
  1000 Polk
  P. O. Box 25569
  Amarillo 79105-269
  806-376-4521

- The Hogg Foundation for
  Mental Health
  The University of Texas
  Austin 78712
  512-471-5041

- Corpus Christi State University
  Library
  6300 Ocean Drive
  Corpus Christi 78412
  512-991-6810

- El Paso Community Foundation
  El Paso National Bank Building
  Suite 1616
  El Paso 79901
  915-533-4020

- Funding Information Center
  Texas Christian University
  Library
  Ft. Worth 76129
  817-921-7664

- Houston Public Library
  Bibliographic & Information
  Center
  500 McKinney Avenue
  Houston 77002
  713-224-5441 ext.265

- Funding Information Library
  507 Brooklyn
  San Antonio 78215
  512-227-4333

- Dallas Public Library
  Grants Information Service
  1515 Young Street
  Dallas 75201
  214-749-4100

- Pan American University
  Learning Resource Center
  1201 W. University Drive
  Edinburg 78539
  512-381-3304

UTAH

- Salt Lake City Public Library
  Business and Science
  Department
  209 East Fifth South
  Salt Lake City 84111
  801-363-5733

VERMONT

- State of Vermont Department of
  Libraries
  Reference Services Unit
  111 State Street
  Montpelier 05602
  802-828-3261

VIRGINIA

- Grants Resources Library
  Hampton City Hall
  22 Lincoln Street, Ninth Floor
  Hampton 23669
  804-727-6496

- Richmond Public Library
  Business, Science, & Technology
  Department
  101 East Franklin Street
  Richmond 23219
  804-780-8223

WASHINGTON

- Seattle Public Library
  1000 Fourth Avenue
  Seattle 98104
  206-625-4881

- Spokane Public Library
  Funding Information Center
  West 906 Main Avenue
  Spokane 99201
  509-838-3361

WEST VIRGINIA

- Kanawha County Public Library
  123 Capital Street
  Charleston 25301
  304-343-4646

WISCONSIN

- Marquette University Memorial
  Library
  1415 West Wisconsin Avenue
  Milwaukee 53233
  414-224-1515

- University of
  Wisconsin–Madison
  Memorial Library
  728 State Street
  Madison 53706
  608-262-3647

WYOMING

- Laramie County Community
  College Library
  1400 East College Drive
  Cheyenne 82007
  307-634-5853

CANADA

  Canadian Center for
  Philanthropy
  3080 Yonge Street
  Suite 4080
  Toronto, Ontario M4N3N1
  416-484-4118

ENGLAND

  Charities Aid Foundation
  14 Bloomsbury Square
  London WC1A 2LP
  01-430-1798

MEXICO

  Biblioteca Benjamin Franklin
  Londres 16
  Mexico City 6, D.F.
  525-591-0244

PUERTO RICO

  Universidad Del Sagrado
  Corazon
  M.M.T. Guevarra Library
  Correo Calle Loiza
  Santurce 00914
  809-728-1515 ext.274

VIRGIN ISLANDS

  College of the Virgin Islands
  Library
  Saint Thomas
  U.S. Virgin Islands 00801
  809-774-9200 ext. 487

IRS identification number. The Foundation Center carries several past years' tax returns. Look up several years and you can:

- Look for trends in grant size.

- Compare shifts in funding patterns toward new areas of interest.

- Uncover patterns in funding amounts dispersed among stated interests.

- See geographic granting patterns.

- Determine if foundation assets are growing and where they come from.

- Find the "pet" recipients, and projects.

CHAPTER 21

Corporate Funding Sources and Research Tools

Although there are over 2.3 million corporations in the United States, your research into corporations that will fund your project will be simplified and narrowed when the following facts are considered:

- Of the 2.3 million corporations in the United States, only 35 percent make any philanthropic contributions at all.

- Of these, only 6 percent contribute over $500 in a year.

- Of the $87.22 billion contributed to nonprofits by private philanthropy, corporations accounted for 5.2 percent or 4.50 billion dollars.

Since we have already discussed why corporations give, you know that corporate plants and factories or vested interests in your geographic area motivate corporate giving. By drawing a twenty-five-mile radius around yourself, you can identify the larger employers (companies with 100 or more employees) and select the group your project can be most easily related to.

A visit to the Chamber of Commerce will greatly aid in this selection process. The Chamber has information on the corporations near you and will share it, including the corporation's number of employees, payroll, and products.

The Foundation Center Publications sheets (pp. 177–179) are not meant to be an inclusive reference list concerning corporations and you need not familiarize yourself with all of them. A visit to your local public library or college library will prove very beneficial and save you money. Your research is based upon two aspects of the corporation:

1. *Profitability:* when profits go up, corporate giving goes up.

FOUNDATION CENTER PUBLICATIONS

Publications of The Foundation Center are the primary working tools of every serious grantseeker. They are also used by grantmakers, scholars, journalists, regulators, and legislators; in short, by everyone seeking any type of factual information on foundation philanthropy. Copies of all publications are available for examination free of charge at any of the regional collections listed in this volume. Publications may be ordered from The Foundation Center, 79 Fifth Avenue, New York, NY 10003. Please include prepayment and complete shipping address. For additional information or to place credit card orders, call toll free 800-424-9836.

Foundation Directory
For over 20 years The Foundation Directory has been recognized as the authoritative guide to the grantmaking interests of major American foundations. The 11th Edition includes descriptions of over 4,400 of the nation's largest foundations. Entries include a description of giving interests, along with addresses, telephone numbers, current financial data, names of donors and key officers, and grant application information.

The Foundation Directory Supplement
In response to many requests from tens of thousand of Foundation Directory users, updated information on grantmaking foundations is now available between biennial editions of the Directory. Information for 1,200 of the 4,400 foundations in the Foundation Directory has been updated for this Supplement, providing new fiscal data, changes in staff, trustees, and officers, changes in addresses and telephone numbers, and changes in deadlines, application procedures, and funding priorities. Together the Directory and Supplement provide current, detailed information on that key foundation universe. $35.00 if purchased separately.

National Data Book
This is the only directory that includes all of the currently active grantmaking foundations in the U.S. 24,261 foundations are listed in one easy-to-use volume with an alphabetical index in a separate companion volume. Foundation entries include name, address, and principal officer, plus full fiscal data— market value of assets, grants paid, gifts received, and fiscal period—and an indication of which foundations publish annual reports. The introduction provides the most comprehensive statistical analysis available of foundation philanthropy. $55.00.

Corporate Foundation Profiles
Comprehensive analyses of approximately 250 of the largest company-sponsored foundations along with summary financial data for over 470 additional corporate foundations are presented for convenient reference in this volume. This is the most complete source of data on the large corporate foundations—

FOUNDATION CENTER PUBLICATIONS (Cont.)

including information on all of those giving more than
$100,000 annually or with assets totaling more than $1 million.   Full
subject, type of support, and geographic indexes are provided.
$55.00

Foundation Grants to Individuals
This is the only publication devoted entirely to foundation grant opportunities
for individual applicants.   The 5th Edition provides full description of the
programs for individuals of about 1,041 foundations, with up–to–date
addresses, program descriptions, interview and deadline information, telephone
numbers, names of trustees and staff, financial data, and sample grants.
$18.00. Released annually in December.

Foundation Grants Index
Lists the grants of $5,000 or more awarded to nonprofit organizations by
major U.S. foundations.   The 16th Edition is the largest index ever, listing
36,320 grants and including a new table of giving interests by type of
foundation – independent, corporate and community.   The volume is
arranged alphabetically by state and an expanded analytical introduction.
Each entry notes the amount and date of the grant.   Indexes to grant
recipients and subject key words and phrases, and a combined subject
and geographic category index are provided. $46.00.   Released annually
in April.

COMSEARCH Printouts
COMSEARCH Printouts are computer–produced guides to foundation grants published
in the annual volume of The Foundation Grants Index arranged in easy–to–use
subject and geographical listings.   COMSEARCH: Subjects includes 67
separate subject listings of grant information which can be ordered as a
complete set on microfiche or by the particular subject area of interest.
COMSEARCH: Geographic lists grants awarded to recipients in 2 cities, 11
states and 7 broad regions.   COMSEARCH: Special Topics includes printouts
of the most frequently requested listings from the Center's reference
databases. COMSEARCH: Broad Topics covers all grants in 24 broad
topic areas.   Series published annually in May; full list of categories
available on request.   Broad Topics $35.00 each; Subjects $17.50 each
paper, $6.00 each microfiche, complete set on microfiche $225.00; Geographics
$28.00 each; and Special Topics $17.50 each.

Foundation Fundamentals: A Guide for Grantseekers
This comprehensive, easy–to–read guidebook presents all of the facts
you need to understand the world of foundations and to identify
foundation funding sources for your organizations. The book includes
tables with information on grants and giving, plus illustrations which
take the reader step–by–step through the funding research process.
Comprehensive bibliographies and detailed research examples are also supplied.
1986 239 pages, ISBN 0–87954–158–X. $9.95.

Other Publications

America's Voluntary Spirit: Readings on Giving and Volunteering
Brian O'Connell, President of Independent Sector, presents 45 of the best
pieces written over the past 300 years on America's national tradition of
giving, volunteering, and not–for–profit initiative. An essential reference
for those who write or speak on the sector's richness and diversity. A

2. You must be able to relate to the values of the funding source.
For instance, many corporations have to recruit young executives; these individuals have educational desires and you may
be able to relate to the career goals of employees (or to the
products they produce, the children of the workers, their re-
tirees, the health costs of the workers, etc.)

Since most executives have families that must relocate, the education system is a big factor in getting the executive to move and
keeping the employees happy once they have relocated. Culture
and the arts may be important to corporate recruiting and the re-

FOUNDATION CENTER PUBLICATIONS (Cont.)

wonderful gift for trustees, volunteers, and others concerned with the extraordinary array of institutions which comprise our independent sector. May 1983, 450 pages, ISBN)-87954-079-6. $19.95 hardbound; $14.95 paperbound.

Philanthropy in an Age of Transition: this collection of essays by Alan Pifer includes topics such as the responsibility of higher education, charitable tax deductions and the financial straits of the nonprofit sector. April 1984. ISBN 0-87954-104-0. $12.50.

Working in Foundations: Career Patterns of Women and Men by Teresa Jean Odendahl, Elizabeth Trocolli Boris, and Arlene Kaplan Daniels. This behind-the-scences look at the world of foundation philanthropy is based on interviews with 60 foundation staff members across the country. April 1985. ISBN 0-87954-134-2. $12.95.

The Board Member's Book by Brian O'Connell is a practical guide to the essential functioning of voluntary boards. May 1985. ISBN 0-57954-133-4. $16.95.

Managing for Profit in a Nonprofit World by Paul B. Firstenberg is a handbook demonstrating how state-of-the-art management techniques used by successful for-profit enterprises can be applied to nonprofit organizations. September 1986. ISBN 0-87954159-8. $19.95.

The National Directory of Corporate Charity. A directory describing the charitable activities of 1,600 major U.S. corporations with an emphasis on direct giving programs in corporations. August 1984. ISBN 0-87954-189-X. $80.00.

Source Book Profiles. Detailed foundation facts on the 1,000 largest U.S. foundations. ISBN 0-87954-1571. $285.00 for 4 cumulative volumes.

tention of personnel. If a corporation has problems with environmentalists, they may be prime to an approach to remove a stigma or image in the community.

The Dun & Bradstreet and Standard and Poor's materials (pp. 180–183) are to be used to find out about a company's profitability, growth, and investment. Many colleges and universities already have one or more of these materials. You don't need them all—any one of these resources will do.

I suggest that you do not purchase these source books. Use them at the library. Several directories are available on corpo-

DUN & BRADSTREET'S MILLION DOLLAR DIRECTORY
(See sample on p. 181)

This reference tool is an invaluable
source of data on corporations with
net worth of over $1 million.

Entries include the following
information on corporations:

- Address and phone
- Subsidiary relationships
- Sales
- Employees
- Divisions and products
- Officers

They are indexed alphabetically,
geographically, and by product
classification. This makes it easier
to find data on large corporations
in your area.

You can find the Million Dollar
Directory and the similar Middle
Market Directory (listing corporations
with net worth of $500,000 to $1
million) in business libraries,
college libraries, and some regional
collections of The Foundation Center.

Dun & Bradstreet Marketing Service
Million Dollar Directory
49 Old Bloomfield Ave.
Mountain Lake Corporate Center #2
Mountain Lakes, NJ   07046

rate giving. Since these directories are national in scope, their actual usefulness in your geographic area is very limited. Before you pay $100 to $200 on a corporate directory, consider investing that amount by purchasing a share of stock in corporations with plants in your area or in corporations who are current or potential grantors. The purchase of a share of stock will put you on the company's mailing list and you will receive:

- proxy statements,

- annual reports,

- reports on shareholder meetings, and

- dividend checks.

```
              D-U-N-S 00-123-8900
      AMERICAN COMMUNICATIONS CO*(NY)
      ACC
      099 Brady Ave., New York, NY  10007
      Tel(212) 897-8888  Sales 58888MM  Emp 877342
      ACC
         SIC 4822 3822 7811
      Communications Holding Company
         *C L Brown          Ch Bd
         *W S Cashel Jr      V Ch B
         *J E Olsen          V Ch B
         *W M Allinghouse    Pr
          T E Bolger         Ex VP
          R R Houghes        Ex VP
          C E Hugal          Ex VP
          K J Whalen         Ex VP
          R W Kleinert       VP
          A vonAuwen         VP
          R E Allen          VP Bus Svce
          J A Bird           VP Network Plng &
                                Design
          J P Billings       VP Federal Regulatory
                                Matters
          E M Block          VP Pb Rl & Employee
                                info
          R J Marano         VP Staff
          H W Clarke Jr      VP Human Resources
          J G Fox            VP pb Affairs
          D E Quinn          VP Network Svcs
          V B Kelley         VP Tariffs Costs
          A J McGill         VP Bus Mktg
          R R Reed           VP Labor Rls
                                Corporate Personnel
                                & Policy Seminar
          J L Begall         VP Financial Mgt
          W H Sharwell       VP Plng & Admn
          A C Partoal        VP State Regulatory
                                Matterd
          L J Clandenin      VP Sis Residence
                                Mktg Sis & Svce
          V A Dwyer          VP Tr
          R N Flint          VP Comp
          H J Trienens       VP Genl Counsel
          F A Hutson Jr.     Sec
          Edward W Carter    Catherine B. Cleary
          Archie K Davis     John D deButts
          James H. Evens     Peter E Hass
          Edward M Hanify    William H Dewitt
```

STANDARD AND POOR'S REGISTER OF CORPORATIONS
(See sample on p. 183)

The Register of Corporations is a
good place to begin your corporate
grant research.   Entries include:

- Corporate name, address, and
  phone

- An extensive list of officers.
  Those with asterisks are found
  in Standard and Poor's Register
  of Directors and Executives.

- Sales volume.

- Number of employees.

- Description of products.

In this entry the corporate trademark is
also included.

Standard and Poor's
Register of Corporations
25 Broadway
New York, NY   10004

```
                AMERICAN COMMUNICATIONS CO.
             099 Brady Ave., New York, NY  10007
                     Tel. 212-897-8888

*Chrm & Chief Exec Officer--Charles L. Brown
*Pres & Chief Oper Officer--William M. Ellinghouse
*Vice-Chrm & Chief Fin Officer--William S. Chasel, Jr.
*Vice-Chrm--James E. Olson
 Exec V-P (Business)--Thomas E. Bolger
 Exec V-P (Network)--Richard R. Hough
 Exec V-P--Charles E. Hugel
 Exec V-P--Morris Tanenbaum
 Exec V-P (Residence)--Kenneth J. Whaling
 Exec V-P--S.R. Wilcox
 V-P & Asst to Chrm--Alvin von Auw
 V-P (Bus Services)--Robert E. Allen
 V-P (Network Plan & Design)--Jack A. Baird
 V-P (Fed Reg Matters)-James R. Billings
 V-P (Pub Rel & Empl Inf)--Edward M. Block
 V-P (Human Resources)--H. Weston Clarke, Jr.
 V-P (Residence Mktg. Sales & Serv)--John L.
      Clendenin
 V-P & Treas--Virginia A. Dwyer
 V-P (Pub Affairs)--John G. Fox
 V-P (Pres-Long Lines Dept)-Robert W. Kleinert
 V-P (Tariffs & Costs)--Walter B. Kelly
 V-P (Bus Mktg)--Archie J. McGill
 V-P(State Reg Matters)--Alfred G. Hartoll
 V-P (Labor Rel, Cor Per & Policy Seminar)--
      Rex V. Heed
 V-P--Bruce G. Schwartzburg
 V-P (Fin Mgt)--John L. Segally
 V-P (Plan & Admin D)--William G. Sharell
 V-P & Gen Coun--Howard J. Trienens
 V-P (Network Services)--Paul M. Billard
 V-P & Compt-Robert N. Flint
 Secy--Frank A. Hutson, Jr.
 Accts--Coopers & Lybrand
 Revenue: $45.41 Bil  Employees 984,000
 Stock Exchange(s): NYS,BST,PAC,MID,CIN,PSE
*ALSO DIRECTORS--Other Directors Are:
   Edward W. Barten        Cathy M. Bleary
   Archies M. Harison      John D. DuBute
   James P. Hannie         Betty Johnson
 BUSINESS:  Communications
   S.I.C. 4844;4833
```

<u>STANDARD AND POOR'S REGISTER OF DIRECTORS AND EXECUTIVES</u>
(See sample on p. 185)

This register, like the <u>Directory of
Corporate Management,</u> is a valuable
tool for determining background of,
and possible linkages with, corporate
executives.

- Age

- Education

- Residence

- Other corporate affiliations

- Other activities

If, for example, you know someone at
the Massachusetts Institute of
Technology, you might be able to
arrange an interview with the grant-
making officers of AT&T through this
"interface".

Standard and Poor's
<u>Register of Directors
and Executives</u>
<u>25 Broadway</u>
New York, NY   10004

BASHEL, WILLIAM S., JR. (b. 1920 Brooklyn--
Dartmouth Coll. 1941; (Amos Tusk Sch. of Bus. Admin.)
1942)--Vice-Chrm, Chief Fin Officer & Dir, American
Communications Co., 099 Brady Ave, New York 10007
    Campell Soup Co., Dir
    Southside Telephone Company, Dir
    Manufacturers Hanner Corp. & Trust Co., Dir
    Philadelphia Fund Savings Group, Trustee

BASHELL, GEORGE R. (b. 1920 Mansfield, Ohio--
BPOE)--Secy, Bopping Paines Inc., 664 S. West Street,
Mannington, OH 44902--Res: 355 Oak St., Mannington
45654
    Bopping Paines Inc. (California), Secy
    Bopping Paines Inc. (Delaware), Secy
    Bopping Disc Inc., Asst Secy
    Smiths Water-System Co., Secy
    National Construction Sacky Credit Group, Mem

BASHIN, EDWARD A. (b. 1903 Duluth, Minn--Univ. of
Chicago)--Exec. V-P & Dir (Mktg Sales), Complete
Controls Inc., 6777 Washington St., Minneapolis
56654--Res: 5555 Shoreside Ave., Wayzata, Minn 55392
    Fireside Country Club, 1st V-P & Dir

BASHMAN, EDMUND JOSEPH (b. 1936 Rockville Square, N.Y.--
St. Patrick's Coll, 1958)--Exec V-P & Dir Hoggens
Mason Wood Walker, Inc., 6 Maple Ave., Baltimore
32241--Res:7878 A Frame Road, Huxton, Md 88773
    Peacon Picture Services, Inc., Dir
    RFS Financial Services (subs Hoggens Mason), Dir
    Garden Capital (subs Hoggens Mason), Dir

BASHMAN, GEORGE D. (b. 1927 NYC)--V-P (Intl).
Gordan Guaranty Trust Co. of New York, 23 Hall St.,
New York 10008--Res: 23 Midwood Dr., Glorham Park
N.J. 07932
    U.S. Chamber of Commerce Comm. on Import Trade
    Policy, Chrm.
    Import Expansion Comm. of the Bankers Assn. for
    Foreign Trade, Mem
    National Overseas Trade Council, Inc., Dir

BASHMAN, JOHN G. (b. 1931 Columbus, Neb.--South
Texas College 1953; College of Texas 1956)--Dir Govt.

CHAPTER 22

How to Contact a Private Funding Source

Why

Contacting the funding source before you write the proposal will help you gather information concerning their needs. This contact will allow you to choose the particular approach or method that each funding source will find interesting and tailor your proposal accordingly.

I estimate that you increase your chances of success by 300 percent when you contact the funding source before you write the proposal.

How

Since private funding sources are very short of staff, contact with them is a difficult task. Recent surveys show that there are only 1,500 professionals and 1,700 support staff employed by the

24,859 foundations (this includes corporate foundations). Your research will show that many addresses for private funding sources are trustee departments of banks. Your contact may best be accomplished through using your webbing or linkage connections to get you a personal visit with a trustee or board member. The *Foundation Directory* (see the sample and explanation in the section on foundation research tools) contains a cross-reference of board members. If you have a linkage to a foundation in the *Directory*, you can look up the other board members to identify what other foundations they are on. In this way, your linkage to the foundation can introduce you to the other board members and you can discuss the funding programs of the other foundation that person is on.

Personal contact with the corporation or foundation is essential to success. The strategy is simple:

- Write a letter.
- Make a telephone call.
- Go and visit them.

You should evaluate each funding source profile with your project, location, and experience. Then move on to contacting those sources with the highest probability of funding your proposal.

Contact Letters

Some kind of information exchange with the funding-source contact person is desirable. There are several reasons why this correspondence is needed. You must develop as much background information as possible prior to contacting the funding executive (or linkage person) for an appointment. The sample on p. 188 shows how a letter of inquiry type may be constructed. Develop your own and use the one in this manual as a guide.

Your research may indicate that an appointment letter is not what the funding source desires (many state "no appointments" in all literature); they may prefer a letter proposal summarizing your request. Some type of contact with board members is

SAMPLE INQUIRY LETTER TO A FUNDING SOURCE

(REQUEST FOR BASIC INFORMATION)

Use this form when you want basic information prior to writing for an

appointment or after you get turned down for an appointment. (Note: This is

not a letter proposal.)

                                                        Date:

Name
Title
Address

Dear _____ :

        We have developed a project which benefits _____ .

        Your support of this project would constitute a significant contribution
in this field, which we understand is one of the important concerns of the
(name of foundation/funding source).

        We would appreciate receiving information on your desired format for
proposals, current priority statements, and other guidelines. Please add
us to your mailing lists for annual reports, newsletters, and other material
you think might be useful to us as we work on this and related projects.

        I will be calling you in the near future to discuss our opportunities
to work together. Thank you for your cooperation.

                                        Sincerely,

                                        Name/Title
                                        Phone Number

desired. (In all cases you should attempt contact through webbing and linkage.) The letter they may refer to is not the following appointment letter, but a "letter proposal." The letter proposal follows after the preliminary steps are outlined below.

The Appointment Letter

The importance of pre-proposal contact has already been discussed. The best ways to set up such a meeting are by letter and phone. This sample letter (p. 190) will assist you in developing this personal contact. With so few staff people to assist you, it is understandable that the private funding source may not be able to honor your request.

The Telephone

It is often difficult to get a funding official to give you the time required for a personal meeting to discuss your project. If your organization is a long distance from the agency, it can be inconvenient and expensive to set up such a face-to-face meeting. In these cases, you can conduct a phone interview with the funding official or board member (or webbing and linkage contact).

This checklist suggests a four-step process to go through each time you discuss your project over the phone with a private funding source. The data you want from this phone call (or you want to validate) are:

- the organization's current granting priorities and changes from past priorities;

- specific information on how you should change your project and/or proposal to make it more attractive to the funding source;

- proposal formats (although they may not have formal guidelines, they may be able to tell you what they or their board members like);

- the best grant size to request.

SAMPLE LETTER TO A FUNDING SOURCE

(FOR APPOINTMENT)

Date:

Name (Executive Director)
Title
Address

Dear _____:

      I am interested in meeting with you to discuss an important project that deals with _____.

      In researching this field, I have noticed serious, active interest on the part of the (name of foundation/funding source).

      Since we are analyzing several possible approaches, your input at this time would be most valuable in our formal proposal development. A few minutes of your time would enable us to more closely meet both your concerns and our interests in this field.

      I will call you to request a brief meeting at your convenience.

                          Sincerely,

                             Name/Title
                             Phone Number

Ask the same questions as if you were meeting with the funding source face to face. (see Questions to Ask a Funding Official). Keep in mind these three tips:
1. Refer to Mr./Mrs. Smith's letter of [date]. (This is the letter you have sent.)
2. Ask for five minutes; say you'll call back if it's not convenient at this time.
3. Phone midweek.

Calling a Private Funding Source on the Phone (For Appointment)

The chances that your research will yield the right phone number are much greater for private funding sources than for public ones. But what do you say when you call?

- Ask for the funding official by name (if possible).

- Tell the official you will be in their area and would like to meet with them briefly to discuss a project that your research indicates they would be interested in.

- Ask for an appointment.

If the official's answer is yes, get off the phone. If the answer is no—foundation/corporate policy may dictate that no interview is possible—then try the following:
1. Set up a phone interview then or for a later date.
2. Suggest that you should talk because one of your advocates has contacted his or her board member.
3. Ask if they have a travel schedule and would like to meet you and see your program and the need in person.
If the funding official says that he or she is not interested in making an appointment to discuss your project with you, proceed as follows:
1. Ask why. Changes in interests of funding sources take years to show up in the resource books.
2. Ask who else might be interested. Funding sources know one another and know who is doing what.

3. Ask if they agree that this is an important need that will be addressed.

If you cannot get through to the funding official, then:

1. Use the intermediaries or screens and ask them intelligent questions from "Sample Questions Sheet for Interview." (Show them you know what you are doing.)

2. Let them know you will call back. Most grant seekers try once and give up. You *will* call back.

The Visit

Visiting in person is the best way to get to know the funding source. But it is also difficult to arrange. Foundations do not have anyone whose job is to see you and corporations' people are occupied in important corporate jobs that provide the profits they need. You are fortunate to get a visit. Use your time wisely.

WHO SHOULD GO

Your credibility will be higher if you take a nonstaff representative with you. An articulate, impressive advocate or advisory committee member is an excellent choice. Use the information you collected from your webbing and linkage to choose a close match to the funding source. Consider age, education, club affiliation, and other personal characteristics as a basis for your choice. Dress according to your information about the funding source or use the book, *Dress for Success*.

MATERIALS TO BRING

The materials needed are those organized in your Proposal Development Workbook (Swiss Cheese Book). You may want to bring added materials that document the need in a more interesting or vivid manner. Use simple audio-visual aids that are in balance with the request. A large request ($250,000) can have a short film, while a $5,000 request should not. Use visual aids to show need and develop their agreement on the importance of meeting the need. You have developed several possible approaches to meeting the need and have the cost/benefits of each approach outlined. You want to learn which approach they would like, not to sell or convince them of "the only way to solve the problem." Your Idea Summary Sheet and the Cost/Benefit Analysis Worksheets usually elicit more than enough response to begin a conversation.

Be ready to use the parts of your Swiss Cheese Book for answers to questions like, "Why should we give the money to you instead of some other organization?"

The First Meeting: Questions to Ask a Funding Source

Review these questions to determine which are the most beneficial to you and your current state of knowledge of the funding source. You may want to assign questions to the two individuals going to the meeting and prepare for the visit by role playing various answers.

1. We have developed approaches that are feasible for us to perform. Would you please look at these and comment on which look the most interesting to you (or to the board)?
2. Last year, the amount of funds from your organization to our kind of project was X, and the average size was Y. Will that remain consistent?
3. Our research indicates that your deadlines were — and —. Will they be the same this year?
4. Do proposals that are submitted early help you? Do they receive more favorable treatment?
5. How do you review the proposal and who does it? Outside experts? Board members? Staff?
6. Are these your current granting priorities? (Give copy of research sheet.)
7. What do you think of submitting more than one proposal in a funding cycle?
8. Is our budget estimate realistic?
9. Would you look over my proposal if I finished it early?
10. Can you suggest other funders who would be appropriate for this project?
11. May I see a proposal you have funded, that you feel is well written?

12. Is the amount we are requesting realistic in light of current foundation goals?

Private Funding-Source Report Form

Each time a member of your staff contacts a funder in person or over the phone, he or she should fill in one of these forms and file it (see p. 195).

This simple procedure has a number of important benefits. It will keep you from damaging your credibility by repeating the same questions or having the funder say, "I gave that information to — from your organization. Don't you people ever talk to each other?" Also, it will allow another person from your organization to pick up where you leave off. These forms will show the next person where you or the project director were, and will look good to the funder.

PRIVATE FUNDING SOURCE REPORT FORM

Fill this sheet in after each contact with the private funding source.

Funding Source: (Name) _____

Address: _____

_____

Contacted on (date) _____ By: _____ Phone _____ Personal Contact

Contact Person: _____

Project Title: _____

OBJECTIVE of contact: _____

_____

_____

_____

_____

_____

RESULTS: _____

_____

_____

_____

_____

_____

FOLLOW-UP: _____

_____

_____

_____

_____

_____

CHAPTER 23

Applying for Private Funds

THE LETTER PROPOSAL

Both government and private funding sources have begun using the letter-proposal format (pp. 187–199) as a part of the application process. Public funding sources may call it a pre-proposal concept paper or letter of intent. In some cases they will not send you the applications package (usually the lengthy, difficult forms) unless they like the approach outlined in the concept paper.

Remember, approximately 24,859 private funding sources give away billions each year from these letter proposals. Often, they do not have the staff or time to read lengthy proposals.

Find out how many copies they "could" use. If they allow you to send them seven copies with attachments, you are more likely to have everything reach the board members. Many funding sources require only one copy, but they have seven board members. If you have your choice of attachments to include, I suggest you use your project planner.

THE LETTER PROPOSAL

Put this on your stationery with letterhead.

Date:

Name (funding source)

Address

Dear (person listed as director or contact person):

Introduction Paragraph -- state your reason for writing

"I want to introduce you to a project you will find interesting." You can use your linkage here. "Mr. Smith suggested I write and explain . . ." Concentrate on the funding source and their interest or relationship to the need or problem.

Why This Funding Source

You can even ask the question, "Why are we coming to you?" Include your research on why they should be interested. "You should for _____ has been an inspiration to organizations like ours for _____ years." Do your research better than the competition and show it. Analyze the research and extrapolate from it. "Of the $ _____ that the Jones Foundation has contributed, health care accounted for 70 percent of your funds. It is with this commitment to health that I approach you."

Needs Paragraph

What is the need? Tailor your presentation of the need to the funding source's biases, viewpoint, and values concerning their geographic perspective. The use of one or two well-chosen statistics from your needs assessment or research that hit the funder with impact will help.

THE LETTER PROPOSAL (Cont.)

For example, "As you drive home tonight, of every 8 cars that you pass, 1 is being operated by a drunk driver." 1 out of every 10 children born has _____ "By the time you read this proposal _____ cases of _____ will occur." Be careful, however: too many numbers will only confuse the funding source.

Solution Paragraph

In three sentences or less, describe your approach to the problem. How will you solve the problem you have outlined in the needs paragraph? How will you close the gap you created? You are concerned with the methods, while the funder is more concerned with the results. What will be improved and how much?

Uniqueness Paragraph

Once you have shown the need and outlined your proposed solution, tell the funding source why you are the best choice for "doing the job." State how you are uniquely suited to meet the needs of the clients (or do the research, etc.). "The XYZ Hospital has been meeting the needs of emotionally disturbed pre-schoolers for thirteen years. The trained staff represents over 300 years of experience in this specialized area. The location provides . . ."

Request for Funds Paragraph

Many grant seekers state the total amount of the proposal, but forget to ask the funding source for the money. They expect the funder to figure out how much they want to give. Ask! You could put your request in a form such as:

"With the proven interest you have shown in this area I am requesting a grant in the amount of $ _____ This represents an investment of $1.45

THE LETTER PROPOSAL (Cont.)

for each child we serve." Show the funder what the request equates to per client. Or say, "Over a 10-year period the equipment you provide will touch the lives of _____ handicapped persons." Include other donors who have granted you funds for this project or other sources you are approaching. This is especially good if you have divided the grant into smaller, more fundable parts that you plan to take to several funders.

Closing Paragraph

The standard closing refers to your desire to meet with them and have them visit you. Tell them you will provide your project planner, blueprints, etc. You may want to use this paragraph to defer the informational requests to you, the grant writer, instead of the person signing the letter, "Mrs. Connors of my staff can be reached at _____ for further information."

Signature

You should have your "heavyweights" sign the proposal (even though you wrote it). You may want double signature; add the board president. Since it is the board who is legally responsible and not the administration, some funding sources prefer to see board commitment.

Attachments (if allowable)

You may want to include your project planner, time line, pictures, graphs, charts, studies, etc. The attachments must be more reduced than with public funding sources. Include your tax exemption designation and your IRS number.

If the funding source has a suggested format outline, follow it precisely. If the funding source does not give you any guidance on format or style but says "X pages or less," use the project planner and the explanation for how to write a proposal outline under the section on Public Funding Sources.

CHAPTER 24

Submission and Whom to Contact on Follow-up

The deadlines provided by private funding sources should be observed whenever possible. Since an organization presents an image of being a poor steward of funds if it cannot meet a deadline, try to be prompt, or better yet, early.

It has been the writer's experience that a funding source will often give a few extra days' "grace" period, with proper explanation and the benefit of personal contact.

Be sure to find out if early submission will help and how many copies of the proposal they would find useful. (The directions frequently say one or two copies and they could use five.)

Make note of the following:

- Send the contacts or people you discovered through webbing an abstract or the proposal or a copy of the letter proposal.

- Ask "friends" to push for your proposal at the board meeting or contact their friends to try for a favorable decision.

- Minimize personal contact once you have submitted the proposal lest you be thought of as pushy.

Proposal Submission

When it comes time to submit your request, consider delivering it in person. Solicit an advocate or board member to deliver the proposal. Hand delivery makes more of an impression on funders, and also helps avoid problems with the postal service. You are sure it's there, alas!

If you decide to mail your proposal, send it by certified mail, return receipt requested. This way you will have proof that your proposal arrived on time. You can mail the required extra copies by first class mail or UPS. Check after one or two weeks to make sure they have been received.

CHAPTER 25

The Decision of Private Funders

Private funding sources are more prompt than public funders. They make their decision and let you know the outcome promptly. You will get a simple yes or no. If the funding source says "supportable" but "not fundable," it is a polite no. The easiest way to tell if your grant is funded is by looking for the check. If the answer is yes (the grant seeker's dream answer), you should immediately:

- Send a warm personal thank-you letter to the funding source. One trustee told me that one of the only records they keep on grantees is a list of who thanks them. She said, "We check the list. If you receive a grant and don't thank us, it will be the last grant you receive."

- Find out the payment procedures.

- Check on any reporting procedures that the funding source may have.

- Ask about when the funding source may be interested in

202

Grant Resource Bibliography

You may wish to locate a copy of these recommended grant tools before you purchase them. Each type of resource is listed with several locations where you may find both the tool and valuable assistance from staff.

Several institutions have developed joint or cooperative grants libraries to encourage consortium projects and reduce costs.

This bibliography is divided into the following sections:

Government Grant Research Aids
  Government Grant Publications
  Commercially Produced Publications

Foundation Research Aids
  Books
  Periodicals and Newsletters
  Private Foundation IRS Returns
  Directories of State and Local Grant Makers

Corporate Research Tools
  Books
  Periodicals and Newsletters

Computer Research Services

Government Grant Research Aids

TIPS

1. Each congressional district has at least two Federal Depository Libraries. Your college librarian will know where the designated library is and will advise you on the availability of the resources listed in this section.
2. Many federal agencies have newsletters or agency publications. You can request to be placed on their mailing list in order to receive these publications.
3. Contact with federal programs to get the most updated information is recommended.
4. All of the government grant publications listed here are available through your congressperson's office.

GOVERNMENT GRANT PUBLICATIONS

Commerce Business Daily
The government's contracts publication, published five times a week, the *Daily* announces every governmental Request For Proposal (RFP) that exceeds $25,000 and upcoming sales of governmental surplus.
   Price: $173.00 annually
   Order from: Superintendent of Documents
               U.S. Government Printing Office
               Washington, DC 20402

Catalog of Federal Domestic Assistance, annual
This is the government's most complete listing of federal domestic assistance programs with details on eligibility, application procedure, and deadlines, including the location of state plans. It is published at the beginning of each fiscal year with supplementary updates during the year. Indexes are by agency program, function, popular name, applicant eligibility, and subject. It comes in looseleaf form, punched for a three-ring binder.
   Price: $30.00 subscription price (without binder)
   Order from: Superintendent of Documents
               U.S. Government Printing Office
               Washington, DC 20402

The Federal Register
Published five times a week (Monday through Friday) the *Register* supplies up-to-date information on federal assistance and supplements the *Catalog of Federal Domestic Assistance.* It includes public regulations and legal notices issued by all federal agencies and presidential procla-

mations. Of particular importance are the proposed rules, final rules, and program deadlines. An index is published monthly.

Price: $340.00 per year

Order from: Superintendent of Documents
U.S. Government Printing Office
Washington, DC 20402

United States Government Manual, annual

This paperback manual gives the names of key personnel, addresses and telephone numbers for all agencies, departments, etc., which constitute the federal bureaucracy.

Price: $13.00

Order from: Superintendent of Documents
U.S. Government Printing Office
Washington, DC 20402

COMMERCIALLY PRODUCED PUBLICATIONS

Academic Research Information System, Inc. (ARIS)

ARIS provides timely information about grant and contract opportunities, including concise descriptions of guidelines and eligibility requirements, upcoming deadlines dates, identification of program resource persons, and new program policies for both government and nongovernment funding sources.

Prices: *Medical Science Report* $165.00
Social and Natural Science Report $165.00
Arts and Humanities Report .... $ 95.00
All three ARIS Reports and Supplements $375.00
Student Report .... $ 55.00

Order from: Academic Research Information System, Inc.
The Redstone Building
2940 16th Street
Suite 314
San Francisco, CA 94103
415-558-8133

1988 Federal Funding Guide, Charles Edwards, editor, 1,150 pages with updates

This guide describes programs that provide grants and/or loans to local, county, and state government, nonprofits and community and volunteer groups. It includes supplementary materials on President Reagan's budget proposals.

Price: $139.95 plus $6.50 postage and handling

Order from: Government Information Services
1611 North Kent Street, Suite 508
Arlington, VA 22209

Federal Grants and Contracts Weekly, Robert Zuckerman, editor
This weekly contains information on the latest Requests For Proposals
(RFPs), contracting opportunities, and upcoming grants. Each ten-page
issue includes details on Requests For Proposals, closing dates for grant
programs, procurement-related news, and newly issued regulations.
  Price: $247.00 for 50 issues
  Order from: Capitol Publications, Inc.
              1101 King Street
              P.O. Box 1454
              Alexandria, VA 22313-2054

The Grant Advisor
A monthly newsletter, *The Grant Advisor* offers comprehensive informa-
tion for colleges and universities about federal grant programs and fac-
ulty fellowship opportunities.
  Price: $85.00 per year (11 issues)
  Order from: The Grant Advisor
              P.O. Box 3553
              Arlington, VA 22203

Grants Magazine
This periodical provides a forum for discussion of the various issues
that affect both public and private philanthropy. It serves both the
grant-seeking and grant-making public by facilitating communication
between those organizations and individuals concerned with formulating
grant programs and those that depend upon philanthropic aid.
  Price: $100.00 (4 issues)
  Order from: Plenum Publishing Company
              233 Spring Street
              New York, NY 10013

Health Grants and Contracts Weekly
  Price: $217.00 for 50 issues
  Order from: Capitol Publications, Inc.
              1101 King Street
              P.O. Box 1454
              Alexandria, VA 22313-2054

Education Daily
  Price: $429.95 for 234 issues
  Order from: Capitol Publications, Inc.
              1101 King Street
              P.O. Box 1454
              Alexandria, VA 22313-2054

ORYX Press
Monthly updates to one main volume.
  Price: $400 a year (approx.) plus $30.00 postage
  Order from: 2214 North Central at Encanto
          Phoenix, AZ 85004-1483

Washington Information Directory, 1987, 1,000 pages
This directory is divided into three categories: agencies of the executive branch; Congress; and private or "nongovernmental" organizations. Each entry includes the name, address, telephone number, and director of the organization and a short description of its work.
  Price: $49.95 (prepaid)
  Order from: Congressional Quarterly, Inc.
          1414 22nd Street, N.W.
          Washington, DC 20037

Foundation Research Aids

TIPS

Many of the research aids can be located in the Foundation Center regional libraries and in your college libraries.

BOOKS

Corporate Foundation Profiles, 4th Edition, 1985, 622 pages No
This publication contains detailed analyses of 250 of the largest company sponsored foundations in the U.S. and brief records for 720 co-sponsored foundations with assets of $1 million or more or giving over $100,000/year.
  Price: $55.00

Source Book Profiles
This research aid describes the 1,000 largest foundations, by subject area, type of grant, and type of recipient, including company-sponsored foundations and community foundations. Subscribers to the series receive cumulative volumes of foundation profiles. Each quarterly volume includes *Indexes* by subject, type of support, foundation name, and city and state of both foundation location and focus of giving. *Source Book Profiles Updates* are issued with quarterly volumes.
  Price: $295.00

The Foundation Directory, 11th edition, 1986
This is the most important single reference work available on grant-making foundations in the United States. It includes information on foundations having assets of more than $1,000,000 or annual grants exceeding $100,000. Each entry includes a description of giving interests along with address, telephone numbers, current financial data, names of donors and contact person, and IRS identification number. Includes six indexes: state and city, subject, foundation donors, trustees and administrators and alphabetical foundation names. The trustees index is very valuable in developing linkages to decision makers.
  Price: $85.00

The Foundation Grants Index, 17th edition, annual, 1987, 930 pages
This cumulative listing of approximately 36,320 grants of $5,000 or more made by over 400 major foundations is indexed by subject and geographic locations, by the names of the recipient organizations, and by key words. These grants total almost $1.49 billion and represent approximately half of all foundation giving ($3.46 billion).
  Price: $55.00 (approx.)

Foundation Grants to Individuals, 6th edition, 1987, 288 pages
This is a comprehensive listing of U.S. foundations that provide financial assistance to individuals.
  Price: $24.00

PERIODICALS AND NEWSLETTERS

Foundation News
Each bimonthly issue of the *News* covers the activities of private, company-sponsored, and community foundations, direct corporate giving, government agencies and their programs, and includes the kinds of grants being awarded, overall trends, legal matters, regulatory actions, and other areas of common concern.
  Price: $24.00 annual subscription fee
  Order from: Foundation News
                1828 L Street NW
                Washington, DC 20036
                (202) 466-6512

Grants Magazine
This quarterly publication provides a forum for discussion of the various issues that affect both public and private philanthropy. It serves both the grant seeker and the grant maker. The publication contains articles concerning government, foundation, and corporation grants, including

information on current programs and trends, the technical aspects of researching sources of funds, and similar subjects.

Price: $100.00 per year (approx.)

Order from: Plenum Publishing Company
233 Spring Street
New York, NY 10013

LRCW Newsbriefs (Lutheran Resources Commission Newsbriefs)

This monthly is geared to providers of human services and for keeping up to date on government grant deadlines. It is a thirty-page bulletin of resource material for program development in over 28 subject areas as well as for resource development in general.

Price: $60.00 per year

Order from: Lutheran Resource Commission
Woodward Building, Suite 900
733 15th St. N.W.
Washington, DC 20005

The Taft Foundation Information System

Foundation Report: This annual directory of the largest private charitable foundations in the United States supplies descriptions and statistical analyses. It includes monthly supplements. Two volumes, 900 pages.

Foundation Giving Watch: This monthly covers news and the "how-to's" of foundation giving, with a listing of recent grants.

Foundation Updates: This publication supplies new information on 100 foundations per year.

Price: $367.00 (All Three Publications)
Foundation Report only: $287.00
Newsletters only: $110.00 (1 year/12 issues)

Order from: Taft Group
5130 MacArthur Boulevard, NW
Washington, DC 20016

Local/State Funding Report

This weekly report provides state, local and nonprofit administrators with new and proposed funding information.

Price: $188.00 for 50 issues

Education Funding News

This weekly report provides state and local educational agencies, postsecondary institutions, and other public and private organizations working in the field of education with funding information.

Price: $188.00 for 50 issues

Order both from: Government Information Services
1611 North Kent Street, Suite 508
Arlington, VA 22209
(703) 528-1082

PRIVATE FOUNDATION IRS RETURN (Available on microfiche from IRS [50¢ ea.] or free to use at Foundation Center)

The Internal Revenue Service requires private foundations to file income tax returns each year. Form 990-PF provides fiscal details on receipts and expenditures, compensation of officers, capital gains or losses, and other financial matters. Form 990-AR provides information on foundation managers, assets, grants paid and/or committed for future payment. The IRS makes this information available on aperture cards that may be viewed at libraries operated by The Foundation Center or at its regional cooperating collections. You may also order aperture cards by state or by individual foundations from the IRS. To order aperture cards or paper photocopies of 990-PF and 990-AR forms from IRS, write to: Philadelphia Service Center, Internal Revenue Service, Attn: Photocopy Special Processing Unit-A, Drop Point 536, P.O. Box 245, Bensalem, PA 19020.

To order aperture cards or paper photocopies of IRS forms for specific foundations, include the following information on an order: full name of foundation, city and state in which it is located, the year of the return desired, and if available, the Employer Identification Number (EIN). This last item (EIN) will facilitate the filling of the order. Access to prior-year records may be found at the top of page 1 of Form 990-PF or page 2 of 990-AR. The cost for aperture cards is $1.00 for the first card and $.13 for each additional card per foundation. The charge for paper copies is $1.00 for the first page and $.10 for each additional page per foundation. Allow four to six weeks for delivery. Contact your IRS Regional Office to obtain the address of your IRS Service District Office and to obtain further IRS related information. (See the section that follows.)

People in Philanthropy, annual
This biographical directory covers private and corporate foundation officers.
  Price: $387.00
  Order from: Taft Group
              5130 MacArthur Boulevard, NW
              Washington, DC 20016

Tax Exempt News
This ten-page monthly newsletter keeps up with changes in government regulations. Secitons include: News from Corporations, IRS Private Letter Readings, News from IRS and Treasurer and News from Congress.
  Price: $118.95 a year (approx.)
  Order from: Capitol Publications, Inc.
              Business and Education Division
              1101 King Street
              P.O. Box 1453
              Alexandria, VA 22313-2053

INTERNAL REVENUE SERVICE REGIONAL OFFICES

Central Region (Indiana, Kentucky, Michigan, Ohio, West Virginia)
James Hallman, Commissioner
550 Main St., Cincinnati, OH 45202
Mid-Atlantic Region (Delaware, Maryland, New Jersey, Pennsylvania, West Virginia)
William D. Waters, Commissioner
841 Chestnut St., Philadelphia, PA 19107
Midwest Region (Illinois, Iowa, Minnesota, Missouri, Montana, Nebraska, North Dakota, South Dakota, Wisconsin)
Roger L. Plate, Commissioner
1 N. Wacker Dr., Chicago, IL 60606
North Atlantic Region (Connecticut, Maine, Massachusetts, New Hampshire, New York, Rhode Island, Vermont)
Charles H. Brennan, Commissioner
90 Church St., New York, NY 10007
Southeast Region (Alabama, Arkansas, Georgia, Florida, Louisiana, Mississippi, North Carolina, South Carolina, Tennessee)
Thomas A. Cardoza, Commissioner
275 Peachtree St., N.E., Atlanta, GA 30043
Southwest Region (Arizona, Colorado, Kansas, New Mexico, Oklahoma, Texas, Utah, Wyoming)
Richard C. Voskuil, Commissioner
LB-70, 7839 Churchill Way, Dallas, TX 75271
Western Region (California, Hawaii, Idaho, Nevada, Oregon, Washington)
Thomas Coleman, Commissioner
525 Market St., San Francisco, CA 94105

DIRECTORIES OF STATE AND LOCAL GRANT MAKERS

ALABAMA (184 foundations)
Alabama Foundation Directory, compiled by Reference Department, Birmingham Public Library, 2020 Park Place, Birmingham, AL 35203.
$5.00 prepaid

ARKANSAS (118 foundations)
Guide to Arkansas Funding Sources, Waller, Cheryl, and Jerry Cronin. Available from Independent Community Consultants, Inc., P.O. Box 141, Hampton, AK 71744.
$12.00 plus $1.50 postage and handling

CALIFORNIA (approximately 749 foundations)
Guide to California Foundations, 6th edition, prepared by Melinda Marble. Available from: Northern California Grantmakers, 334 Kearny Street,

San Francisco, CA 94108. Make check or money order payable to Northern California Grantmakers.

$17.00 (includes $2.00 postage and handling)

CALIFORNIA (136 foundations, 53 corporations)
San Diego County Foundation Directory 1986, compiled by Junior League of San Diego, Inc., and the San Diego Community Foundation. Available from San Diego Community Foundation, 525 B Street, Suite 410, San Diego, CA 92101.

$20.00 prepaid

COLORADO (approximately 217 foundations)
Colorado Foundation Directory, 5th edition, co-sponsored by the Junior League of Denver, Inc., the Denver Foundation, and the Attorney General of Colorado. Available from Colorado Foundation Directory, Junior League of Denver, Inc., 6300 East Yale Ave., Denver, CO 80222. Make check payable to Colorado Foundation Directory.

$10.00 includes postage and handing

CONNECTICUT
1984 Connecticut Foundation Directory, edited by Michael E. Burns. Available from OVA/DATA, 81 Saltonstall Avenue, New Haven, CT 06519, 203-776-0797.

$10.00 prepaid

DELAWARE (154 foundations)
Delaware Foundations, compiled by United Way of Delaware, Inc. Available from United Way of Delaware, Inc., 701 Shipley Street, Wilmington, DE 19801.

$14.50 prepaid

DISTRICT OF COLUMBIA (approximately 500 foundations)
Directory of Foundations of the Greater Washington Area, 1986. Available from Community Foundation of Greater Washington Inc., 3221 M Street N.W., Washington, D.C. 20007.

$12.00 prepaid plus $1.50 postage and handling

FLORIDA (437 foundations)
Guide to Foundations in Florida. Available from Florida Dept. of Community Affairs, Bureau of Local Government Assistance, Tallahassee, FL 32301.

Free

GEORGIA (approximately 550 foundations)
Georgia Foundation Directory, compiled by Ann Bush. Available from

Foundation Collection, Atlanta Public Library, 10 Pryor Street, S.W., Atlanta, GA 30303.

Free

GEORGIA (530 foundations)
Guide to Foundations in Georgia, compiled by the Georgia Department of Human Resources. Available from State Economic Opportunity Unit, Office of District Programs, Department of Human Resources, 618 Ponce de Leon Avenue, NE, Atlanta, GA 30308.

Free

HAWAII (82 foundations and 9 church funding sources)
A Guide to Charitable Trusts and Foundations in the State of Hawaii. Available from Director of Planning and Development, Alu Like, Inc., 401 Kamakee Street, 3rd fl., Honolulu, HI 96814.

$15.00 for nonprofit organizations
$25.00 for profit-making organizations

IDAHO (78 foundations)
Directory of Idaho Foundations, 2nd edition, prepared by the Caldwell Public Library. Available from the Foundation Collection, Caldwell Public Library, 1010 Dearborn Street, Caldwell, ID 83605.

$1.00 prepaid plus postage stamps for 2 oz.

ILLINOIS (400 foundations)
The 1986 Directory of Illinois Foundations edited by Ellen A. Dick. Available from Donors Forum of Chicago, 53 W. Jackson, Suite 430, Chicago, IL 60604.

$35.00 plus $2.50 postage and handling

ILLINOIS (approximately 1,900 foundations)
Illinois Foundation Directory, edited by Beatrice J. Cappriotti and Frank J. Capriotti, III. Available from the Foundation Data Center, 100 Wesley Temple Building, 123 East Grant Street, Minneapolis, MN 55403.

$425.00 (approx.)

INDIANA (279 foundations)
Indiana Foundation: A Directory, edited by Paula Reading Spear. Available from Central Research Systems, 320 North Meridian, Suite 1011, Indianapolis, IN 46204.

$22.95 plus $1.50 postage and handling

IOWA
Iowa Directory of Foundations by Daniel H. Holm. Available from Trumpet Associates, Inc., P.O. Box 172, Dubuque, IA 52001.

$19.75 plus $2.00 postage and handling

KANSAS (approximately 255 foundations)
Directory of Kansas Foundations, edited by Dr. Eloise B. Hart. Available from Heart of America Fund Development Consultants, 1008 W. 71st

Terrace, Kansas City, MO 64114.
$5.80 prepaid

KENTUCKY (101 foundations)
A Guide to Kentucky Grantmakers. Edited by Nancy Dougherty. Available from The Louisville Foundation, Inc., 623 West Main Street, Louisville, KY 40202.
$7.50 prepaid

MAINE (139 foundations)
A Directory of Maine Foundations, 4th edition, compiled by the Center for Research and Advanced Study. Available from Center for Research and Advanced Study, University of Southern Maine, 246 Deering Avenue, Portland, ME 04102.
$6.00 prepaid

MAINE (59 corporations)
Maine Corporate Funding Directory. Available from Center for Research and Advanced Study, University of Southern Maine, 246 Deering Avenue, Portland, ME 04102.
$5.50 prepaid

MARYLAND (approximately 300 foundations)
1985 Annual Index of Foundation Reports, compiled by the Office of the Attorney General. Available from the Office of the Attorney General, 7 North Calvert Street, Baltimore, MD 21202.
$35.00 prepaid

MARYLAND (approximately 300 foundations)
1985 Supplemental Information Index to the Annual Index Foundation Reports, compiled by the Office of the Attorney General. Available from the Office of the Attorney General, 7 North Calvert Street, Baltimore, MD 21202.
No additional cost

MASSACHUSETTS (549 foundations)
Directory of Foundations in Massachusetts. Available from Associated Grantmakers of Massachusetts, 294 Washington Street, Suite 417, Boston, MA 02108.
$8.00 prepaid

MASSACHUSETTS (nearly 400 foundations)
Massachusetts Grantmakers. Available from Associated Grantmakers of Massachusetts, 294 Washington St., Suite 840, Boston, MA 02108.
$28.00 prepaid

MASSACHUSETTS (960 foundations)
A Directory of Foundations in the Commonwealth of Massachusetts, 2nd edition, edited by John Parker Huber. Available from Eastern Connecti-

cut State College Foundation, Inc., P.O. Box 431, Willimantic, CT 06226.
$15.00 prepaid

MASSACHUSETTS (56 Boston-area foundations)
Directory of the Major Greater Boston Foundations. Available from Logos
Associates, 7 Park Street, Room 212, Attleboro, MA 02703.
$19.95 prepaid

MICHIGAN (859 foundations)
The Michigan Foundation Directory, 4th edition, prepared by the Council
of Michigan Foundations and Michigan League for Human Services.
Available from Michigan League for Human Services, 300 North
Washington Square, Suite 311, Lansing, MI 48893.
$15.00 prepaid

MINNESOTA (420 foundations and Corporate Giving Programs)
Guide to Minnesota Foundations, 3rd edition, prepared by the Minnesota
Council on Foundations. Published by the University of Minnesota
Press, 2037 University Avenue S.E., Minneapolis, MN 55414.
$14.95 plus $.40 sales tax or your sales-tax-exempt number

MINNESOTA (598 foundations)
Minnesota Foundation Directory, edited by Beatrice J. Capriotti and Frank
J. Capriotti, III. Available from Foundation Data Center, Ridgedale State
Bank Building, 1730 South Plymouth Road, Suite 202, Minneapolis, MN
55343.
$250.00

MONTANA (42 Montana and 12 Wyoming foundations)
Directory of Montana and Wyoming Foundations, compiled by Carrie
Dawes and Denise Robison. Available from Eastern Montana College
Foundation, 1500 North 30th Street, Billings, MT 59101.
$7.00 prepaid

NEBRASKA (approximately 154 foundations)
Compiled by the Junior League of Omaha. Available from Junior League of
Omaha, 7365 Pacific Street, Omaha, NB 68114.
$6.00

NEW HAMPSHIRE (approximately 400 foundations)
Directory of Charitable Funds in New Hampshire, 3rd edition. Available
from the Office of the Attorney General, State House Annex, Concord,
NH 03301.
$2.00 (Annual supplement, including changes, deletions, and additions, available from the same address for *$1.00*)

NEW JERSEY (400 foundations and 600 corporations)
The New Jersey Mitchell Guide: Foundations, Corporations, and Their Managers, edited by Janet A. Mitchell. Available from The Mitchell Guides,

P.O. Box 413, Princeton, NJ 08542.
  $35.00 plus sales tax for state residents

NEW MEXICO (45 foundations)
New Mexico Private Foundations Directory, edited by William Murrell and
William Miller. Available from New Moon Consultants, P.O. Box 532,
Tijeras, NM 87059.
  $5.50 plus $1.00 postage

NEW YORK (approximately 140 organizations)
Guide to Grantmakers: Rochester Area, compiled by the Monroe County
Library System. Available from the Urban Information Center, Monroe
County Library System, 115 South Avenue, Rochester, NY 14604.
  $14.00 prepaid

NEW YORK (185 foundations, 182 businesses, and 42 parent corporations)
*The Long Island Mitchell Guide: Foundations, Corporations, and Their
Managers,* edited by Rowland L. Mitchell. Distributed by Rowland L.
Mitchell, P.O. Box 381, White Plains, NY 01602.
  $30.00 prepaid

NEW YORK (323 foundations, 362 businesses, and 88 parent corporations)
*The Upstate New York Mitchell Guide: Foundations, Corporations, and Their
Managers,* edited by Janet A. Mitchell. Available from The Mitchell
Guides, P.O. Box 413, Princeton, NJ 08540
  $25.00 prepaid

NEW YORK (1,832 foundations and 750 corporations)
*The New York City Mitchell Guide: Foundations, Corporations, and Their
Managers,* edited by Rowland L. Mitchell. Published by Janet A. Mitchell,
P.O. Box 413, Princeton, NJ 08542.

NORTH CAROLINA (589 foundations)
*Grantseeking in North Carolina: A Guide to Foundation and Corporate
Giving,* compiled and written by Anita Gunn Shirley. Published by North
Carolina Center for Public Policy Research, P.O. Box 430, Raleigh, NC
27602.
  $35.00 plus $2.50 postage and handling

OHIO (1700 foundations)
Charitable Foundations Directory of Ohio, 7th edition. Available from
Charitable Foundations Directory, Attorney General's Office, 30 East
Broad Street, 15th floor, Columbus, OH 43215.
  $6.00 prepaid

OHIO (38 foundations)
Guide to Charitable Foundations in the Greater Akron Area. Available from
Grants Department, United Way of Summit County, P.O. Box 1260, 90
North Prospect Street, Akron, OH 44304.
  $7.50

OHIO
The Source: A Directory of Cincinnati Foundations. Available from Junior League of Cincinnati, Regency Square, Apt. 6-F, 2334 Dana Ave., Cincinnati, OH 45208.
$10.32 includes postage, handling and state sales tax or $9.85 for out-of-state orders.

OKLAHOMA (224 foundations)
Directory of Oklahoma Foundations, edited by Thomas E. Broce. Available from University of Oklahoma Press, 1005 Asp Avenue, Norman, OK 73019.
$22.50 plus postage

OKLAHOMA (221 foundations)
Oklahoma Foundations Directory, edited by Dee Reid, published by Philanthropic Resource Associates, Inc. Available from Foundation Research Project, P.O. Box 1146, Oklahoma City, OK 73101.
$22.00 plus $2.00 postage and handling.

OREGON (approximately 329 foundations)
The Guide to Oregon Foundations, 3rd edition. Available from The United Way of the Columbia-Wilamette, 718 Burnside, Portland, OR 97209.
$15.00 plus $.50 postage

PENNSYLVANIA (2267 foundations)
Directory of Pennsylvania Foundations, 2nd edition, compiled by S. Damon Kletzien, editor, with assistance from Margaret H. Chalfant and Frances C. Ritchey. Available from *Directory of Pennsylvania Foundations,* c/o Friends of the Free Library, Logan Square at 19th Street, Philadelphia, PA 19103. Make check payable to: Friends of the Free Library of Philadelphia.
$18.50, plus $1.11 for PA sales tax if applicable

PENNSYLVANIA (194 foundations)
Pittsburgh Area Foundation Directory. Available from Community Action Pittsburgh, Inc., Planning and Research Division, Fulton Building, 107 Sixth Street, Pittsburgh, PA 15227.
$10.00

RHODE ISLAND (91 foundations)
Directory of Grant-Making Foundations in Rhode Island. Available from the Council for Community Services, 229 Waterman Street, Providence, RI 02906.
$8.00 prepaid plus $1.00 postage and handling

SOUTH CAROLINA (approximately 400 foundations)
South Carolina Foundation Directory, 3rd edition, edited by Guynelle Williams. Available from Guynelle Williams, Reference Librarian, South Carolina State Library, P.O. Box 11469, Columbia, SC 29211.
$10.00

TEXAS (approximately 200 foundations)
The Guide to Texas Foundations, 2nd edition, edited by Jed Riffe. Available from Marianne Cline, Dallas Public Library, 1954 Commerce Street, Dallas, TX 75201.
  $10.00 prepaid

VIRGINIA (approximately 500 foundations)
Virginia Foundations, available from the Grants Resources Library, Hampton City Hall, 9th Floor, 22 Lincoln Street, Hampton, VA 23669.
  $10.00 prepaid

WASHINGTON (approximately 968 foundations)
Charitable Trust Directory, 2nd edition, compiled by the Office of the Attorney General. Available from the Office of the Attorney-General, Temple of Justice, Olympia, WA 98504.
  $4.00 prepaid

WEST VIRGINIA (approximately 99 foundations)
West Virginia Foundation Directory, compiled and edited by William Seeto. Available from West Virginia Foundation Directory, Box 96, Route 1, Terra Alta, WV 26764. Make check payable to: West Virginia Foundation Directory.
  $7.95 prepaid

WISCONSIN (643 foundations)
Foundations in Wisconsin: A Directory 1982, 6th edition, compiled by Susan H. Hopwood. Available from The Foundation Collection, Marquette University Memorial Library, 1415 West Wisconsin Avenue, Milwaukee, WI 53233.
  $15.50 prepaid plus sales tax or Wisconsin tax exempt number

WYOMING (45 foundations)
Wyoming Foundation Directory, prepared by Joy Riske. Available from Laramie County Community College Library, 1400 East College Drive, Cheyenne, WY 82001.
  Free, $1.00 postage for out-of-state orders.

WYOMING (12 foundations). See MONTANA.

Corporate Research Tools

The current trend is for corporations interested in corporate giving to establish foundations to handle their contributions. Once established as foundations, their Internal Revenue Service returns become public information and data are compiled into the directories previously mentioned under Foundation Research Aids.

Corporate contributions that do not use the foundation are not public information, and research sources consist of:

- information volunteered by the corporation
- product information
- profitability information

BOOKS

Annual Survey of Corporate Contributions, annual
This survey of corporate giving is sponsored by the Conference Board and the Council for Financial Aid to Education. It includes a detailed analysis of beneficiaries of corporate support, but does not list individual firms and specific recipients.
Price: $15.00 for Education Members
      $25.00 for Associates
      $75.00 for Non-Associates
Order from: The Conference Board
            845 Third Avenue
            New York, NY 10022
            212-759-0900

The Corporate 500: Directory of Corporate Philanthropy, 6th Ed.
This volume gives information on the contributions programs of the 500 largest American corporations. Entries include: areas of interest; analysis of trends and priorities; geographic areas receiving funds; activities funded; eligible organizations; policy statements; contribution committee members; financial profiles; sample grants and applications procedures. It is published by the Public Management Institute.
Price: $290.00
Order from: Gale Research Company
            Book Tower
            Detroit, MI 48226
            800-223-GALE

Corporate Foundation Profiles, 1985, 622 pages, 4th Ed.
This comprehensive analysis of over 250 of the largest company-sponsored foundations includes subject, type of support, and geographic indexes. It also includes financial data for over 470 additional corporate foundations. (Reissued from *Source Book Profiles.*)
Price: $55.00
Order from: Foundation Center
            79 5th Avenue
            New York, NY 10003

The Corporate Fund Raising Directory, 1986-87 edition
This directory provides information on the giving policies of several
hundred of America's top corporations. It includes name, address and
phone number, contact person, primary and secondary areas of
corporate giving, best time to apply, corporate policy on appointments,
typical grants, total amounts of grants, geographic limitations and other
relevant information, including guidance and advice to grant seekers.
  Price: $39.95 plus postage and handling
  Order from: Taft Group
          5130 MacArthur Blvd.
          Washington, DC 20016
          800-424-3761

PERIODICALS AND NEWSLETTERS

Directory of Corporate Affiliations, 1987
This directory lists divisions, subsidiaries, and affiliates of 4,000 com-
panies with address, telephone, key persons and employees, etc. Over
40,000 listings. Included is a separate geographical index.
  Price: $349.00 plus handling and delivery
  Order from: National Register Company, Inc.
          3004 Glenview Rd.
          Wilmette, IL 60091
          312-256-6067

Dun and Bradstreet's Million Dollar Directory, 3 volumes
The three volumes list names, addresses, employees, sales volume and
other pertinent data for 160,000 of America's largest businesses.
  Price: $1,195.00 for 3 volumes
  Order from: Dun and Bradstreet Marketing Services
          49 Old Bloomfield Ave.
          Mountain Lake Corporate Center, #2
          Mountain Lakes, NJ 07046
          800-526-0651

Standard and Poor's Register of Corporations, Directors and Executives,
annual
The register provides up-to-date rosters of over 400,000 executives of
the 46,000 nationally known corporations they represent, with their
names, titles, and business affiliations.
  Price: $425.00 for one-year lease, includes 3 supplements
  Order from: Standard and Poor's Corporation
          25 Broadway
          New York, NY 10004

Taft Corporate Directory, 1987, 845 pages
This directory provides detailed entries on 550 company-sponsored foundations.
Included are nine indexes.
   Price: $297.00 plus $15.00 postage and handling
   Order from: Taft Group
               5130 MacArthur Boulevard, NW, Suite 200
               Washington, DC 20016
               800-424-3761

Taft Corporate Information System
   Directory: see above
   Corporate Giving Watch: This monthly reports on corporate giving developments. $127.00 a year
   Price for the entire system: $397.00 per year plus $15.00 postage and
                        handling.
   Order from: Taft Group
               5125 MacArthur Boulevard, NW, Suite 200
               Washington, DC 20016
               800-424-3761

Computer Research Systems

There is a wealth of information available through data-base and information-retrieval systems. Check with your librarian and your grants office to locate those data bases you may already have access to.

Congressional Information Service Index (CIS Index)
   Congressional Information Services, Inc.
   4520 East West Highway, Suite 800
   Bethesda, MD 20814
   301-654-1550
CIS covers congressional publications and legislation from 1970 to date.
It covers hearings, committee prints, House and Senate reports and documents, special publications, Senate executive reports and documents, and public laws. It includes monthly abstracts and index volumes and annual cumulations. Non-computer grant related materials are also available from CIS, including the CIS Federal Register Index, which covers announcements from the Federal Register on a weekly basis.
   Price: $595.00

The Dialog Information Retrieval Service
   3460 Hillview Avenue
   Palo Alto, CA 94304
   800-3-DIALOG

Educational Research Information Center (ERIC)
This data base provides a complete file on educational materials from the Educational Resources Information Center. Coverage includes reports and periodical literature in education and education-related areas; career education counseling; early childhood education; educational management; exceptional children; information resources junior colleges; languages and linguistics; reading and communication skills; rural studies; social science education; teacher education and tests and measurements ERIC comprises two machine-readable files which correspond to two separate printed products: *Resources in Education* and *Current Index to Journals in Education.* Entries cover the period from 1966 to the present. It is prepared by the National Institute of Education in Washington.

Federal Assistance Program Retrieval System (FAPRS)
The FAPRS lists more than 1,100 federal grant programs, planning and technical assistance. All states have FAPRS services available through state, county, and local agencies as well as through the federal extension services. Initially, the program operated through cooperative extension and may have moved. For further information, write to:

1. Your congressperson's office; they can request a search for you, and in some cases, at no charge.
2. Federal Domestic Assistance Catalog Staff
   General Services Administration
   300 7th Street S.W.
   Washington, DC 20407

Foundation Center Data Bases
The *Foundation Directory,* the *Foundation Grants Index,* and the *National Data Book* are each available for approximately $60.00 per hour through *Dialog.*

The Sponsored Programs Information Network (SPIN)
The Research Foundation of S.U.N.Y.
P.O. Box 9
Albany, NY 12201
(518) 434-7150
This is a database of federal and private funding sources. Contracts for 100, 200 or 500 sources are available for $1,000, $1,700, and $2,200 respectively.

Index

225

DAVID G. BAUER ASSOCIATES, INC.
3368 Governor Drive Suite F-182
San Diego, CA 92122
(716) 271-5879

GRANTSEEKING MATERIALS

ORDER THE FOLLOWING MATERIALS FROM MACMILLAN PUBLISHING COMPANY:

The "How To" Grants Manual – Text, forms and worksheets to improve grantseeking skills. Designed as a "stand alone" grants aide, or to accompany the WINNING GRANTS tape series.	$20.00 Order from Macmillan Publishing
The Complete Grants Sourcebook for Higher Education – 465 pages of research on funding sources for higher education. Excellent source of information on funders and their higher education expenditures.	$85.00 Order from Macmillan Publishing
The Complete Grants Sourcebook for Nursing and Health – A practical gide that includes an in-depth analysis of 300 funding sources for nursinga and health.	Order from Macmillan Publishing

Macmillan Publishing Company
ATTN: Robert Oppedisano
866 Third Avenue
New York, New York 10022
Order toll Free 800-257-5755
In AK, HA, NJ Call 609-461-6500

ORDER THE FOLLOWING MATERIALS FROM DAVID G. BAUER ASSOCIATES, INC.:

Proposal Organizing Workbook	Per Set $9.95 Plus Shipping
Set of 30 Swiss Cheese Tabs 10 or More Sets	Per Set $8.95 Plus Shipping
Project Planner	Per Pad $8.85 Plus Shipping
Pad of 25 worksheets for developing your workplan and budget narrative. 10 or more pads	Per Pad $7.95 Plus Shipping
Grants Time Line	Per Pad $3.95 Plus Shipping
Pad of 25 worksheets for use in developing time lines and cash forecasts 10 or more pads	Per Pad $2.95 Plus Shipping

---

GRANT WINNER – Software package of 4 diskettes for IBM-PC or compatible. Includes a user's manual and a copy of The "How To" Grants Manual. Organizes grantseeking techniques according to the Bauer System. Provides space to store four proposals simultaneously and copies of worksheets presented in The "How To" Grants Manual. $215.00 includes shipping. To Order write or call: Department C, 80 S. Early St. Alexandria, VA 22304 / 703-823-6966. Questions? Call 619-758-5213 9-5 Pacific Time.

WINNING GRANTS – A series of 10 videocassettes providing a systematic approach to developing a successful grant winning system and a method to assist you in meeting your organization's training needs. Sponsored by The American Council on Education and The University of Nebraska. Call 800-228-4630 for a preview tape. Questions? Call 619-758-5213 9-5 Pacific Time.

CONSULTING/SEMINARS

Use David Bauer and his enthusiasm to increase skills and interest in grantseeking at your institution or organization. Call David G. Bauer Associates, Inc. for fee information and to find out when David is able to include you in his travel schedule. 716-271-5879,

PLEASE NOTE THAT ALL PRICES ARE SUBJECT TO CHANGE WITHOUT NOTICE.

NEW YORK RESIDENTS ADD 6% SALES TAX OR INCLUDE TAX EXEMPT NUMBER WITH ORDER.